MILE 445

Hitched in Her Hiking Boots

Claire Henley Miller

ISBN: 1530854067
ISBN 13: 9781530854066
Library of Congress Control Number: 2016906365
CreateSpace Independent Publishing Platform
North Charleston, South Carolina

For my beloved Big Spoon

AUTHOR'S NOTE

This book chronicles my adventure on the Pacific Crest Trail and beyond. It reflects my trail journal and memory of that adventure, as well as my research and opinions. The names and identifying details of many of the individuals and places in this book have been changed.

For those with eyes that see what's not seen.
That explore what is beyond.

—*Caleb Miller, "What's Not Seen"*

TABLE OF CONTENTS

CHAPTER 1
STARTING LINE

I cannot rest from travel: I will drink
Life to the lees...

—*Alfred, Lord Tennyson, "Ulysses"*

The sun rose as I boarded my plane at the Chattanooga Metropolitan Airport. Fear crept within me like a thorny vine as I inched down the narrow aisle to my seat. Scooting past a man in a suit working on his laptop, I sat down and buckled up. My fingers shook. I had never done anything on this scale before. The flight attendant's voice pierced through the overhead speaker, describing to the passengers how to fit yellow oxygen masks over our faces and inflate the life jackets stashed under our seats in the event of a dire fate. The plane started moving as she spoke, backing away from the gate and crawling for the airstrip, where it began coasting, gaining momentum until the wind roared around it and lifted it off the ground.

I released my breath. Up there in the pale-pink sky, my inner vine budded in peace. I'm ready for this, I thought. I'm ready. Over the last four months, I had trained like a soldier for the journey ahead. Nothing, though, could have prepared me for what would happen.

It was Tuesday, April 21. I was on my way to California to thru-hike the Pacific Crest Trail, also referred to as the PCT. First proposed in 1926 and not to be established as a National Scenic Trail until 1968, the PCT is a foot and equine path that spans 2,650 miles from Mexico to Canada, carving through the mountains of California, Oregon, and Washington. As a thru-hiker, by definition, I was setting out to complete the whole thing in one continuous walk—a journey that would take five months.

I changed planes in Chicago and watched from my Plexiglas window as the earth changed from rolling green hills to dusty brown plains to cracked ground ripping through orange, barren lands. Charcoal-colored mountains made of granite sculpted the wall between Arizona and California. Then came San Diego, a place of sweeping sea and golden hills. My plane landed on a runway next to the Pacific Ocean, where a fleet of ships swayed in the harbor. Once off the plane, I dodged past the airport crowd toward baggage claim to pick up the musty gray suitcase I'd bought for five dollars at a thrift store the day before. The moment I arrived, it slid around the baggage carousel and before me. I grabbed the faux-leather luggage and unzipped it just enough to peek in. My backpack, gear, and trekking poles were still safely stored inside.

Alone in the heart of what felt like a huge hurry, I clung to my ugly old suitcase. Among the California fashionistas, I stuck out like an outdated style in my un-flattering hiking clothes—white polyester button-down, gray nylon pants, and gray hiking boots with hints of green. The outfit made me look like a sun-bleached rock.

"Or a frumpily dressed businesswoman," said Buffalo, a guy about my age—twenty-five or so—with tangled brown locks like the matted hide of a buffalo. He picked me up from the airport that sunny after-noon. I was waiting outside when he pulled up to the passenger pickup in a silver Prius with yellow pom-poms waving out the back windows.

"For easy identification," Buffalo had said of the bright, clustered streamers when he'd called to tell me he was on his way.

He wore a ripped, sweat-stained T-shirt with a paper name tag peeling off the front that read Volunteer in big, bold letters.

"You've got to be the cleanest, most well-dressed hiker I've picked up today," he said as he loaded my suitcase into the trunk.

"I'm Claire," I said, changing the subject, my cheeks heating up and flushing.

Buffalo looked me up and down. "Well, *Claire*, you're very clean." He laughed as if he knew something I didn't. "Just don't expect to stay that way."

Buffalo, I learned in the car, had thru-hiked the PCT the year before. He was from Minnesota, but because he'd loved his time on the trail so much, he'd signed up to help drive this year's trekkers—known as the Class of 2015—from the San Diego International Airport to the home of famous trail angels Scout and Frodo. Trail angels, I would soon discover, were very special people who out of sheer generosity assisted hikers by providing them with things like homes to sleep in off the trail, rides to and from town, warm meals, cold drinks, hot showers, and laundry facilities.

Scout and Frodo were some of the best. A married couple in their early sixties, Scout (a retired lawyer) and Frodo (a biochemistry teacher) had thru-hiked the PCT in 2007. They had spoken with several people from all over the country who had hiked the trail with them that year and were disappointed to learn that their comrades had had a disorienting experience upon their arrival in San Diego. This was because their fellow backpackers were unfamiliar with the big city and had a hard time finding affordable transportation to the southern terminus of the PCT, fifty miles east in the rural town of Campo.

"Unacceptable," Scout and Frodo thought. "Hikers shouldn't spend the first day of the most fantastic trip of their lives in a gush of worry."

As a result, these San Diego residents (whose kids were now grown and out of the house) had dubbed their home Hikertown. They began hosting northbound hikers at the start of the thru-hiking season (from mid-April to mid-May), giving those who weren't from the area a welcoming place to stay and helping them tie up any logistical loose ends before shuttling them at dawn to the trailhead.

I learned of Scout and Frodo several months earlier through my guidebook, *Yogi's Pacific Crest Trail Handbook*, as well as through my Internet research. Amazingly, the trail angels offered their services for free. They understood that the majority of thru-hikers quit their jobs to hike the trail, so one of their hopes in running Hikertown was to help people pinch pennies where they could. The angels took this seriously, saying in an interview that injuries and money were the two main things that forced a hiker off the trail. I even read one story about how Scout had tracked down a young man to return the twenty-dollar bill he'd slipped into the Prius's center console when the couple dropped him off in Campo. Seeing as I, too, would quit my job to walk in the wild, I had e-mailed the couple in January, using the address provided in my guidebook, to ask if they would host me when I arrived in April.

They didn't hesitate to respond with a very comforting yes. After that, we'd stayed in touch, exchanging the necessary details that ultimately led to Buffalo's fetching me from the airport a mere five minutes after I stepped out of the sliding glass doors into the California sun.

"I hope you're not planning to carry that suitcase on the trail," Buffalo said, shattering the awkward silence that had settled between us as he sped up the I-5.

I laughed nervously. "My backpack is in the suitcase. You know, to protect it from getting damaged on the flight."

Although it was obvious this guy meant no harm, I realized that I was scared. I mean, I was a girl alone in a car with a complete stranger who looked and smelled like a stray dog and went by the name of Buffalo. Of course, with all the research I had done on long-distance hiking, I knew that Buffalo wasn't his real name—just like Scout and Frodo weren't Scout's and Frodo's real names. In real life, Scout and Frodo were Barney and Sandy Mann. But they answered to Scout and Frodo in the trail community because in this world they, like Buffalo, were no longer in real life but in hiker life.

And in hiker life, you went by a trail name.

Most every thru-hiker received one at some point during his or her journey. One's fellow hikers typically came up with it after unearthing something unique or funny about that person, a quality so defining that he or she had no choice but to be called by it.

For example, it took but one glance to see that Buffalo had been dubbed Buffalo for the mess of dark hair that covered his eyes and shrouded his shoulders like the tousled pelt of a bison. I looked over at him from the passenger seat. He was wild looking, scraggly—an unwashed beast of a man. But there was kindness in his caramel eyes, and even though he poked fun at me, he made it clear it was all for play.

As the eleven-mile drive to Scout and Frodo's proceeded, I warmed up to my disheveled driver, picking his brain with my burning questions, such as, "Is it hard to find a place to set up camp every night on the trail?"

"Not at all," Buffalo replied. "There are designated sites all along the trail that you can sleep at if you choose. Your maps should have them listed with their mile markers. Or you can be like me and wander off the trail a little ways to find your own spot away from everyone else."

"Everyone else? Did you see many people on the trail?"

"Oh, yeah. In the beginning, at least. And you will, too. You're starting at the height of hiker season. I think there's something like two thousand thru-hikers going for it this year. Anyways, I did the same thing as you— started alone but was in the mix of people immediately.

I actually paired up with three others my second day out there. Ended up hiking the whole thing with them. People click like crazy on the trail."

These words relieved me. Although I was a loner by nature and had been on several solo backpacking trips back East, I still feared the prospect of being totally alone for days at a time, isolated in the unforgiving wild.

"Were you ever scared?" I asked as Buffalo turned into an attractive neighborhood where tall, healthy palm trees shaded the yards.

"Oh, sure. Plenty of times." He slowed to twenty-five miles per hour. "Got caught in some violent desert storms that shook me up. Almost stepped on a rattlesnake a time or two. Skirted the edges of twelve-thousand-foot cliffs through snow in the High Sierra. That was sketchy as hell." He reached the end of the cul-de-sac and pulled into a driveway that had been freshly pressure-washed. "But it was good for me—the incredible challenge. It kept me on my toes, kept me alert." He shut off the engine, turned, and looked me in the eyes like an animal. "Ah, and when I made it through those trickier times, I felt so triumphant, so empowered, so *alive*. The trail has that effect. It wakes you up and opens you to possibilities beyond your craziest imagination. It wrecks you for life. But in the best way."

I didn't understand what Buffalo meant when he said the PCT would wreck me. But I didn't have time to contemplate it that afternoon at Hikertown. A flag with the triangular green-and-white Pacific Crest Trail emblem proudly waved over the front door. The emblem pictured an evergreen before an alpine peak, with the name of the trail written over it. I followed Buffalo inside the red-brick home, where a crowd of eager hikers buzzed. According to the last e-mail I'd received from Scout and Frodo the day before, I was one of thirty-seven hikers they would host that night, a new record for them in their eight years as trail angels.

Several factors played into this uncommonly high number of people. First, as Buffalo had said, it was the height of the hiker season, meaning that because northbound hikers (those walking from Mexico to Canada) had a window of time to complete the trail before the autumn snows of Washington washed it out, now was when most thru-hikers started, the strategy being to get through the Southern California desert before the height of summer struck, allowing enough time for the snow in the Sierra to melt before entering its domain, all while hiking an average of twenty miles a day to finish the trail before the harsh northern weather made it impossible to pass.

Furthermore, due to the shockingly low snow accumulation in the Sierra Nevada over the past winter along with the major publicity the trail had recently received from Cheryl Strayed's memoir-turned-movie *Wild: From Lost to Found on the Pacific Crest Trail*, the PCT called for three times the amount of foot traffic this year than the year before. In fact, because of the anticipated in-creased demand, this season marked the first in which a limit had been placed on the number of thru-hikers al-lowed to start the trail on the same day. In other words, to preserve and not overcrowd this National Scenic Trail, only fifty people had permission to take off from the Mexican border per day. I had applied for my long-distance hiking permit months in advance to secure my coveted spot. This made me one of fifty who would start the PCT the next day—Wednesday, April 22. And because no other trail angels in the area had gained as much popularity as Scout and Frodo, the majority of these fifty had flocked to Hikertown. It was like slipping into an earth-toned circus.

The living room was flooded with people perform-ing yoga or sitting cross-legged amid an eruption of backpacks of all colors and shapes. One group sitting in a closed-off circle stared at me as I shuffled in.

"I'd set that down before you get the trail name Suitcase," a barefoot male with beaded dreadlocks remarked.

Good Lord, I thought, my backpack is in the suitcase—to protect it from getting damaged on the flight! But I laughed the comment off, quickly set down my geeky va-lise, and looked around the room. I must have been the only person who'd thought it a brilliant idea to guard my pack from the merciless airport conveyor belt. Looking closer, I saw that I was also the only one wearing a collared shirt—my pure white, never-before-worn, long-sleeved, button-down REI designed to protect me from the SoCal desert rays.

I felt foolish, like the new kid in school who didn't get the gist of things. Then the front door opened, and another volunteer walked in followed by a tall, blue-eyed boy wearing the same shirt as me—only his was the color of a robin's egg. He didn't carry a suitcase, but he did have an awkwardly shaped duffel bag slung over his shoulder. Our eyes met before I swept a glance at his bag. His backpack has to be in there, I consoled myself.

I wasn't so out of place after all.

"Come with me," Buffalo said, waving me on a tour of the house. He showed me the guest bathroom first, stating that because of California's severe drought, Scout and Frodo expected their guests to be conscious of and conservative with how much water we consumed.

"With that in mind, they ask that you do the following regarding the use of the toilet," Buffalo said and then cleared his throat for the public service announcement. "If it's yellow, let it mellow. If it's brown, flush it down."

In the kitchen, Buffalo taught me that if I was ever hungry at Scout and Frodo's, then something was wrong. "Don't hesitate to help yourself to anything in here at any time," he said. It was one o'clock, I hadn't eaten lunch, and my hunger was amplified because my body believed it was actually four o'clock. It hadn't yet adapted to the three-hour time change from east to west.

A crumb-scattered tray on the granite counter with one remaining ham and cheese sandwich caught my eye. I looked at the sandwich and then back at Buffalo. He nodded. I chowed down.

Two white event tents billowed up from the Astroturf in the backyard. Several hikers were there, relaxing in the shade of the tents or spread out on the bright-green lawn beneath the cobalt sky. Some were sorting through gear and organizing packs—getting as ready as possible before starting the trail the next day. Buffalo told me that the majority of hikers would sleep in the backyard— in their sleeping bags beneath the tents. But because of the large number of people Scout and Frodo were hosting that night, there wasn't enough space for everyone.

"You and the other solo females will stay next door with neighbor Beth. She'll be here a little later and will take you and the rest back to her house after dinner. In the meantime, use the backyard to get your suitcase—I mean backpack—ready for tomorrow," Buffalo said with a laugh.

Back in the living room, he gave me a high five and then left to round up more hikers. I scanned the house. My peers were everywhere—filling water bottles, stretching leg and back muscles, and mingling with each other. I remembered reading in my guidebook what Buffalo had helped confirm in the car: that the majority of PCT hikers started alone and formed partnerships along the way. I was alone now—alone in a crowd, but alone. I walked my suitcase to the backyard, unzipped it all the way, and exploded my sixty-eight-liter backpack and its contents onto the plastic turf.

I'd owned my pack for a couple of years. A Utah-based company called Ultralight Adventure Equipment (or ULA) hand sewed it to specifically fit my petite, five-foot-four frame. Basically, it was an indestructible nylon sack with an aluminum internal frame that weighed in at forty-one ounces when empty. Its trim was stitched with a rich, royal color called purple blaze. On past backpacking trips to the Colorado Rockies and the Great Smoky Mountains, I used the large black zipper pockets on the hip belt to stow granola bars, toilet paper, my headlamp, pocketknife, whistle, and phone—which I used as my camera—for easy access. In the front external mesh pocket that spanned the length of the pack, I kept things I needed throughout the day, like my maps, compass, guidebook, bandanas, journal, pen, water filter, hat, and—just in case—my purple rain jacket. I hooked my rubber camp shoes to the Velcro loops at the top of the mesh pocket. For water, I carried four one-liter Smartwater bottles because of their lightweight durability, sleek design, and pleasing price tag, fitting two next to each other in my pack's sturdy side pockets that angled in a way that made it possible to grab and replace the bottles without having to unstrap.

My pack was fashioned with a rolltop closure that opened to everything else. Loading it up from the bottom, my strategy was to stuff my navy Marmot sleeping bag (made of premium goose down and rated to keep me warm in at least fifteen degrees Fahrenheit) in first. I would stack my red MSR one-person tent on top of the sleeping bag, followed by my red blow-up sleeping pad, which I'd then position next to a blue dry bag, one that would protect my striped teal thermals, black down jacket, two pairs of merino wool socks, fleece hat, nylon gloves, sky-colored workout top, and gray running shorts from getting wet.

Atop the dry bag lay a clear three-liter Platypus bladder (for extra water storage) and a blue cuben-fiber food sack. Other than food, the sack housed several Ziploc bags (to hold and seal trash); an aluminum cook pot (that also served as my bowl and cup); a compact, collapsible stove plus a fuel canister, titanium spoon, lighter, and matches.

Then came my first-aid/repair/personal hygiene kit: a Ziploc gallon freezer bag filled with safety pins, a sewing needle, thread, duct tape, Band-Aids, Neosporin, ibuprofen, bar soap, a razor, comb, toothbrush, toothpaste, hair ties, and a bell-shaped silicon menstrual cup that I would use during my period instead of tampons, as it was reusable and could allegedly capture my blood all day before I needed to dig a hole, dump it out, rinse it with water, and stick it back in.

It was called the Diva Cup, and although I was tentative about trying it when I first read about it in my guidebook, I would soon discover that it made for much less mess in the woods by eliminating my having to pack out used tampons during my time of the month.

Now, I stared down at the crunchy turf with all of these gear items spread before me like a melted rainbow. Among them lay my multicolored bandana patterned with cosmic stars, suns, and iridescent strips of the northern lights. I'd had this bright piece of cloth for years—bought it at a Chattanooga outfitters store called Rock Creek—and took it with me every time I went backpacking. I called it my lucky bandana. Given the number of times it had been washed, its pinks, purples, blues, yellows, and greens still hadn't faded. I picked it up, clenched it with my teeth, and drew my long, dirty-blond hair into a ponytail. Then I folded the bandana and tied it around my head, enhancing my drab ensemble—a ritual I would perform most every morning to come on this trip.

"Cool bandana," said the short, skinny woman next to me. She was bent over on her knees, wearing a tan visor and what looked like an army uniform, sorting through her equipment.

"Thanks," I said, sitting down next to her to go through my own gear, now seeing more clearly the fine wrinkles webbing the skin of her sun-shielded face. She couldn't have been younger than seventy.

"Name's Helen," she said, briskly sticking out her hand.

"Claire," I said, grasping her bony shake, surprised by the strength in her delicate fingers.

Side by side, we prepared our packs. Helen was all smiles, revealing that she was a dialysis nurse from California who had hiked the six hundred miles of trail through the Sierra but never the seven hundred miles of desert leading up to it.

"I'm no spring chicken," she said, laughing, "so now's my time to give it a go." She lifted her age-spotted fist to the sky.

Girl power in the elderly flesh.

Minutes later, the moment of truth arrived—weighing my pack to see how heavy a load I'd be carting my first day on the trail. Hoisting onto my back the whole of everything I would need to survive in the wilderness for the next five months, I headed to the digital hanging scale nailed over the kitchen doorway. A gray-bearded Australian man standing by helped me lift and hook my pack onto the scale. Along with the things like my sleeping bag that I'd always carry, my pack also contained four days' worth of food and six liters of water—consumables that would deplete the heaviness of my load after each use until I made it to town.

I let go of my pack and waited as the numbers on the scale shot up. The backpacking rule of thumb was to lug no more than one-third of your body weight so as not to put too much stress on your bones. Considering that I weighed 120 pounds, I didn't want to see a number bigger than 40 appear on the scale's electronic readout. I closed my eyes and reopened them. The small black device flashed the final digits in red: 38.

"Not bad, mate," the Australian said, his accent like an upbeat song. "I'm up to seventy backbreaking pounds. Have to make some bloody adjustments."

He helped me take down my pack and then left to modify his bulky cargo.

"You look the part, kid," someone said from behind me as I strapped my new livelihood back on. I turned to see a tall, fit man clad in jeans and a plaid shirt. He had white hair and a full mustache that blanketed his upper lip. A woman my height with short brown hair and gentle motherly curves walked up next to him, a casserole dish resting in her hands. I recognized the two from a picture in my guidebook—Scout and Frodo. After months of communicating with these angels through my computer, it was wonderful to finally be in their presence.

"And you look like Scout and Frodo."

They nodded, Scout's salt-and-pepper mustache lifting with his smile. This seemed to be the theme here: although there was much to be done, everyone at Hikertown wore the grandest of smiles. Even Buffalo in all his subtle mockery had been infectiously cheerful.

I introduced myself and thanked the couple for their unprecedented hospitality.

"We're just doing what we can," Scout said.

"And that's really all we can do," Frodo added, winking at Scout before joining the volunteers in the kitchen to help make dinner.

I asked Scout what I should do with my suitcase. He led me to the garage and showed me the giveaway pile he said he would take to Goodwill the next day. The pile was designated for things hikers needed in order to get to San Diego but wouldn't need on the trail, like street clothes and duffel bags—and now my clunky suitcase.

Frodo summoned Scout to come take out the trash. I walked out the open garage door, away from the hectic bustle, and sat on the brick curb in front of the house. From my pack I pulled my waterproof journal and black pen and wrote down everything that had happened so far—a habit I would maintain throughout the trail. When I finished writing, it was time for dinner: a feast of roast chicken, couscous, and potato salad. The boy in the blue button-down stood a head taller than everyone else in the kitchen line. He was a few people behind me, and I had the slight feeling I was being watched as I dished a big spoonful of potato salad onto my paper plate.

That feeling faded, however, when I took a seat out on the Astroturf among the tribe of hikers and could no longer be distinguished from the rest. I sat next to a woman named Liz, a spunky lesbian with short auburn hair shaved down to coarse stubble on both sides.

I asked her what had brought her out here. She said she was a traveling nurse from Michigan who, after completing the Appalachian Trail the previous year, had worked at a hospital near Joshua Tree National Park to save up money and get a taste of the desert landscape before hopping on the PCT.

"I'm made for this stuff," she said, referring to long-distance hiking. "I'm forty-two years old, and I guess I should be settled down. But the trail is where I belong."

Her navy shorts showed her rock-hard legs, but her checkered shirt failed to hide her stout stomach.

"I lost so much weight on the AT that I purposely gained thirty pounds for this trip by eating doughnuts and Doritos—and drinking beer every day over the last three months." She tilted back her head and gave a good laugh.

"That's one way to do it," I said, laughing along, noticing the sag in her paper plate from her hearty meal.

With the setting of the sun around seven thirty, the air cooled. I slipped on my down jacket and then joined the crowd Scout and Frodo had gathered by the white tents after everyone had finished dinner.

"We want to talk to you about being ambassadors of the trail," Scout began. He was a whimsical man who spoke with floating hand gestures. Having served since 2008 on the board of directors of the Pacific Crest Trail Association—the organization dedicated to preserving and protecting the PCT—he went on to say how hiking the trail and then working for it had opened his eyes to the sheer beauty and power of the human spirit. "Which, mark my words, comes fully alive through the beauty and power of the wild," he said. His eyes glinted like the night's first star when he uttered the word *wild*.

"There are eighteen hundred thru-hikers this year," Frodo, a more direct speaker, declared. "That's more people on the trail than in any other year to date. It is crucial—*crucial*—that each one of you walks with the knowledge that the trail is an intricate life of its own, one we must steward and help grow rather than invade and destroy. This being said, Scout and I urge you to treat the trail, as well as each other, with kindness and respect. Pack out your trash. Don't cut switchbacks. And please, for everyone's sake, don't use the bathroom near water sources. Kindness and respect, people. They are the keys to a flourishing society."

In closing, Scout said, "You're all about to do something few people will ever do. Setting out on the PCT, out into the splendor of the great unknown, will be the most extraordinary experience of your lives." He paused, as if remembering his own time on the trail. "Over half of you won't make it all the way," he said, his tone dropping to a serious note. "Yes, that's right—statistics show that over half of aspiring PCT thru-hikers drop out of the trail for this reason or that."

Not me, I thought confidently.

"Nevertheless," Scout continued, "no matter how many or how few days you get on the trail, you must be adamant about—you must be *deliberate* in—savoring every single step. Because this is your journey of a lifetime. Don't dare miss it."

With these final words, it was time for bed. As Buffalo had said, a woman named Beth rounded up the solo women and walked the seven of us across the street to her home. She showed us to the den, where she had scooted the couch against a bookshelf to make space on the hardwood floor for us to spread out our sleeping pads and bags. I rinsed my face and brushed my teeth in the bathroom before making up my pallet. A watercolor painting of a rugged wooden cross rising from a sun-drenched mountaintop hung next to the mirror. The symbol of both sacrifice and victory, I thought, carrying this notion with me that night as I lay my head to rest.

In the waning darkness of predawn, the solo females and I met the other hikers in Scout and Frodo's kitchen for a fruit, frittata, and fresh-from-the-oven blueberry-muffin breakfast. I squeezed into the last seat at the dining-room table and ate in meditative silence. Today is the day, I thought again and again. The day I've been preparing for. The day I'll begin my walk.

After breakfast, a nine-car caravan transported everyone to the trailhead. It was a one-hour drive down

I-8E through the layered bouquets of green and rocky hills to Campo.

"I can't believe I'm finally here," I said out loud when I touched the wooden monument marking the southern terminus of the PCT. Four rectangular towers ranging in size from two feet to seven feet tall made up the monument. It was weathered and rough, inscribed with the words: "Pacific Crest National Scenic Trail. Established by Act of Congress on Oct. 2, 1968."

I pressed my hand against its splintery surface for several seconds, taking in the wide, mountainous view. The sun rose over a pale-yellow field in the distance, where the blades of a hundred wind turbines spun in the steady breeze. A border patrol band zoomed by on ATVs, kicking up a cloud of dirt that seeped between the holes in the metal fence separating the United States from Mexico.

I felt a stirring sense of urgency. It was time. Time to get on the trail and walk. I buckled my backpack to my waist and chest, adjusted the straps, and then grasped my lime-green trekking poles.

I hugged Scout and Frodo good-bye. The other drivers of the nine-car caravan started to pull away.

"Happy trails!" Scout called as I headed down the hill from the monument toward the small opening for the trail. Fifty yards later, I faced a narrow, gritty path embedded with footprints stretching a long, long way before me. I stared it in the eyes, filling my lungs with the cool, dry air, feeling my heart flutter like humming-bird wings.

This was it.

There was no turning back now.

I set foot on the trail.

CHAPTER 2
ADZPCTKO

I walked at an elevation of 2,915 feet. Over the next twenty miles, the trail would rise to 3,500 feet above sea level. That's how far I needed to hike my first day out there if I wanted to make it in time for dinner at the ADZPCTKO—the Annual Day Zero PCT Kickoff being held over the next two days at Lake Morena County Park.

Twenty miles on day one.

I had never hiked more than fourteen miles in a day, and I prayed to God to strengthen me. But after mile 1, which was marked by a green-and-white PCT emblem nailed to a tree—one of the few markers I'd see throughout my time on the trail—my feet already hurt.

"God, strengthen me. Dear God, strengthen me," I chanted as I walked.

The morning was cloudy and cool, encompassing the slim, dusty trail and the surrounding desert beauty. Yucca and cacti sprang up from the hills alongside the springtime petals—yellows, purples, and reds—starting to burst from the brush.

The smells of sage and sand traveled with me as I coiled along exposed rock mountains that looked out on auburn valleys below. I hiked alone but passed—and was passed by—other hikers the entire day. One hiker I came up on was Liz, whom I'd met at Scout and Frodo's the night before. It was midmorning, and the nurse was on her knees off to the side of the trail, bandaging up another female hiker around my age, who introduced herself as Jen.

Jen wore a red windbreaker and had her shoes and socks off as Liz doctored the blisters that had already begun to form on Jen's big toes.

"Other than water, foot care has to be your top priority out here," Liz, the veteran long-distance hiker and health-care professional, preached for Jen and my edification. "If your feet go, you're a goner. I stop every hour or two to shake all the sand and debris from my socks and shoes. I wash my socks whenever I come across a natural water source too, and then wear my spare pair while the wet ones dry. You just safety pin them to the outside of your pack."

I slipped off my pack and sat next to a cactus. My shirt was plastered to my back with sweat. I pulled off my green-and-gray Oboz (they were a couple of years old and let in lots of dirt) as well as my socks to do as Liz said.

A cloud of filth floated in the air when I gave my socks a good whip.

"Maybe you should stop every half hour," Liz said, breathing in my crud.

The sun burned through the clouds at noon. Now I understood the difference between heat and *desert* heat. It was like a sauna you couldn't escape—a thick, dry hotness that made it hard to breathe. I put on my tan ball cap, donned my polarized sunglasses, and rolled down my white sleeves to deflect the blazing rays from my skin. By mile 14, which I reached after eating a lunch of tuna salad at a spot between spiky bushes, the trail took a sharp right turn onto a remote dirt road. Just a few days before, I had read about several unmarked junctions on the trail that tended to disorient hikers and throw them off course. One in particular was coming right up: a blind left turn off the dirt road notorious for being overlooked and getting thru-hikers lost on their first day.

I walked slowly on the road so I wouldn't miss the turn. Something hummed in the distance. I looked up. A man riding a red moped was zipping my way. He stopped at the side of the road before me and stood to reveal his long, emaciated form. No one else was around. I had to walk past him. He lit a cigarette and sucked in the smoke, standing on a cliff that faced a desolate mountain where a vague zigzag of the trail carved through.

"You gotta take that hairpin turn just beyond that small yellow sign down there," the man said as I nervously approached him. He wiped his sooty hands on his worn-out jeans, speaking in a voice that was surprisingly shy. "Most you folks miss it. I've been meaning to bring some spray paint."

He turned to view the mountain, gently inhaling his tobacco and then releasing its strong aroma into the sizzling air. I thanked him for his help and walked on, remembering what I'd read in my guidebook several months back: "If you've lost your faith in humanity, go hike the PCT."

Beyond the faint yellow sign, I turned left to descend a steep grade into Hauser Creek. The creek ran dry due to California's record-breaking drought, which had been evaporating water from the land for four years. At the campground next to the ghostly creek, two rangers stood in their forest-green uniforms, speaking to two other hikers and checking permits.

I reached into my pants pocket for the folded-up piece of paper that declared my permission to be on the PCT on this day and showed it to the rangers when I stepped up to them.

"Want an Arizona Tea?" the tanned hiker in a jade-colored shirt asked, holding out an unopened can that was wet with condensation.

"Sure," I said. "Please."

The tea represented my first run-in with trail magic—the spontaneous gifts hikers received on the trail.

"I'm Tortoise," said the guy who'd given me the sweet tea. "So named because I'm slow but steady. And this is Kinetic. Now, this guy can move." Tortoise looked up at his bushy-haired friend, who was actually walking in place. As I sipped my cold, sugary drink, Tortoise and Kinetic related to me what they had just told the rangers: that they were thru-hikers who had already been on the trail for a month. They said they'd been at mile 450 in the town of Agua Dulce and had hitchhiked back to Lake Morena the day before to attend the ADZPCTKO, which in their words was a "badass party" going on five miles ahead.

"We'd planned to take a zero today, you know, since it is the *Annual Day Zero* for the PCT, but we decided to do a little trail-angeling instead," Kinetic said.

A zero, I had learned from my research, was a day on which hikers walked zero miles in order to rest and recuperate. It was a day off—like a Saturday—and the ADZPCTKO served as the official zero of the thru-hiking season for hikers to celebrate, learn about the trail, and meet.

According to Tortoise, he and Kinetic had bought all the Arizona Tea earlier that morning at the convenience store close to Lake Morena. They'd loaded their packs with the cold cans and had been walking the stretch of trail near the campground all day to hand out the drinks and boost the morale of the first-day hikers who were almost finished with what has been said to be the hardest twenty miles of the trail.

"But it's only the hardest because your body isn't used to walking that much yet, especially for those who haven't experienced the desert," said one of the rangers.

I had five miles left before making the county park, where I'd reserved a campsite months ago for the kick-off. I'd figured that since I was taking this trip solo, it would be wise to place myself in the mix of what was referred to as the "hiker bubble." Being in the bubble meant I was in with the pack—the mass who commenced the trail around the same time. This appealed to me far more than the alternative: walking about the western wilderness utterly alone. Now, as I stood in the mix of Tortoise, Kinetic, and the rangers, I was grateful for my decision, considering how difficult the last fifteen miles I'd just hiked had been and how much more difficult they would have been had I seen no one to encourage me on. Especially since painful hot spots on the outside of my right big toe and on the back of my right heel had now begun to burn. If I wasn't careful, these red irritations would grow into blisters—small but powerful injuries that could pluck a person off the trail for days at a time. I looked down at my hiking boots. They can't be the problem, I thought. They were broken-in, comfortable, and exactly my six-and-a-half shoe size.

Which I'd soon discover was the problem.

Anyhow, at this point, I didn't think anything of it. My boots were fine. It was like the ranger said: my hot spots resulted from my body's not being used to daylong hiking in the desert.

These ruminations prompted me to ask where everyone was from. One of the rangers said he had lived here in Southern California all his life. The other came from Seattle.

"We're from Chattanooga," Tortoise said.

"Wait. *Where?*" I asked, disbelieving what I'd just heard.

"Chatt-a-noo-ga. It's in Tennessee. I know, weird name, right?"

"That's what I thought you said." I beamed. "Crazy. Of all the places you could be from, and you're from Chattanooga. I'm from there, too. Born and raised."

"Hell, yeah!" Tortoise hollered as Kinetic called, "Represent!"

"Don't think that's a coincidence either," Kinetic said and winked. "Coincidences don't happen out here."

Soon after the guys and I made our hometown connection, Liz arrived at Hauser Creek, tired but upbeat. When Tortoise and Kinetic offered her a tea, I took to the trail and journeyed on. Up, up, up a switch-backed mountain I climbed for five straight miles in the dead of day, sweat pouring out of me like a monsoon. It felt like someone was hammering my feet—with every step, the hot spots seared as if nails were being driven in. From where my pack hung, my shoulders felt as if they had been body-slammed by a heavyweight wrestler. Twenty miles, it turned out, was a long way to walk with a backpack.

In fact, I was so out of breath when I reached the top and saw a parched Lake Morena below that when I exhaled "Hallelujah!" I didn't know if the word would come out. Now, at dusk, I practically fell into Lake Morena County Park, my body as weak as a reed withered by daylong wind. Hundreds of hikers roamed the park, as did a handful of helpers wearing neon-orange vests. A grayhaired woman mixing lemonade in a Rubbermaid cooler pointed me in the direction of the main tent where I needed to sign in. I hobbled to the end of the park and received my registration for Campsite 73. Then I hobbled all the way down the dark paved road lined with sites and a multitude of compact tents.

By now, my feet were screaming at me to get off of them. I was worn out and sore, but I managed to pitch my freestanding tent despite the unruly wind that kept trying to blow up my rainfly like a kite. With the tent finally staked in the hard ground, now I could lie down to rest.

However, just as I was crawling in, Tortoise strolled up to my site.

"Look who I found," he said with great enthusiasm. "Another Chattanoogan."

He pointed to the young guy next to him, who stood at a lanky height with small black ear gauges and long, curly hair partially covered by his blue tie-dyed buff.

"I'm Crunchmaster," he said, smiling like the cutest kid.

"Grab your jacket and join us for dinner," Tortoise said. Desert evenings came with much cooler weather.

"I don't know," I said, sticking halfway out of my tent. "I'm so tired. Earlier today, I thought I'd want to eat. But now I'm just going to skip dinner and go to bed."

"Oh, come on," Crunchmaster said, waving me to get up. "It's not like it'll take all night. You need to refuel your body, anyways."

"Crunchmaster's right. One of the last things you want to be out here is calorie deficient," Tortoise added.

"Okay, fine," I said, defeated by the friendly peer pressure. "But then I'm turning in."

Two long rows of tables parted the field across from the campsites. They supported several foil pans of overstuffed burritos and moist brownies that melted in your mouth. In my extreme fatigue, I hadn't realized how hungry I was until I actually saw and smelled the food. Crunchmaster and I grabbed a burrito and a brownie each and then picked a spot on the sharp grass to sit down. Tortoise followed, holding a fat burrito in each hand.

"Hiker hunger, man. It's real. Catches up to you around week three. The endless gnaw," he said, diving into the tortilla-wrapped beef.

"So, why are you hiking the PCT?" I asked Tortoise as he chewed.

He swallowed. "Back home, I was an EMT. Pretty exhilarating stuff in the beginning. But after a few years of it, I wanted out. All that trauma and pain. It consumed my life—the dark tragedies. Then I met someone, a beautiful girl. She reopened my world to the light, you know. We got engaged." Tortoise spoke slowly and profoundly, his half-eaten burrito slumping over his hand. "She dumped me not long ago. That ripped me to my soul. The tragedy was now mine." He took a deep breath. "So, that's why I'm here. To heal. To step beyond this dark time in my life, taking my time in this good and natural world to return to the light."

"Dude," Crunchmaster said. "Heavy."

"Really," I said, stunned by such open honesty from this stranger.

"What about you, Crunchmaster man? What drew you here?" Tortoise asked, shifting the focus from himself.

Crunchmaster—who I learned was twenty and had been on the trail for the last two days before hitching a ride out of the town called Mount Laguna to make the kickoff—said he'd hiked the Appalachian Trail after graduating high school instead of going to college like he was "supposed" to.

"The AT's where I got my trail name, because I was always eating chips on the trail, making a lot of noise or something when I chewed."

He went on to say that during that 2,200-mile haul from Georgia to Maine, he realized this was where he belonged—the trail, for its great challenge and freedom.

"So, I worked for my dad after finishing it to save money for the PCT. He's all for what I'm doing, says I'm living my young life. But I've dealt with tons of naysayers. They've told me again and again I need to go to school and get a degree so I can get a job. I haven't let it get to me too much, though. They don't see what I see. They don't see that the trail *is* an education. That it *is* a job. Man. And it's the hardest one I've ever had, too, that demands daily overtime." He spread out his long arms as if to envelop the mountains ahead. "Worst of all, they don't care. All they see is what's right in front of them. They don't try to look *through* any of it. They don't try to *make* something of it for themselves." He paused, taking in the scenery. "Ah. But I've found liberty in this life I love, in doing something I believe I was made to do, even if it doesn't fit in with the mold. Dude, I'd take what the trail has to give me any day of the week over a steady paycheck."

With his arms opened so wide, I noticed the text of a tattoo sticking out from his jacket sleeve on his right wrist.

"What does your tattoo say?" I asked.

Crunchmaster pushed up his sleeve.

"I can do everything through Him who gives me strength," I read the black ink up his arm.

"Awesome, man!" Tortoise exclaimed. "Keep following your soul."

Crunchmaster gave a thumbs-up. "Your turn," he said, looking at me. "Why are you hiking the PCT?"

I took a moment to think, gazing out on the fuchsia sunset over the yellow peaks. There was so much I could tell. Like how over the last two years, I'd worked in a gray cubicle—five feet deep, five feet wide—for a major insurance corporation in Chattanooga. And how I was advancing in the job, getting paid well, and making my way financially. But how—though I worked with wonderful people—this job didn't cut it for me. How staring all day at two stark computer screens and answering the phone to angry customers demanding higher benefits wasn't my dream.

My dream was to travel and write books. To explore and tell the tale. Instead, I was sitting eight hours a day, five days a week, in a stuffy box with no windows—the only sound in that airless space the shrill and ceaseless phone.

I was suffocating in there and turning too numb to feel it, tricked by what society called my success. Then the New Year rolled in, and I soon turned twenty-five. I've lived a quarter of my life, I thought. Twenty-five percent of it.

That's when it struck me like a harsh bell. Life—my precious life—existed like a still, hollow shell.

So, I decided to do something about it. I decided to make a change. To fill that shell up with a creature of zeal. Having grown up hiking and camping with my parents and two younger siblings in places like the Blue Ridge, Appalachian, and Great Smoky Mountains, I viewed the outdoors as a second home and decided to go on a thru-hike, choosing the PCT in order to pluck myself from my asphyxiating box and place myself on the ridges of some of the grandest mountains in America, where no matter where I turned, my world would be wide open.

I knew the West offered this, because I had moved to Colorado in 2012 after receiving my bachelor's degree in creative writing at the university in Chattanooga. I did the ski-bum thing for a winter, working as a waitress and lift-ticket girl who lived in shoddy employee housing and who skied down the dazzling Aspen Mountain on my lunch break every day.

This season in my life shot me to the highest level of the great outdoors I had yet attained. And it served as the kindling for my desire to hike the PCT when one sunny day, a coworker at the ticket office told me he'd hiked a portion of it before winding up in Aspen.

"And it brought me fantastically to life," he'd said of the trail.

These words went with me when I moved back to Chattanooga the following summer. I wasn't sure what to do, which was how I ended up in my corporate box: my safe little stall. As I worked, I lived at home to save money. For what, I didn't know—until my twenty-fifth birthday flashed by, and that idea of life on the PCT started consuming my mind.

I can actually do this, I thought one January morning at work. I can actually quit my job and go do something amazing, something I really want to do.

Walk among the wild.

As a birthday gift to myself, I bought *Yogi's Pacific Crest Trail Handbook*—the hefty forty-dollar guide referred to by hikers as the bible of the PCT. From that point on, I woke hours before work in the early morning darkness, brewed a big cup of coffee, and sat at my writing spot at the kitchen table (next to the window with a sunrise view) to prepare.

With highlighter in hand and laptop at arm's length, I determined when I should leave for the trail, which direction I should walk, what to put in my pack, and what to wear from head to feet. I studied how to train for twenty-mile days and how to fuel my body accordingly—with one liter of water every four miles and four thousand calories a day with foods like tuna, granola, nuts, pasta, chocolate, jerky, and beans. I learned what towns to resupply in and by what method: either at the general stores or by mailing prepackaged boxes of food to the post offices I'd pass along the way. I tracked the desert water and Sierra snow reports and analyzed thru-hiking logistics, like how to hike in hundred-degree SoCal heat (ideally at morning and dusk, resting midday in the shade), and how to hike in High Sierra snow (with ice axe, crampons, and careful steps), and how to hike in town (by sticking out a thumb).

The months went by, and I discovered more, like how to properly poop in the woods by digging a seven-inch hole two hundred feet off the trail and packing out my sullied toilet paper every single time. I read up on rain gear, repair kits, and water purification systems—for quality was essential, yet every ounce I'd carry mattered on a long-distance hike. I learned where in the Sierra I'd need to carry a bear canister—a bulky container with a locking lid designed to keep bears out of food. I memorized leave-no-trace practices, like camping on durable surfaces and leaving my site looking untouched. Furthermore, I read about the diarrheal results from ingesting giardia—the parasite found in fecal-infested water. And I studied how to identify the alluring yet poisonous poodle-dog bush—the purple-flower shrub in Southern California infamous for inflicting blistering rashes and even respiratory distress upon those who touched this pungent plant.

My rigorous research persisted, and I confirmed the indispensable value of duct tape, bandanas, safety pins, and the Ziploc bag.

But the most important thing I confirmed from the eye-straining, mind-draining, soul-enriching research was this: I could do it. I could hike the PCT.

Thus, after work, I began to physically prepare by hiking a rugged, two-mile grade up Lookout Mountain that was deceptively called the Kiddie Trail. With each paycheck, I purchased the gear I needed from local outfitters as well as from REI online. I already owned my backpack, tent, and sleeping bag, which I'd bought while living in Colorado to backpack within the Rockies. Now, I was working with what I had to design the lightest, most durable, most effective way to pack, seeking answers to questions like: Should I carry cash or credit with my ID? Should I brush my teeth with toothpaste or tooth powder? Should I dig a hole with a trowel or trekking pole when it came time to poop?

My preparation was demanding. Just thinking about it wore me out further as I now sat amid all I had worked for. However, Crunchmaster's question wasn't about my preparation but something deeper: the why behind my journey.

I remembered feeling scared the day I handed in my two-week notice—like a child riding her bike without training wheels for the first time. This seals the deal, I'd thought, the great unknown of the PCT opening before me once I quit my stable job.

I'd either crash or soar.

But why this route? Why renounce something secure for something so far away and feral?

I knew.

It was because I had made that job my life. As one who always strove for excellence in whatever I was doing, I let that job rule my days as the telephone screamed on, demanding my total submission. But that job was no life, no loving master. Rather, that job was a cell slowly smothering my soul. And if I didn't break out, it would have been only a matter of time before it dimmed my soul completely. If I continued to work my way, year after year, toward retirement from that job in which I never felt a deep, resounding calling, it would have been only a matter of time.

The PCT was my calling.

The PCT would free me, open my way to a quest.

But a quest for what?

"Life," I told my fellow Chattanoogans as the sunset lit up the sky. "I'm hiking the PCT for life, all for life, and nothing else."

CHAPTER 3

GODSPEED

The rosy sky had darkened to indigo by the time Kinetic joined our powwow in the field.

"Small trail," he said when he learned that Crunchmaster, too, came from the land of the Southeast.

Crunchmaster stood and placed his hands on his hips. "And our tribe shall be called the Four-two-threes!" he proclaimed, naming us after Chattanooga's area code.

The boys left to check out the various events going on, like the talk on the PCT's geology. I returned to my tent, lathered Neosporin onto my new blisters, and fell sound asleep. The next morning, I awoke aching but eager to get back on the trail. I reconvened with the Four-two-threes beneath the gray clouds for coffee and oatmeal at a picnic table in the field. Several vendors had taken over the space, selling things like backpacks, stuff sacks, and dehydrated meals. To avoid the crowd of shoppers, after a second round of coffee, the Four-two-threes and I walked to Lake Morena Grocery—the burger joint and convenience store up the road a quarter mile. There, Tortoise and Kinetic, whose stomachs were bottomless pits, ordered milkshakes and burgers to eat outside on the front porch.

I took a seat in a white plastic chair next to Crunchmaster at the patio table, enthralled by the old man on the nearby curb playing his didgeridoo. It was the first time I'd ever heard the wooden wind instrument, which resembled a mammoth's ivory tusk. Its profound bellows seeped inside my sore flesh like a deep massage.

"It's beautiful," I said, turning to Crunchmaster.

"Really," he said, as captivated as I was.

Back at the campground, the female voices in the bathhouse echoed against the cold tiles as I took what was called a navy shower—a bathing method for conserving water. The sign in the stall instructed hikers to wash this way due to the drought. First, I turned on the water in the cave-like hollow to rinse off my naked self. Next, I shut the water off, soaped up, and then turned the water back on to wash away the suds. I dried off with a bandana, reading the laminated paper tacked up next to the navy shower bathing rules.

"Watch your thoughts; they become your words. Watch your words; they become your actions. Watch your actions; they become your character. Watch your character; it becomes your destiny," the paper read.

Destiny. I pondered this powerful facet of life as I wrung out my sopping hair into the drain. It was something I believed in as much as one's power to choose. And it was destiny, I knew, just as much as choice that had led me to where I was now. It was the combination of fate and action that had put me on this track.

The kickoff would continue one more day, but I packed up that afternoon to leave Lake Morena. I was eager to get going. Eager to be on my way. As I collapsed my tent and stuffed everything inside my pack, the Four-two-threes practically begged me to stay, using the fact that it looked like rain as a good excuse for me to hunker down for another night.

But it was time for me to move on, and that was what I said.

They gave me brotherly hugs and wished me Godspeed.

"Who knows, maybe I'll catch up to you guys," I said.

This was unlikely, though. After the kickoff, the Four-two-threes would get rides back to where they'd left off on the trail. Because they were many miles ahead of me, we all knew we'd probably never cross paths again this trip.

Nevertheless, the faces of all three—Tortoise, Kinetic, and Crunchmaster—brightened when I said this.

"We hope!" they exclaimed as I walked through the field to the trail.

⊷⊷

It was nightfall when I arrived at Boulder Oaks Campground six miles past Lake Morena. It was about to rain, so I rushed to set up camp at my sandy site across from two other hikers, refill my water containers at the nearby spigot, and make a pasta dinner on my camp stove at the picnic table beside my tent.

After dinner, I rinsed my food pot and brushed my teeth several feet away from where I'd sleep, a method for keeping wildlife from sniffing around my camp. Then I replaced all the items I didn't need for bed in my backpack, laid that under my rainfly vestibule, and nestled inside my tent. With the sun gone, the desert air was cold. But the thermals I wore as pajamas and my feather-filled sleeping bag warmed me. Huddled within the down like a caterpillar in a cocoon, I pressed my headlamp on to review the water report I'd obtained the day before at Scout and Frodo's. Both trail angels and hikers updated the logistical spreadsheet online daily, revealing which mile markers had running-water sources either on or near the trail. I read that the next reliable source from where I was wouldn't come until Burnt Rancheria Campground at mile 42, sixteen miles ahead. This meant I needed to carry four liters of water the next day to ensure I'd have enough between founts.

Damn, that's nine added pounds, I thought as I turned off my headlamp, considering the blisters that now bubbled on both my feet and how the weight of my pack disturbed them.

The sky spat raindrops onto my tent before throwing down a steady pour. The deep croaks of toads would have serenaded me to sleep had it not rained all night, making my nylon rainfly sound like a waving piece of foil. It continued to rain in the morning, making me think as I emerged from my soggy tent, Whoever said there was a drought in the desert lied.

I boiled water for instant coffee in the dirt beneath my vestibule and then slowly sipped the hot morning drink from my cook pot, savoring its comfort before slipping my rain jacket on over my clothes and breaking down camp in the wet cold.

Not a sliver of sun graced the trail that day, only fog and the incessant drizzle. However, in the morning, I had the muddied path to myself, and there was something beautiful—mystical—about the mountains I climbed encased by the cool mist. Surrounding me were lush green peaks and white-flowered slopes that could only be seen every few minutes when the wind momentarily wiped away the gray. I hiked up the slippery ridge, rising to 6,000 feet in elevation over the course of the day.

The dripping beauty of where I was distracted me for a time. But by noon, the blisters on my heels and toes flamed like a fire that the rain just couldn't put out.

Relief came at mile 30, at the trail crossing on Kitchen Creek Road. As I entered the gravel pull-off where the trail shot me out, I saw a parked car and some hikers bunched beneath a beach umbrella, all sitting in folding chairs.

"Welcome to the Kitchen Creek trail magic station!" cried a man wearing a royal-blue baseball cap and mustard-yellow poncho as I walked over. "And please help yourself!"

Beneath the umbrella, I took a seat in the last available chair and gazed at the goodies in the blue cooler at my feet. Cheese, salami, strawberries, and white wine arose from the ice for the taking.

I followed the lead of the other hikers and stuck my hand in the cooler for some food. The man who had made this trail magic happen said his name was Phil. I spoke with him as I ate several slices of salami I'd wrapped with Swiss followed by a handful of the sweet and juicy strawberries. Phil said he lived in the area and had hiked this section of trail many times.

"I'd love to do the whole thing one day, but I can't right now because of my three-year-old boy at home. So, I live vicariously through you all. Try to dish out the magic where I can. I mean, it's just so rewarding to see you people this happy over cheese."

"Thank you," I said, washing down my lunch with a swig of wine. "This is only my third day out here, but this means so much."

I used this break to take off my shoes and socks and doctor my blisters with Neosporin, Band-Aids, and, for added protection, duct tape. My socks were wet, which wasn't helping my wounds. I rummaged through my pack for a dry pair, slid them on, and shortly got on my way.

"Safe journey!" Phil called as I crossed Kitchen Creek Road to reconnect to the trail.

"Thanks again for the cheese!" I said, delighted by his pure benevolence.

The rest of the day's walk wound through a forest of scented pines, where fat pine cones textured the ground and yellow-hooded orioles swept from branch to soaking branch. The rain subsided in the evening when I reached the microscopic town of Mount Laguna where the Burnt Rancheria Campground resided. Without setting up camp, I marched straight from the campground a small way down Sunrise Highway to Pine House Café and Tavern.

Inside the log-cabin restaurant, a cheerful fire crackled in the stone fireplace in the foyer. I unstrapped my damp pack and set it along with my trekking poles next to the others by the fire. In the dining room, I joined the cluster of slouching hikers, who sat with fatigue on their faces as they chewed their dinner at the long, communal table. I sank into a wooden chair, exhausted like the rest, conjuring enough energy to order a burger and fries before falling silent to the hushing weariness in my bones.

No one else said too much, either.

We simply sat in quiet camaraderie and ate.

A man wearing a white cowboy hat and standing before the bear hide that hung on the back wall played gentle tunes on his acoustic guitar. The soft songs nearly sent me to sleep as soon as I finished my meal. I snapped awake, however, when a boy just starting to sprout a blond mustache took a seat next to me and asked, "Did you hear about the big storm coming in?"

"No," I said. "What storm?"

"I was just at the outfitters down the street. Some locals said that tonight and tomorrow call for a giant storm not far up the trail. Sixty-mile-per-hour winds, they said. Shit, that's near hurricane status. They said hikers should stake out here until it passes."

"Wow," I said. "Scary. Thanks for the beta."

I left the tavern after paying my bill and returned to Burnt Rancheria. A large, grassy lot had been designated for thru-hikers to camp at a cost of $2.50 a night. The lot was next to the bathrooms and coin-operated showers. I pitched my tent on a patch of dirt away from the pines—my deliberate stab at not getting crushed in the event the wind grew so fierce that it knocked over trees. The storm was building, I could tell. The clouds were filling like water balloons as they dashed across the sky. I grabbed my soap and thermals and then ran to the camp host's RV to exchange some dollars for quarters.

"I'd hunker down in the bathrooms tonight if the storm gets too bad," the old man advised as he filled my hands with coins.

It cost me two dollars for an eight-minute shower, and it was worth every cent. I watched the sand and dirt that had caked my calves and feet over the last twenty-two miles run into the drain as the steaming water soothed my sores and cricks. It would be a long, rainy, cold, and windy night. But in the heat and rejuvenation of the shower as the eight minutes ticked by, I didn't care.

All was well within those eight minutes.

CHAPTER 4

AND THE WINDS, THEY RAGED

It was a turbulent night. The wind shook my tent like an angry man and made the aluminum pole propping up my shelter creak like fragile bones. I hardly slept. Leaving my tent up and zipping my backpack inside it, I ambled down the highway to Laguna Mountain Sport and Supply early in the cloud-covered morning to restock on stove fuel. As I shuffled through the shop, the female clerk at the cluttered outfitters asked me how I'd fared in the windstorm.

"Fine," I said. "A little freaked out at times throughout the night, but all in all, okay."

Checking out, I asked her what the weather looked like for the day.

"The storm's supposed to ramp up again this afternoon, but if you're wanting to hit the trail, you're safe to hike the next four and a half miles to Laguna Campground. There's tree cover the whole way on that stretch. But don't go any farther after that. It turns into a bare ridge."

Good, I thought. I can go a little way today, at least.

Having other errands to run before leaving town, I walked across the glossy, wet street from the outfitters to Laguna Mountain Lodge and Store. I needed to resupply on food. A few other hikers were already there, shopping at the general store that catered specifically to their dry-goods needs. I grabbed a basket at the front door and then stopped at the counter next to the cashier to sign the red composition notebook serving as the trail registry. "Claire Henley," I wrote, adding the date, "April 25, 2015." Some of the hikers who'd signed it before me had left little funny or inspirational notes. I thought up one to write, too, scribbling it below my name: "The world is not a home, but a path."

Next, I rummaged through the ripped hiker box beside me on the floor. This was like a thrift store consolidated into a cardboard box (or crate or bin) where hikers could donate food and gear they didn't want or need anymore for other hikers to freely claim. I snagged two unopened and slightly smashed Blueberry Crisp Clif Bars, placed them in my basket, and then scanned the aisles. Foods like Knorr Pasta Sides, Peter Pan Crunchy Peanut Butter, packets of StarKist Tuna, flour tortillas, Pop-Tarts, almonds, and Snickers chocolate bars progressively filled my basket. To my dismay, everything was double the price it would have been at a normal grocery store, which didn't exist in this secluded hub of San Diego County.

Ironic.

Now that I was making no money, I was spending more on food than ever before.

Back at the campground, I consolidated my processed nutrition for the next sixty-eight miles into airtight Ziploc bags, refilled my water, and broke down camp. With everything I owned balanced on my back, I returned to the Pine House Café and Tavern for one last real-world meal before my five-day sweep beyond society.

Hikers clustered inside the restaurant, a safe haven in which to wait out the looming storm. The only seat open at the long, communal table was at its head. So, I sat there after removing my pack, regarding everyone, whose heads were bent as they read their menus. Everyone except the boy in the bright-blue shirt sitting at the opposite head. He stared at me like a direct ray of sunshine as soon as I plopped down. That's that guy from Scout and Frodo's, I thought. The one with the duffel bag. I returned his blazing gaze for a second before averting my eyes, the reality of staring starkly at a stranger searing them.

"Good, you made it. Now we can begin," he called to me down the table, his voice calm and smooth.

The head-bowed hikers looked up.

Begin what? I wondered. Who is this guy?

I forced myself to observe him. His skin was the color of bronze, and he had platinum-blond hair. The white light streaming through the window beside him accentuated his muscular forearms and made him appear to glow.

"Sorry I was late," I coyly replied.

He nodded.

I opened my menu.

A stressed-out, pear-shaped waitress took my order. By the time my barbecued chicken sandwich and side salad came out, I had learned that every hiker at the communal table planned to stay in town until the storm passed. The boy in the bright-blue shirt said he'd splurged on renting a cabin at Laguna Mountain Lodge because the forecast called for torrential rain. The hut could hold up to six people. He said he'd already rounded up four others to split the cost with him. "That makes five hikers who'll be there tonight so far," he calculated. Then he asked me from across the table to be number six.

I thought it over as I wrote out a tip on my credit card slip, tempted to avoid the storm altogether in the cozy cabin that, the boy said, came with a fireplace.

But something deep inside urged me to move on. I couldn't say what. All I knew was that I was on a journey now. I desired to keep going.

"No, thanks," I told the boy a second time when he caught up to me outside the restaurant to ask again if I wanted to stay at the lodge. Now that he stood by my side, I clearly saw how handsome he was. He was a foot taller than me and strong, with rugged facial features and sandy stubble that evenly covered his prominent jaw. His eyes were watercolor blue—similar to mine, but milkier.

He smiled when I shot down his offer, revealing his two shadowy dimples, one carved within the peak of each cheek.

"Maybe I'll see you up the trail then," he said, fitting his full-brimmed hat to his head.

"You never know," I said.

And we walked our separate ways.

⚓

The wind grew mad on the trail, kicking up dirt and thrashing branches. Maybe I should've stayed back, I thought worriedly when the rain began firing down like bullets. I only had three miles left to go before reaching the next campground. And because the tunnel of trees I walked through shielded me from the wind, I kept on.

But two miles later, things got very bad. The trees opened to a high and exposed ridge—the type of terrain I should have verified on my map after the outfitter's clerk told me this stretch was solid trees. Standing on the edge of the woodland wall and facing the bare, black doom ahead, I could actually see the wind as it whipped up with tremendous force, crashing over the ridge in heavy gray torrents like lethal rogue waves.

I took a deep breath and stepped onto the ridge. The wind struck me on my side, and I stumbled near the drop-off, where it kept beating me as if we were at war.

I sprinted back into the forest and yanked out my map. Why didn't I review this back in town? I berated myself. The pictured topography clearly showed that this short stretch included an uncovered ridge.

I cursed myself for being so naïve. For believing the clerk without a doubt.

I traced my finger on my map. It revealed a spot big enough for one tent at a place called Foster Point a half-mile ahead. I weighed my options. I could either go back the three and a half miles I had just hiked to Mount Laguna, or I could risk the small distance to the site.

"Keep going. Keep going," a voice inside me said.

I listened, charging the dark, windy ridge with my head ducked down, stabbing my trekking poles into the trail to steady my every step.

It was woman against the wild. I wondered as I walked if I'd make it out of the battle alive.

At Foster Point, there were no trees in sight, and the wind still raged like a god unleashing his wrath. I'll be blown off this mountain if I camp here, came the realization, and I wished with all my heart that I'd turned back when I'd had the chance.

"God, help me!" I cried, not knowing what to do.

A violent gust of wind forced me to look down at the trail.

My heart stopped.

Written in the sand at my feet were my directions.

"Hike On!" read the bold inscription.

And so I did.

Several yards later, the trail descended the ridge and then shot back within the shelter of the safeguarding trees. I saw a headlamp shining not far ahead through the shadowy forest, assuring me that the Laguna Campground was close.

"Thank you, Jesus!" I said through a heavy exhale when I stepped off the trail onto the road, welcomed by the entrance sign to tonight's home.

Although it was late afternoon, it was as dark as midnight when I staggered into the storm-torn site for thru-hikers. The rain and wind persevered as a timeworn man named Velcro helped me throw up my tent next to his. The other tents around us rattled, weighed down by the hunkered bodies inside. Velcro was still outside, he said, because he'd arrived mere minutes before me.

"I saw your headlamp through the trees. The light gave me hope to continue," I yelled over the storm's boom as we rushed to stake in my tent.

"I never had my headlamp on," Velcro shouted. "And there wasn't anyone out here when I got in."

I shuddered.

"But I know I saw a light."

"Maybe it was an angel," the old man voiced. "They're real, you know."

We double-anchored my tent with rocks.

"Thank you for your help," I cried as Velcro scurried inside his tent.

"That's what we hikers do!" he called through his trembling tarp.

Soaking wet, I zipped myself up in my shelter, stripped off my clothes, and burrowed deep within my sleeping bag. I went to bed without dinner, miraculously falling asleep amid the furious wind and rain that roared like maniacs all night.

But before the gentle arms of slumber cradled me, I remembered my saving light.

Maybe it was an angel, I thought. Maybe…it was God.

CHAPTER 5
BATTLE OF THE BLISTERS

The early morning bequeathed quiet and calm. I poked my head out of my tent while it was still dark. Stars flooded the cloudless sky—a dazzling relief that augured well for the day to come.

I boiled a cup of coffee, drank it down, and then boiled another cup. The storm had passed, and I had made it through.

"Thank you, God," I whispered.

Everything I owned was wet. At sunrise, I surfaced into the day wearing my running shorts and blue short-sleeved shirt and spread my backpack, sleeping bag, white shirt, and pants on the nearby stumps and branches to dry. Velcro had already cleared out, along with most of the other hikers. One man was still there, scattering his saturated gear on the site's picnic table, wearing nothing but a camera around his neck and a makeshift kilt fashioned out of a tatty gray tarp.

He looked middle-aged—short and dark with a hairy chest, and he had curly black hair that stuck up from his head as if he'd been electrocuted. We struck up a conversation, and I found out he was an artist from Oakland who went by the trail name Splat.

"Neat name," I said. "Who came up with it?"

"I did, man," he replied, his voice smooth and cool.

"Huh. What's the significance?"

"Well, nothing, I guess. It's the name of the main character in my comic, the place where I—or rather Splat—can call out all the bullshit in our world and get away with it."

I shifted my sleeping bag onto the next stump over, which was now in the sun's spotlight.

"What do you mean? What kind of bullshit?"

Splat lifted his chin to the beautiful sun and closed his chestnut eyes.

"I'm sure you know," he said, keeping his face pointed up. "You must know, if you're out *here.*"

Interesting, I thought. The bullshit in our world. The lies we believe about what it means to live—like making lots of money in order to quench our deepest desires through bought stuff, thus complacently ticking off one day after the next while never fully being satisfied and always longing for more.

"Is that why you're out here, then?" I said. "To escape from it?" I was referring to the bullshit—the way of life we were brainwashed to live that was really just a bunch of phony and hype.

"Partially." He laughed. "Mostly, it's because I'm between jobs. I design sets and create special graphics for the film industry. But I don't have any movies lined up. Hiking the PCT seemed like the right thing to do in the interim. I love nature, man. Draw a lot of inspiration from it. And coming on this trail, seeing California—the state I've lived in my whole life—in this new light just kind of worked out. Some might say it was meant to be."

He shook the water off his tent and wrung out his clothes.

"A godfather of a storm last night, huh?" Splat remarked. "Were you okay?"

"I think so," I said, laughing. "I should've just hunkered down in Mount Laguna like everyone else. Would've saved me some stress."

"I don't know, man. When I was getting water down by the pit toilets earlier, the camp host came by and told me a bunch of hikers ran for Pine House Café last night. Apparently the storm got so rough the restaurant opened its doors. People were sleeping under the tables." He looked me in the eyes. "I can't believe you hiked through it, though. You deserve the trail name Badass."

"More like Dumbass," I said, and Splat ripped a lion's roar of a laugh, tossing his black mane back.

"But thank you," I said, laughing along. "Not sure Badass quite fits me, though."

"Oh, yeah? Well, that's what I'll know you by, at least."

Splat packed up and left while I let my things continue to dry. Meanwhile, I reviewed my map and determined to hike to the on-trail tent site at mile 64, seventeen miles ahead. I was now at an elevation of 6,000 feet. The day's hike would drop me to 3,500.

With an almost dry pack suspended from my shoulders—wet socks and bandanas safety-pinned to the outside—I began my day of travel. It was midmorning, and I immediately felt the sting of my blisters as I walked along in my wet boots. Fortunately, the trail offered a jaunt through the colors and scents of purple nightshade, Indian paintbrush, and California poppies that for a time directed my thoughts to beauty over pain.

Then the desert took over, and cracked ridges dominated the path, the sun spilling down like lava, my feet simmering to a boil.

When the sun was directly above me, I came upon a collection of red and yellow rocks in the middle of the trail. I stopped and read what they spelled out. Mile 50. Not bad, I thought. Fifty miles down. It was my first major milestone on the PCT and the farthest I'd ever walked in one trip. I beheld the colorful rocks, drinking the moment in and summoning a line from Luci Shaw—one of my favorite poets—to my lips: "My blood has drunk color from the stones as if it were the meal I needed."

I chanted these words to myself over the next three miles as blood built up in my blisters. For lunch, I paused at the Pioneer Mail Picnic Area right off the trail, where a hiker I'd met at Pine House Café sat reading a book in the sliver of Cleveland National Forest's sparse yet delicious shade.

His name was Lancelot—a young guy with a bandana-wrapped head and unusually long fingers folded around his psychological thriller. I sat down in the dull grass next to him and removed my boots and socks, the blisters on the back of my heels and the ones puffing out from my toes bulging with light-orange liquid and burning to the touch.

Lancelot noticed my foot injuries, closed his paperback, and said, "It's time."

"Time for what?" I asked, a tremor in my voice.

"Time to pop those nasty pests."

"How do you know?"

"Because I've been there. I actually got my trail name because I've"—he paused for effect—"lanced a lot of blisters."

Gross, I thought to myself before asking him, "How many?"

"Thirty-five. On the Colorado Trail last summer."

"You got thirty-five blisters?" I asked, gazing down at my four, horrified at the prospect of acquiring more.

"But they all went away after I performed the necessary surgery that yours, I can see, now need."

My blisters hurt so badly that I figured I had nothing to lose. I rummaged through my first-aid kit and pulled out the sewing needle. A mixture of blood and ooze gushed down my soles once I'd poked each swollen boil with the silver barb. A burning sensation like salt being rubbed into raw flesh followed.

Fuck! I wanted to yell. This fucking hurts, Lancelot!

But I bit my lip and took the scorching pain.

Within a minute, the burning shrank to a faint pricking sensation. I applied Neosporin to the frayed flesh, bandaged the wounds with the moleskin I'd bought in Mount Laguna, and eased my socks and shoes back on.

"Your feet will kill for the rest of the day, but those blisters should turn to calluses by tomorrow," Lancelot said.

Great, I thought sarcastically. Thanks for telling me ahead of time.

I had twelve miles left to hike. Had I known how true Lancelot's prophecy would be, I would have waited until camp that night to pop my blisters.

For the rest of the afternoon, I walked on the balls of my feet, tiptoeing down the mountain like a bandy-legged bird so as not to put any pressure on my throbbing lesions. When I reached the tent site at sunset, I couldn't have been more relieved. It was an open field located in a verdant valley within pale, rising peaks. Purple clouds swept over as I set up my tent near the edge of the grass, away from the others who were gathered on the logs around the unlit fire ring (as Southern California had a fire ban in effect because of the drought), talking backpacking gear and food.

The traveling nurse Liz was among the group. I had crossed paths with her more than once, the last time right before I left Mount Laguna. She ran over to me as I blew up my sleeping pad to see how I'd managed in the monstrous storm.

"It was crazy, but I made it through," I said. "Now my *real* problem is these damn blisters."

Having already changed into my airy camp sandals, I peeled back the moleskin to show Liz—who had been trail-named Saltlick for her finger-licking love of all salty foods—the sloppy damage.

To my dismay, I found that the blisters hadn't calloused but had returned, fully loaded and ready to fight.

"It's normal for them to keep coming back," Saltlick said. She then advised me to keep popping the pussy beasts and nursing them with Neosporin until they went away.

Later that night, I made instant mashed potatoes for dinner, which I ate on a log in the company of the hikers, sitting next to a happy-eyed, energetic female who went by the trail name Pandora. She was a few years older than me, tall and muscular with sun-streaked hair and navy eyes, wearing shorts and a fitted periwinkle top beneath her black down jacket. Saltlick, who sat across from us on the ground, said she'd paired up with

Pandora in Mount Laguna, naming her after the online radio station because she tended to burst out in song throughout the day.

Pandora, I could tell right away, was the type who'd tell you like it is. When I showed her my blisters, she said flat out, "You need to go a size up in your shoes."

"How can you tell?" I asked, since at that point I wasn't wearing my boots.

"Oh, you know," she said in her Iowan accent, "that's generally why thru-hikers get blisters. That's what made me get them last summer on the John Muir Trail. I was wearing the same size shoe I always do, and my feet got destroyed."

"Huh. Do you know why that is?"

"Oh, yeah. Because your feet swell when you're walking all day, so if you're wearing shoes that normally fit, they're going to become too small, causing your heels and toes to rub against them like it looks like yours have. But going up one size fixes that," she nodded vigorously.

"Something to consider," I said, scrutinizing my charred feet. "My boots *are* my normal size."

I stuck with Saltlick and Pandora the next day, my blisters ablaze as if the iron-hot ground were branding them with each step. The sun consumed the sky, roasting every ounce of air as we walked deeper and deeper into the vastness of the baking desert. Those we passed said they planned to hitchhike into Julian once they reached Scissors Crossing—a distinguished junction on the trail where Highway 78 and County Road S2 intersected. Known for San Diego County's 1870 gold rush, Julian was located twelve miles off the PCT down the highway. Word on the trail was that the local bakery, Mom's Pies, served a free slice of apple pie to every thru-hiker who stopped in. All you had to do was show your PCT permit, and voilà! You got pie.

This sounded fantastic. I was wounded, and now, after walking all day in a draining, hot abyss, I was hungry too. Pie would make things better. Oh, yes...free pie.

But Saltlick had other plans, saying as we approached Scissors Crossing at mile 77 that she had read in her guidebook about a place called Stagecoach Trails RV Resort, located four miles off-trail in the opposite direction from Julian.

"It has cheap lodging, laundry facilities, showers, and a pool!" she advertised. "A desert oasis, and everyone else is going to town. I bet we'd have it all to ourselves."

"What about the pie?" I asked, honestly concerned.

"No pie that I know of. But there's ice cream."

I weighed my options. Ice cream by the pool, or pie in a confined space filled with hiker stench...

"I vote RV resort," Pandora said.

"Me, too," I said. "That actually sounds amazing."

A handful of hikers stood on the side of the highway, thumbs raised as they fished for a hitch westward. Pandora, Saltlick, and I walked across the desolate road to go east, making this my first-ever hitchhiking experience.

The road before us was silent and empty. Nevertheless, a minute after we'd perched ourselves in hitch position, a pickup truck came up and stopped.

"Stagecoach Trails?" the Latino driver asked, having rolled down his window.

"That's us!" Pandora said.

The driver motioned us to hop into the back.

We kept our packs on as we squeezed next to each other in the bed of the work truck crowded with tools. The wind blew through my greasy hair as the driver transported us to the RV park. As Saltlick had predicted, we were the only ones there—except for Splat, of all people, who was eating an ice-cream sundae on the front porch of the main office when we arrived.

Painted props resembling stagecoaches were parked throughout the deserted grounds. A group of matronly women wearing bonnets and long prairie dresses ran the park. After we'd paid for a saloon-style cabin, one of these women showed us to the hiker box in the women's bathroom, where a wide variety of hotel toiletries were stashed.

"Please wash up first if you intend to use the pool," the woman said, eyeing my grimy fingernails and dirt-splotched shirt.

Splat, Pandora, Saltlick, and I shared the cabin— essentially a shack with four twin beds priced at forty dollars a night. We bathed in the bathhouses and then combined our rancid laundry into one load before lounging by the pool in sports bras and shorts—the crude kilt for Splat—as the sun went down. The washing machine in the utility room worked overtime.

I licked my mint-chocolate-chip ice cream and read from the Steven King novel I'd grabbed from the library shelf in the main office, all while soaking my battered feet in the wonderfully cold pool. Like Pandora had recommended, I would buy a new pair of boots one size up the next time I got into a legitimate town.

But for now, with the power of the pool and a clean pair of socks on the way, my brutal blisters had met their match.

CHAPTER 6

THE TRAIL-NAME CHRISTENING

"Need a ride back to the trail?" the shaggy-haired, tie-dye-shirted driver of a red minivan asked us as we walked along the side of County Road S2.

It was the morning after our RV-park stay, and although Splat had slept in, Pandora, Saltlick, and I awoke before the main office opened to get back on the trail. A hitch hadn't looked promising. We'd waited on the side of the vacant road for several minutes before deciding to hike the four miles back to the PCT. That's when the red van appeared from over the asphalt horizon, driving in the direction opposite to where we needed to go.

We shot up our thumbs anyway as the van passed, jumping for joy when it stopped a little beyond us and turned around.

After confirming the driver's question with a resounding yes, he hit a button that opened the automatic side doors.

"Name's Devil Fish," the driver said after we crawled in the van and he started coasting down the road, his long red hair waving out the window.

"Oh!" Pandora exclaimed, excited yet perplexed. "Are you a hiker too?"

Devil Fish took a sip from a can of Red Bull. "Last year I was," he said. "This year, I'm paying forward all the trail-angeling I got when I was on the trail. I mean, if it hadn't been for my trail angels, I would've found myself stranded time after time on lone highway roads, just like you three looked to be back there." He laughed. "So, anyway, I've been following the bubble since the kickoff, giving rides to hikers when I can."

"Aw," Pandora said. "Your name should be changed to Angel Fish."

"It should!" agreed Saltlick and I.

Devil Fish flashed us a smile in the rearview mirror. "You know the rules. Once your trail name finds you, there's no changing it. It becomes just as real as your real name. It becomes part of who you are."

He pulled over at the trailhead, let us out, and wished us well before driving on to Julian to round up more hikers.

The sun had already burned away the crisp morning air as we took to the trail, stepping into the granite mountains of the San Felipe Valley. Feeling rejuvenated from last night's rest, I set a solid pace, hiked ahead of Saltlick and Pandora, and soon caught up to the hiker named Flaco—a gangly man with fine brown hair and Appalachian Trail emblems sewn to the army-green canvas of his long sleeves. I had run into Flaco a couple of times since starting the trail but hadn't spoken to him yet. As with most hikers I'd met and conversed with on the trail, this gnarled-faced man instantly dove beneath the superficial surface of small talk and into the depths of his life as we hiked toward the naked sun, dodging the flowering cacti and skirting the rocky edges of steep cliffs.

Flaco was a farmer from South Carolina. He stopped on the trail to show me his earth-stained hands. "That's how I got my name. Not through hiking or nothing. The Mexicans I work with always call me that. Flaco. Means skinny. When I did the AT for the first time, I just stuck with it," he said with a familiar southern drawl.

"How many times have you hiked the AT?" I asked.

In answer, Flaco said, "I used to be married. To a beautiful woman I loved, and we had a beautiful daughter. We were happy, I thought. But then my wife left me for someone who made more money. Took our daughter with her. That's when I hiked the AT for the first time, about twenty years ago or so. I've hiked it two more times since then, which is why I'm on the PCT. For a change of scenery."

"Where's your daughter?"

"I don't know," Flaco said, the pain of this truth cutting short his words. "I don't know. We hardly speak. She's twenty-eight now. Twenty-eight. You know, you remind me of her. Brave but kind. Last time I saw her was in a photograph she mailed me. She's so beautiful. My girl." Flaco wiped his eyes. "I keep her picture and return address in my breast pocket. I want to send her a letter. But I'm scared."

I waited a moment before sensitively suggesting, "Maybe you could start with a postcard. When we get to Warner Springs? I know, for me, writing down my thoughts always brings peace."

"I could do that," Flaco said. "That's something I could do."

And, as if eager to connect with his daughter, he picked up his pace, quite literally leaving me in the dust.

I didn't mind. I was glad to be alone, to have the trail to myself for a while as I walked along the mountain's crest through fields of white boulders and red anthills, among green hummingbirds sucking nectar from cacti and yellow spotted lizards sunning on the trail. There was no breeze, and the sun was high. Sweat flowed from my every pore. The wild bushes and scraggly cacti growing in spurts up the path offered zero shade. At least my white collared shirt shielded my torso and arms from the roasting rays. But my uncovered hands were getting fried. Nothing blocked them from the sun. They cooked to a blackened crisp.

At mile 91, I unlocked and passed through the third gate in a wire fence built to keep cattle in. I had already entered through the first and second gates and was thrilled to achieve the third, as it was known among the trail community for its generous water cache.

Typically stocked at road crossings, water caches were unnatural water sources stashed by trail angels on the long stretches of trail that were notorious for being dry. For this span in particular, thirty miles extended from mile 68 before another natural water source would spring up. Thus, water caches were godsends because they broke up the arid haul and allowed hikers to re-supply sooner on water. However, because they were un-natural, they were not to be relied upon because they depleted over time if no one replenished them. And when you were on the trail—outside society and cell phone service—you had no way of knowing if someone had maintained a water cache until you got there to see for yourself.

The Third Gate Water Cache was the exception: of all the caches I'd come across, this would be the only one I'd trust to be there because of the unmatched fame it had received as a solid source.

A split wooden sign beyond the gate read "Water" in white lettering with an arrow pointing down a steep dirt side trail. I set my pack down next to the low-lying junipers across from the sign and pulled out my emp-ty water bottles. The path to the cache was at least a quarter-mile long and led to a rugged dirt road, where

I spied a bright-blue tarp draped over a big, boxy structure against some scraggly trees near the side of the road. I advanced to the tarp and lifted it. Gallons upon gallons of store-bought jugs were stacked in the shade of the tarp in a mass of milk crates. A sign hanging from a branch asked hikers to finish off one jug before opening another and not to take more than three liters of water per person. Using the plastic funnel tied to a string from another branch, I filled three of my four bottles with the water that was still cool and then drank one bottle down right there, reveling in the instant gratification of not having to apply my water filter to purify this elixir of life.

I poured the remaining water from my jug over my starry bandana, wiped my salty face, and tied the wet cloth back over my head. Then I smashed the emptied jug with my foot, threw it away in the recycling bin by the tarp, and tramped back up the spur trail, cradling my water bottles in my shirt like newborns.

Sitting against my pack beneath the scattered shade of the junipers, I ate some dried mango and was about to close my eyes for a nap when Saltlick and Pandora showed up, followed by the boy from Mount Laguna who'd asked me to stay in the cabin.

Although I hadn't thought of him since that time, a piercing sensation of both tension and delight leaped within me at the sight of him.

I sat up promptly.

"Tell me there's still some water left," Saltlick said, plunking her pack next to mine, perspiring and breathless from the climb up to the third gate.

"There's a gold mine of water down there," I said, watching the boy as he took a seat on a flat rock a few feet away.

"Those are some tan hands you have there," he said to me, settling himself comfortably.

Pandora and Saltlick regarded my sun-fried skin, which glowed in stark contrast to my white sleeves.

"Whoa! They look like a Native American's hands," Pandora remarked, dropping her pack next to Saltlick's.

"Yeah, I know," I said. "I haven't really been keeping sunscreen on them."

"That's intense," Saltlick said. "Be careful they don't burn."

A few minutes later, she and Pandora headed for the cache. "You coming too, Big Spoon?" they called to the boy as they stepped down the side trail.

"Be down in a minute," he answered.

"So, your name's Big Spoon?" I shyly asked.

He had taken off a boot and sock and was examining the enormous blister on his big toe.

"I guess so. That's what everyone's calling me."

"How'd you get it?"

"My shoes. I need to go a size bigger. My toes rub against the front when I hike, causing this massive annoyance of a blister."

I laughed. "I have the same problem. But I didn't mean how you got your blister. I meant how'd you get your name?"

"Oh, oh, right...my name." A look surfaced on his sweat-shining face that told me this wasn't his favorite story. "I got it in Mount Laguna on the night of that storm. It was when everyone was going to sleep, and one girl—her trail name's True—rolled her sleeping bag out on the cabin floor. I was in a bed and offered to give it to her. But True kept refusing until another hiker yelled out, 'What are you so afraid of? He could be the little spoon.' You know, like in spooning with someone." His cheeks popped in red. "But look at me. Do I look like the little spoon?"

I regarded his tall body and shook my head.

"Right. So, anyway, in the cabin to defend myself I called back, 'Actually, I'm the big spoon!'" He sighed. "Unfortunately, the name stuck."

"I like it," I said. "It's clever."

"Really? You do? I think it's kind of lame," Big Spoon said. "I was hoping to get a name that revolved around fire. Campfires are my specialty. But everyone keeps calling me Big Spoon." He swept his thumb over his bloated blister and then pulled his pocketknife from his khaki-colored pants. "Do you have a trail name yet?" he asked.

"No, I'm still Claire."

Big Spoon nodded, flipped open his knife, and pressed the pointed end of the blade into the center of the blister, quick and calculated, calm in his efforts to repair his irritated wound.

"Just like that, huh?" I commented as Big Spoon wiped his blade with his red bandana while letting the open sore drain onto the dirt.

He slid the knife back in his pocket and looked me in the eyes. There was something about this stranger. He seemed so solid and assured.

"Yep," he said. "Just like that."

━≺┼≻━

When dusk reduced the day's heat, I hopped back on the trail to make the tent site at mile 94 by sunset. Pandora, Saltlick, and Big Spoon were still resting beneath the scratchy junipers when I set off. *I hope he follows me,* I wished of Big Spoon as I ascended the trail, slightly sickened by this schoolgirl crush that seemed to have crashed into me out of nowhere.

Of course, his following me was a ludicrous dream. He was doing his thing; I was doing mine. We were both solo hikers in the bubble.

So it came as a pleasant surprise when five minutes later, I heard someone coming up behind me, turned to see who it was, and found none other than Big Spoon.

"Feel free to pass me," I said, stepping to the side of the trail, betraying my desire to spend time with him.

He walked by.

Figures, I thought.

And just as this flitted through my mind, he turned around and faced me.

"Mind if I hike with you?" he asked.

"Oh, no. No, not at all," I said, too weak to wrestle down the smile that took over my face.

We walked together over the next three miles, me behind Big Spoon and his overstuffed gray-and-red pack with his binoculars strapped to the side—a weighty item no thru-hiker carried.

At first, we stepped in silence, each in our own retrospective world to which the mind tended to transport walkers as we progressed up the long and narrow path.

Then, at the top of a 4,000-foot peak, Big Spoon spoke. "Do you believe in soul mates?"

His bold question stunned me.

"I do," I said, relieved we were still walking so he couldn't see me blush. "Do you?"

"I do."

The silence returned.

"Why do you ask?" I finally blurted, disappointed by his answer.

"Well, you see, I'm a mechanical engineer," he began, "and I do a lot of step-by-step analyzing, not only in my line of work but also in my life. I'm from Jersey but lived in Florida over the last year, where I met my girlfriend."

My heart sank. Of course he had a girlfriend.

"We have one of those on-again, off-again relation-ships," he continued. "One of those don't-know-what-you-got-till-it's-gone ordeals. And now, with all this time to think on the trail, I'm trying to figure out if she's really the one I'm meant to be with."

"Uh-huh," I said, my voice lacking its initial luster. "I see."

Not detecting my displeasure, Big Spoon went on. "I mean, we hit it off great in the beginning and did neat things together, like hunt for fossils in Florida's rivers. It probably sounds strange or nerdy, but I'm a fossil hunt-er. That's what led me to Florida in the first place. A lot of people don't know this, but it's loaded with fossils."

I like fossil hunting, I thought. I'd never done it, though, nor had I ever heard of such a thing. But it was something I could see myself enjoying—throughout my life, I had searched riverbanks and creek beds for beau-tiful stones.

"Back to my girlfriend..." Big Spoon said, interrupt-ing my fantasy of his and my hunting fossils together. "I've had my doubts. Then again, I've thought, isn't that part of any relationship—having doubts at some point or another? When I really think about it, though, she's more of a friend than anything—a buddy to do stuff with. But then I think, isn't that good for a relationship? Granted, she stayed in Florida, and I came out here. So I think, doesn't that say something? I just don't know how to know if she's the one."

It was obvious that this was tormenting him.

"You'll know when you know," I said tersely, and he sighed.

"That's what everyone says. I don't like that, though. How do you *know* when you know?"

"I don't know." I laughed, thinking back to my past few relationships, which although loving and strong, had all ended with doubt.

"So, what do you do then? You know, to sort this stuff out?" Big Spoon asked in earnest.

"Well, I'm a writer," I said, "which is part of the reason I'm out here—to pursue my craft in a place that inspires me. So, with stuff like what you're talking about, I write about it. I put it before me on the page so I can see it clearly, for what it really is."

Big Spoon stopped abruptly, turned, and penetrated me with his dreamy blue eyes.

"I just thought of your trail name."

"You did? What is it?" I asked perhaps too eagerly.

"Tan Hands."

"Tan Hands?" I reiterated, unenthused.

"Yeah, you know, since your hands are scorched... and you're a writer, too."

"Huh, Tan Hands. I don't know, Big Spoon."

"You don't have to accept it if you don't like it," he said, a little offended.

"It's not that I don't like it," I consoled, although I wasn't too fond of the name. "It's just...it's...I don't know, not really my—" And before I could finish my jumbled thought, Big Spoon made a revision.

"How about just Hands, then?"

"Oh...huh. Hands. Hands." I rolled it around on my tongue. "That's a little better, I guess. 'Hi, I'm Hands,'" I practiced, neither confirming nor denying the name.

The night's campsite resided on a ridge overlooking the mass of mountains that seemed to melt to shadows as the sun sank into them. Big Spoon stayed at the same site, pitching his tent on the other side of the bushes where I pitched mine, as close to the cliff's edge as he safely could.

"I'm going to find a place to use the bathroom. So don't worry if I'm gone for bit," he called to me over the bushes.

"Okay," I called back, smiling to myself. There was no hiding anything on the trail.

When he returned, he took off his blue shirt—asking me if I minded before he did so, and after I coolly said, "Go right ahead"—revealing his chiseled abdomen.

Saltlick and Pandora joined Big Spoon and me not long afterward. They set up their tents, and then the four of us sat on the cliff to make and eat our bland pasta dinners as the sky altered from red to purple to black.

"Claire got a trail name today," Big Spoon said when the stars began to show.

"Boom!" Pandora cried. "What is it?"

"Yeah, girl, what is it?" Saltlick asked, her nightly cigarette hanging from her lips.

"Hands," I said. "I've been christened with the trail name Hands."

The crew cheered.

"Not bad," Saltlick said.

"Oh, it totally fits!" said Pandora.

And I knew my new name fit, too, when later, as I closed my eyes to sleep inside my tent, my companions called out, "Good night, Hands!"

CHAPTER 7

WARNER SPRINGS SHUTDOWN

The next morning, Big Spoon packed up and left before Pandora, Saltlick, and I rose from our tents. I was glad. I had spent only a day on the trail with him, but he felt like a total distraction from my course to Canada.

So long, Big Spoon, I thought as I uprooted my tent stakes from the ground.

The next town, Warner Springs, was sixteen miles ahead. I planned to reach it that day, but Saltlick, who liked to say she was on more of a "pleasure cruise" than a long-distance hike, intended to stop for the day eight miles ahead at Mountain Valley Retreat—a lavish campground one mile off-trail where hikers could sleep in tepees and soak in the hot tub and eat a prime-rib dinner made by the camp host, all for the low cost of twenty-five dollars.

"No way I'm missing that," Pandora said as she chewed on a granola bar before getting going.

"Come with us, Hands," Saltlick urged. "I know you want to be all tough and go alone and whatever, but this'll be fun."

It was true. Although I had greatly enjoyed Pandora's and Saltlick's company over the last couple of days, I maintained the mentality of making this trek solo, which hindered my willingness to compromise.

"Thanks, but I want to get to Warner Springs today," I said. "I have a resupply package at the post office there that I'm wanting to pick up."

"Suit yourself," Saltlick said, putting on her pack.

"If you wait for us, we can meet you there tomorrow," Pandora said, a hint of hope in her tone.

Do they want me in their group or something? I wondered of this funny yet wonderful pair.

"Okay," I said, flattered. "I can do that. See you both tomorrow at Warner Springs."

I hiked ahead, determined to return to the comforts of civilization after having spent several days on the arduous trail. Historically, Warner Springs had never offered much in terms of hotels and restaurants. But it did provide a community resource center—run by two old ladies—where hikers could pitch their tents and purchase refreshments such as pie, Coke, and five-dollar burgers. I fantasized over the big, juicy burger as I swept through the flat yellow fields that led to the tumbleweed town of abandoned buildings. But my dream melted to mush when I arrived at the resource center in the afternoon and found that the kitchen had been shut down.

"Happened yesterday," one of the old ladies said after I entered the air-conditioned lobby and asked her about the burger. "Yep, the County of San Diego decided to drop by for a little health inspection." She spat these words with spite and then revealed that because she and her coworker, Martha, had failed to find the permit records for electrical, sewer, and plumbing, the county closed the center's kitchen.

"Real pity, too," the old lady said. "All the proceeds from the food and drink went to Warner Springs' underprivileged families."

"That's terrible," I said, doubly concerned for the families as well as the obstacle this created to my eating a real meal.

At least hikers could still sleep outside beneath the giant oak. I claimed my spot in the grass next to the fence that delineated the property line, set up my tent, and threw my backpack inside. Then I got a hitch to the post office with the local sheriff, who, lacking crime to fight in this ghost town, spent his time transporting hikers.

At the post office, I picked up the resupply package I had prepared the month before after learning that Warner Springs provided little to nothing in terms of hiker resupply. I'd had my dad mail the box to this location a week before I arrived to ensure it would be here when I got in. It contained dry foods for my next seventy-mile haul to Idyllwild. Nothing in it, though, could compare to fresh meat.

More people had arrived at the center by the time the sheriff dropped me back off there. It looked like a miniature circus with the colorful array of tents springing from the grass. Hikers sat at the picnic tables, rummaging through resupply boxes and trading prized food items like Oreos and Snickers. As soon as I stepped out of the cop car, I smelled the salty oil in the air—unmistakably, sizzling ground beef. *Could I be so hungry that I'm smelling things now?* I wondered, setting my box near my tent and then following the aroma behind the building.

Sure enough, a band of hikers was there, hovering over a charcoal grill, taking turns flipping patties. Among the hikers stood Big Spoon. He held a notepad and pen and nodded me over when he saw me.

"What's going on?" I asked. "I thought we couldn't get burgers."

"Technically, only the kitchen is closed," Big Spoon said with a sly smile. "So, because everyone's been pretty bummed about the situation, the women over this place fired up the charcoal grill about an hour ago and gave all the burger makings to the hikers around at the time. It's still five bucks if you want one. That guy over there, Chug, is collecting the cash. I'm taking orders," Big Spoon said, indicating his pad and pen. "We're basically running a black market. Would you like cheese or no cheese on your burger?"

"Cheese, lots of cheese," I said, my mouth watering.

Although he tried to be discreet, I saw him write my name and order above every other hiker on the list. Five minutes later, someone called out "Hands!" and I claimed my tasty prize.

I ate on the paved parking lot against the fence, away from the noisy crowd, relishing every bite of my long-awaited burger in peace. After eating, I showered in the wooden shack next to the center. The water was cold, but it was still hot enough outside that I didn't mind. I put on my running shorts and blue shirt and then rinsed my filthy socks, pants, and white shirt (which had taken on a brownish-yellow hue from dirt and sweat) with the hose next to the shower. I hung these garments to dry on the fence that doubled as the communal clothesline.

It felt strange—overwhelming, actually—to be around so many people again. On the trail, I saw people every day, but never so many all at once for an extended period of time. At sunset, I stepped away from the herd and took a seat on the white bench in front of the center to sort through my resupply box—the nuts and pastas and chocolate—before it got too dark.

As I organized the food and placed it in my food sack, Big Spoon came over and sat next to me on the bench.

"Why aren't you over there with the posse?" he asked.

"I'm not part of the posse," I said. "I'm a lone wolf." And I howled into the sky.

"No, I'm a lone wolf," he argued. "You're not a lone wolf. You have Saltlick and Pandora."

"Do you see them anywhere?"

He looked around. "No."

"Really, I'm a lone wolf who wanders with a select few," I said. "Here, have these. They're extras I don't need from my box." I handed Big Spoon a packet of cherry Gatorade powder and a Hershey's chocolate bar.

"Oh, awesome. Thanks!" he said, taking the treats.

I was about to get up to go to my tent when Big Spoon told me that he and Splat—who'd arrived in Warner Springs not long after me—were going to cowboy camp on the field beyond the fence to get away from the crowd. Cowboy camping was when you slept on the ground without a tent.

"It's a good night for it. There's no clouds, and the stars are going to be great," Big Spoon said, seemingly hinting for me to join them.

This sounded wonderful.

But I simply said that I hoped he and Splat had a good night and then left to go to bed. After all, I couldn't let myself fall for Big Spoon. He had a girlfriend. I had been on the PCT only a week. Not to mention that the reason I was even out here was to reclaim my young life of wide-open adventure after spending the last two years stuffed inside a corporate cubicle. I knew then that I couldn't let myself become the person who stayed at her society-deemed "good" job for years and years and years until the ripe old age of retirement because of its "desirable" yet unfulfilling pay, career path, benefits, and vacation time. That job wasn't my life. That job was the system's idea of my life. But my life—my very own life— I'd reclaimed when I'd stepped on the PCT. And now that I had, I couldn't let myself get tangled up and tied down in a romance in which I had no business being tangled up and tied down in the first place. I needed to stay focused on the trail.

I struggled to fall asleep in my cramped spot, as many hikers stayed up late talking and laughing and drinking the handle of whiskey someone had packed in his resupply box even though alcohol wasn't allowed on the premises.

In the morning, I felt the bags sagging beneath my eyes. I crawled out of my tent and took a seat at the nearby picnic table with Purple Princess and Donezo, the comical gay couple from Texas, who with their energetic charm had scored a loaf of banana bread from the old ladies in charge.

"Have some bread!" offered Purple Princess, so named because all his gear and clothing were purple. Donezo—a black-haired, tan-skinned Apple computer programmer who'd gotten his name for his famous phrase, "I'm done with this trail. I'm just so done!"— handed me a slice. As he did so, a gray-bearded man in a pickup truck pulled into the parking lot. He stepped out of his truck, clasping two brown paper bags. "Fresh apple pie! Come and get it!" he yelled for all to hear. Apparently, the man had caught wind of the fact that health inspectors had closed down the resource center's kitchen. Being a local, he knew how much hikers relied on this place for fresh food. So that morning he'd driven to the nearest McDonald's—an hour away in Julian—and bought the place out of its baked apple pies.

Hikers swarmed the bighearted man like flies. Purple Princess, Donezo, and I sprinted over to him too, which was unnecessary since there was plenty of pie to go around. When we returned to the picnic table, we found a raven pecking at the banana bread.

But what did we care?

We had pie.

Pandora and Saltlick showed up around lunchtime, raving about how great a night they'd had at the retreat.

"We had the place all to ourselves, so the camp host, Miranda—she was so cool—just let us do whatever we wanted. She gave us beer, cooked us an incredible meal, and let us hang out in the hot tub for hours. She even gave us a free yoga lesson. It was amazing! We missed you though, Hands!" Pandora went on and on.

Minutes later, she and Saltlick hitched a ride with the sheriff to the post office, returning shortly afterward with their resupply boxes. As they organized their goods, I walked over to the picnic table, where Big Spoon was going through the items he'd scored from the hiker box on the center's front porch.

We wouldn't be lovers, I'd decided. But we could at least be friends.

"Are those Jelly Bellies?" I asked.

"They are. Someone left an unopened bag in the hiker box. Can you believe it?" Big Spoon said, opening the jelly beans and handing me the bag, telling me to take some.

"My posse's here now. We're heading on in a bit," I said, picking out my favorite flavor—orange.

"You are? In this heat? I'm not leaving until evening when the weather cools. Splat, Roadrunner, and Key Lime are doing the same. We're going to night hike to beat the heat of the day. You should come with us."

Roadrunner—whom I'd originally met as Jen the first day of the trail—and Key Lime were girls my age who were really cool. But Pandora and Saltlick had become my pack. Unreasonably, I felt jealous that Big Spoon had chosen to hike with them over us.

"I thought you were a lone wolf," I curtly replied.

"A lone wolf who wanders with a select few," he said, smiling.

"Good one," I had to laugh. "Well, Pandora and Saltlick are pretty set on leaving this afternoon. I've decided to go with them," I said, popping the orange jelly bean into my mouth.

"Until we meet again, then," Big Spoon said.

"Until we meet again."

The hike that day was dreadfully hot. The three of us made it only ten miles past Warner Springs to mile 120 before calling it a day and setting up camp in a small clearing beside the trail. By hiker midnight, which sounded at nine in the evening, Saltlick, Pandora, and I were in our tents.

I had nearly fallen asleep when I heard footsteps coming up the trail and saw the golden dots of headlamps shining through the fabric of my tent. Three of the dots bobbed on, but one dot stopped and scanned the clearing. "Is that Hands?" uttered the one who'd stopped.

"Is that Big Spoon?" Pandora called back.

"We're going on up the trail a bit farther. Trying to reach a hundred and thirty tonight," Big Spoon said. "We're aiming to make Idyllwild not tomorrow but the next day."

"That's great for you guys. Thank you, good sir, for the play-by-play," Saltlick's sarcasm was in full force. "Now, let us get some sleep."

"Okay. Just wanted to let you all know where we'll be," Big Spoon said. "Good night, everyone. Good night, Hands."

"Good night, Big Spoon!" I called back, watching the light of his headlamp disappear up the trail.

"He wanted to let *you* know where *he'd* be," Pandora said to me through her tent.

"Yeah, he's got it bad for you," Saltlick chimed in.

It hit me then—like it hadn't before—that with Big Spoon now ahead of me on the trail, I may never catch up to him again.

CHAPTER 8

A DAY IN THE DESERT WITH THE TALLYHOS

Time worked differently on the trail. Instead of being measured by clocks on the wall, it was measured by the sun in the sky. It was more natural this way, more true. Half the time, I didn't even know what day of the week it was until someone looked down at a digital watch and told me. Simply, when the SoCal sun rose, I rose with it, walking the whole day through until it disappeared again.

Pandora and Saltlick did the same. The sunrise after we left Warner Springs, we emerged from our tents, rolled up our sleeping bags, and slipped on our clammy clothes. Breaking down camp was a quick game of multitasking—eating breakfast while restuffing packs.

Today we had a view of smooth, blue mountaintops and wildflower valleys as we collapsed our tent poles and folded up our durable homes. Prairie dogs poked their heads up from their earthen dwellings to see what was going on as we examined the map and counted the miles to the next water source. We only had so much time to hike in the crisp morning air before the sun burned it all away.

"We could call ourselves the Tallyhos? You know, after the cry the hunter makes when he sees a fox? 'Go get 'em!' is what it means," Saltlick suggested as she brushed her teeth, a line of white foam dribbling from her mouth.

It was either that or her earlier idea: the Honeybuns.

"I like it," Pandora said. "We can yell out when we see each other on the trail—'Tallyho! Tally-tally-ho!'"

"It think it works," I said. "We're the Tallyhos."

And with our group name decided, Saltlick, Pandora, and I became an official team.

"Tallyho!"

"Tallyho!"

"Tallyho!" the three of us shouted before taking to the trail.

We set our own pace and walked alone, although every couple of miles, we stopped to break and meet back up in the meager shade. During this time, we'd take off our shoes and air our feet, careful not to rub against any poison oak. We'd hydrate ourselves and shake out our socks. I'd stretch and flex my shoulders and legs. Saltlick would wipe the salt deposits from her face with her bandana. Pandora—always ready with a song—would belt out her best impersonation of Bette Midler.

After our midmorning break, we regained the trail. I took the lead, looking all around as I walked through the dome-shaped hills strewn with white boulders. Collared lizards darted across the path when I stepped by; the horny toads froze in place. I nearly stepped on a rattlesnake. It lay across the trail, sunning—its oranges and grays blending in perfectly. I shrieked and jumped back the moment I almost crushed it. The snake remained very still, silent, and undisturbed by my presence. My heart beat rampantly against my chest. Only yesterday in Warner Springs, I'd heard about a boy who went to a rock to eat a snack and sat on a rattlesnake that was coiled up and camouflaged. He got bit on the hand and had to backtrack several miles to town—the poison flowing through—to seek medical help.

After a minute, the rattlesnake lying across the trail still hadn't noticed me. I made noises and jumped up and down. Nothing. Is it dead? I wondered. I extended my trekking pole and stepped as far back as I could before tapping him with the point of the pole. Still nothing. A second passed by. Then came a slight sticking out of the black, slimy tongue. I stepped back farther. Then came the rattle. It went off like a set of maracas—loud and rhythmic and sharp. "St-St-St-St-Stay away!" the rattle harshly warned. The snake then slithered slowly off the trail into the junipers. I waited until I could no longer see it, and then I ran—the sound of the rattle shaking in my mind.

At mile 127, the Tallyhos and I reconvened to resupply on water. A water tank with a spigot was positioned a quarter mile off-trail down a dirt road. Brightly painted signs lined the way to the water, saying things like, "Give your dogs a break! Shelter, Shade, and Food at Trail Angel Jose's!"

The sign at the water tank had a blue arrow pointing farther down the abandoned road. After replenishing our water, we followed the sign. A minute later, we were walking down steep cinder-block stairs to enter what appeared to be a secret hiker society. We arrived on the grounds of a yellow stucco home surrounded for miles by the vast, brown lands. Large white canopies ballooned up from the yard, giving all who sat beneath them daylong shade. Many of our fellow hikers were there, waiting outside by the restaurant-sized griddle and practically drooling as Trail Angel Jose, a hefty Hispanic man in a grease-splotched apron, served up pancakes, fried potatoes, sausage links, and fried eggs.

Johnny Cash blared from the old-fashioned record player in the nearby garage. I liked this place, and it was lunchtime. I grabbed a PBR from the cooler by the griddle and then waited in line for the grub. The beer ran cold and pure down my dry throat. I gulped the beverage to the last carbonated drop as Jose loaded my paper plate with his fatty, fantastic food. I topped my pancakes with sliced strawberries and bananas and smothered them in syrup. Then I grabbed a second beer and took a seat with the Tallyhos at the plastic card table beneath one of the canopies. The brothers from Oregon (Shades, Pogo, and Sticks), the boy from North Georgia (Pretzel), and Splat were already there.

"You look great!" Pretzel—a burly-bearded, short-shorted hiker I'd met near Mount Laguna and hadn't seen since—said as I sat down. "The trail's given you that good, ruddy shine." He had his sculpted leg elevated on the table—shoe off, grimy toes exposed—because of the shin splint that had held him captive at Trail Angel Jose's over the last two days.

"Thanks, man!" I said. Then I asked, as nonchalantly as I could, if anyone had seen Big Spoon.

"Just missed him," Splat said, fiddling with his camera.

"Yeah, he was just here with Roadrunner and Key Lime, but they headed on," said Pretzel.

A passing cloud of disappointment shaded my otherwise happy disposition.

"Oh, okay. That's cool," I said, my words betraying my thoughts.

The day rolled on as we ate, drank, and told stories from our lives. Saltlick recounted the days she'd lived on a sailboat with her then girlfriend in her hometown of

Traverse City. "Those were the golden days," she said, remembering the person she'd previously described to me as her true love who had broken her heart. "Who needs the ocean when you have Lake Michigan?" she said.

Pandora—an Iowa native who had been living in Albuquerque and working for a major engineering firm—remembered the New Mexican green chiles she and her friends would pick from the farm and roast to make a big meal from. "The chiles are so unique, so true to the flavors of New Mexico," she said, licking her lips, revealing that it was the taste of these local peppers as well as the camaraderie of this tradition that had made it so special.

I told of my love for Tennessee's green, rolling hills. They weren't anything like the desert hills—grand and jagged and hard. No. The hills of Tennessee were subtle and smooth. "You can always find a place in the shade."

In the afternoon, several hikers napped on the ground or swung in the tattered hammocks to wait out the blistering heat. A dark-haired boy called Poet observed the scene from afar with his journal and pen. Splat tiptoed from hiker to hiker as they slept, snapping candid pictures of them with his old-school camera. I returned to the griddle for seconds, dropping seven dollars into the donation jar by the cooler on my way. As Trail Angel Jose—the owner of a food-processing-equipment company—served me another egg, I asked him how he'd become an angel.

"Because you people kept coming by," he answered with great charisma.

About an hour later, the Tallyhos and I hugged big-bellied Jose good-bye and then put in eight more miles beneath the merciless sun before stopping at sundown at a sandy site. Beneath the nearly full moon, we pitched tents, lit stoves, and ate our trail dinners—tasteless compared to Jose's cooking.

The air was cool and serene. Pandora brought up New Mexico's green chiles again—how she would hand-select the peppers and then roast them in a special metal wheel that spun over an open flame.

"What's today?" I asked.

"Friday, May first," said Saltlick after pressing a button that made her watch glow.

I had been on the Pacific Crest Trail for ten days. Saltlick and Pandora made their way to bed, but I remained outside, gazing up at the golden moon, wondering what was going on in the world I had left behind.

Yet somehow I knew.

That world, like this one, kept spinning, spinning, over the open flame of life.

CHAPTER 9

NO TALLYHO
LEFT BEHIND

The next morning, Saltlick, Pandora, and I strode into the pale stone and dark pines of the San Jacinto Mountains. The prospect of reaching Paradise Valley Café sixteen miles ahead drove us. A mile off-trail on CA 74, the café was hailed for having the most heavenly burger on the PCT, motivating Pandora and me to hustle through the scorching heat for this allegedly divine meal.

Saltlick lagged behind. She wasn't feeling the hiking today, which she told us when we took a break at mile 144, the halfway point to Paradise.

"Go ahead. I'll meet you guys at the café," she said to Pandora and me, remaining seated at the side of the trail as we strapped our packs back on.

Eight miles later, in the early afternoon, Pandora and I came up on the highway, where a white catering van was parked at the pull-off by the trail. A stout man stood next to the van, watching us as we walked toward him.

Oh, great...our kidnapper, I thought, even though I had learned by now that it was normal for some trail angels to hang out by the trailheads to give hikers rides.

"You ladies looking to go to Paradise?" the man asked, as if delivering a tacky pickup line. His tan arms stuck out from his white Paradise Valley Café T-shirt.

"Who isn't?" Pandora responded with her quick and humorous wit.

The man opened the van's back doors and ushered us and two other hikers who had just arrived into the cell-like space. We rocked back and forth with our clunky packs as the man—who turned out to be the café owner who'd been transporting hikers to and from the café all day—took us to the highway-side heaven.

The café was the main attraction in the pit-stop town of Mountain Center. As the owner let us out of the van, Pandora told him that Saltlick should be coming up soon.

"I'll keep an eye out for her," he said and then took off back down the highway.

Paradise Valley Café was hiker friendly, meaning hikers could relax here freely without being snubbed for what looked and smelled to be our total homelessness. Pandora and I set our packs on the patio, kicked off our shoes, and took a seat at a spacious table beneath a big umbrella. A mixture of locals and hikers dined outside. The waiter took our order, Pandora and I both choosing the Mother Load—two beef patties, American cheese, and bacon. The burgers came with fries, and we also ordered chocolate milkshakes. Waiting for our food, we listened to the old man next to the patio play his gentle keyboard tunes, an upturned ball cap next to his feet for any and all to slip him cash and coins.

The burgers arrived, stacked high upon our plates like an architectural feat of greasy nutrition. They were the biggest, the juiciest, the most loaded with cheese and bacon and beef burgers I'd ever had the privilege of trying to fit inside my mouth. Pandora was more civilized and used a knife and fork. And although the portions were generous beyond belief, we scarfed the heavy sandwiches down to the last gritty crumb and slurped up our milkshakes until our straws made a loud sucking noise that made people turn their heads.

"I'm going to be sick," Pandora said, clasping her stomach after swallowing her last fry.

She left to go to the bathroom, during which time more hikers staggered in, none of whom were Saltlick. I went to the bathroom after Pandora to scrub the dirt off my face and arms, hoping Saltlick would be there by the time I came out.

"She's still not here," Pandora said when I sat back down at our table.

We ordered a beer to bide the time, asking every new hiker who filed out of the white van if they had seen our friend.

No one had.

By dusk, Pandora and I were worried.

"Did she have enough water on her?" I asked.

"Plenty, as far as I know," responded Pandora.

"Do you think she got lost?"

"But how? The trail's so well defined."

We tried to call her on her cell phone, even though we knew it was hopeless—there was rarely ever any reception on the trail.

"What if she got bit by a rattlesnake?" I said after hanging up the phone, my imagination starting to stretch.

"Or what if she—" But before Pandora could finish her worst-case-scenario thought, someone behind us butted in.

"Stepped off the trail to rest in the shade and fell asleep for several hours?"

We turned to see who it was.

"Saltlick!" Pandora and I cried, hopping up to give her, who wasn't one for hugs, a smothering embrace.

"Thank God!" I said. "We were so worried."

"What happened to you out there?" Pandora demanded.

"Guys, I'm sorry," Saltlick said, wearily taking a seat. "I just didn't feel like hiking today. So, when I saw this incredible shade under a pine, I couldn't resist. I didn't mean to fall asleep."

"God, Saltlick," Pandora said. "We're just glad you're okay. But from now on, all the way to Canada, no Tallyho leaves another Tallyho behind."

"Yeah, really. No Tallyho left behind," I repeated.

And the three of us made a pact.

It was dark out by the time Saltlick finished her burger and beer. The owner offered the confined yard behind the café to hikers to pitch tents and stay the night, announcing cheerfully to the crowd that any nonhiking customers bothered by this could simply leave. But the trail had become our home. Thus, the Tallyhos and I walked the mile back to the trailhead to make our beds in a mossy field just beyond the road.

We slept beneath the light of the full moon and woke with the first light of the sun to continue to Idyllwild at mile 179. A wildfire from the summer of 2013 had wiped out a good portion of this strip, causing sixteen miles of it to still be closed. As a result, hikers had the option of making Idyllwild by either doing a seventeen-mile road walk on the highway from Paradise Valley Café or hiking ten miles on the PCT to where the closure began at mile 162 and then dipping down a muddy eight-mile back road that dripped into town. Several hikers simply hitched the seventeen-mile road walk from Paradise to Idyllwild. But, because the Tallyhos and I wanted to walk as much of the trail as was available, we chose the back road detour.

Saltlick took the lead, followed by Pandora and then me, as we hiked up miles of jagged rock that gradually morphed into a forest of fine-scented pines. On this muscle-burning climb, I chatted with Pandora and learned why she had come to the PCT.

"I had become an angry person," she said to me. Saltlick was too far ahead to hear. "I had a great position at a great job in this really cool place. But I got burned out, tired of the routine, and I turned mad—so mad that I started treating my coworkers the way I felt inside, which isn't what I'm about." She breathed heavily as she spoke while walking up the grade. "Then last summer, while my boyfriend and I hiked the two hundred miles of the John Muir Trail, I discovered how freeing this life of motion in the mountains is and how happy it made me. That's how I decided to hike the PCT. I wanted more, so I quit my job without having any certainty that I'd be able to come back to it. And now, here I am." She turned and looked at me for a moment, her blue eyes filled with peace. "My boyfriend, John, is holding down our fort, watching our two senile cats while I'm gone. He's the best for letting me do this without making me feel bad about it. I miss him. But I'm so glad I'm here. This life is empowering, you know. I mean, I'm daily realizing what I'm capable of as the trail throws different challenges my way. And it's fun, too! Teaming up with you and Saltlick has really enriched this whole experience. I feel like myself again. I feel restored."

"Making a change seems to do that for a person," I said, feeling much the way Pandora had described.

"And, yeah, I agree. Having friends out here makes the trail so much better."

We caught back up to Saltlick at the summit of the ridge, breaking for a minute at an elevation of nearly 7,000 feet. From there, we could see that the land on one side of the mountain thrived with thick, green life but dwindled on the other with sickly, charred trees.

"From the wildfire," Saltlick said. "Two years later, and the trees are still dead."

"Wow," Pandora said, and I did too, for this land of death was bleak and immense.

At dusk, we reached the log-cabin town of Idyllwild, our feet as raw as uncooked ground beef after the detour down the hard and punishing back road. It was Sunday night, and the town was winding down. Fortunately for us, we nabbed the last available cabin at the Idyllwild Inn on Village Center Drive, the three of us splitting the cost, paying thirty dollars each for our accommodations, which included a queen-size bed and pullout couch.

As soon as we stepped inside our cabin, I collected everyone's dirty clothes and started a load of laundry in the main lodge's utility room. Pandora washed our cook pots and spoons in the kitchen sink, and Saltlick walked to the general store before it closed to buy a six-pack and potato chips.

After these chores, I showered, regarding my lightened hair and roughened skin in the bathroom mirror before stepping into the steaming shower to perform the laborious task of scouring the dirt from between my toes, washing the grime out of my hair, and shaving the coarse hairs that had grown like groves on my now grossly muscular legs and under my stinking armpits.

Pandora and Saltlick showered too, taking a total of thirty minutes each to cleanse their sullied selves. With our hair combed and our freshly laundered clothes donned, the three of us decided to have a little fun and go out on the tiny town that lay tucked in the San Jacintos.

Most everything was closed, but that evening, Idyllwild bustled with packs of hikers ambling about. For dinner, the Tallyhos and I met up with a big group at the only restaurant that was open—Good Times Pub and Grill. Purple Princess and Donezo—the couple that had shared their banana bread with me in Warner Springs—sat among the group. It had been only a few days since we'd last seen each other, but meeting them now felt like a grand reunion. As I sipped my Blue Moon—the refreshing beer I often craved on the trail—I wondered just what it was about the trail that created this undeniable bond between strangers in such a short amount of time.

"Oh, honey, you know. It's our common ground that an uncommon number of people take," said Purple Princess, a student of environmental sustainability, when I brought up the subject. He had a chili-bowl cut of bright, blond hair, a grizzly beard I could tell he didn't normally flaunt in the "real world," and rock-solid legs, which jutted out from his purple shorts.

"It's a path of kindred souls," he continued. "And, God, it's so raw, and we're so exposed. We have to dig a new hole to shit in every day, for Jesus's sake! There's no covering up what you're about to do when you step off the trail with toilet paper."

Donezo overheard this and laughed. "Ain't that the truth, baby!" he said, patting Purple Princess's back.

"But the beautiful thing is," Purple Princess went on, "that no matter what brought us out here, and no matter where we came from, we're doing this fucked-up, life-changing thing of walking over two thousand miles on this ridiculously hard and amazing terrain together. Girl, no wonder we connect on that deeper level."

"Wow, babe. That's beautiful," Donezo said. "You're so deep."

It is beautiful, I thought. It's like Saltlick, Pandora, and me. Never could I have expected to partner up with this duo. After all, Saltlick was forty-two and Pandora was thirty-four. We were all from different parts of the country with very different backgrounds. Yet the higher forces on the trail had brought us together. We became friends—lifelong friends, it seemed—in only a matter of days. It was magical. But it was real. Saltlick and Pandora had become my family.

I awoke in the morning next to a sleeping, open-mouthed Pandora in the bed—Saltlick slept on the couch—with a mild headache from the beer. But because I had plenty to do before the Tallyhos and I hit the trail that afternoon—like finally buying a bigger pair of hiking boots to cure my blistered feet—I got an early start, informing Saltlick, who was on the porch puffing on a cigarette as I left, my plans to go to the outfitters up the road, the grocery store across the street, and the public library to print off an updated water report.

"Sounds like you got it all mapped out," she said, her hazel eyes still hazy with sleep.

However, after purchasing groceries and a hundred-dollar pair of low-rise Keens—size seven and a half—I decided to return to the cabin to load up my pack before swinging by the library.

Saltlick and Pandora were on the couch organizing their things when I arrived.

"Guess who we just saw?" Pandora playfully asked.

"Who?" I had no idea.

"Well, we were walking back from the diner where we had breakfast, and in the cabin down from ours, Splat was sitting out on the deck."

"Oh," I said. "That's cool."

"So, you know, we talked to him for a minute or two, and then Big Spoon popped out from the living room."

"Oh?" I was more interested now.

"Yeah. Apparently he and Splat split a cabin last night because Big Spoon ordered some new shoes online or something that won't arrive at the post office until tomorrow," Pandora spat this out in one breath. "But wait! Do you know what the first thing he said to Saltlick and me was when he saw us?"

"What?" I tried to sound unenthusiastic but was very eager to know.

"He said, 'Where's Hands?' Not 'Hi, Saltlick. Hi, Pandora. How are you two today?' None of that. Just 'Where's Hands?'"

"What'd you tell him?" I quickly asked.

Saltlick rolled her eyes.

"Oh, you know, just that you were running some errands and that you might be at the library."

"But I haven't gone to the library."

"So, why don't you go the library, then?" Saltlick said in her sarcastic way.

I packed my pack like a bandit on the run and set off, striding beyond Idyllwild Inn in my new boots to the other side of the street and down the paved drive to the library.

"Look who it is," came a familiar voice from the computer station as I approached the front desk for a guest pass.

I turned toward the voice and saw Big Spoon sitting at a computer that faced the library entrance, a big smile on his golden face.

He was waiting for me, I fancied, taking a seat at the computer opposite him after I'd received my pass.

We looked at each other over the barricading screens. Although I already knew the answer based on what Pandora had said, I asked Big Spoon in my inside voice what he was still doing in Idyllwild.

"The shoes I've been hiking in are too small, and they tore up my feet with blisters. I actually hiked the last forty-seven miles in my rubber Crocs because of it," Big Spoon said in his normal voice. The librarian promptly shushed him. He leaned closer to me and continued in a whisper. "So, on Saturday when we got into Idyllwild, I went to buy a new pair of shoes, but the outfitters didn't carry my size. I wear a fourteen normally, but out here I need a fifteen—wide. I had to order online, and the shoes won't get in until tomorrow. So I'm stuck here until then."

"Those are some big feet you have, Big Spoon," I said and laughed, and the librarian shushed me. "What about Roadrunner and Key Lime? Where are they?" I whispered.

"They left this morning."

"Oh, I'm sorry."

He shrugged. "It's fine. I'm a lone wolf, remember?"

"I remember. But it's nice to have friends."

"It is," he said, looking into my eyes. "You've got a good group, Hands."

"Thank you," I said. "No Tallyho left behind."

Naturally, he gave me a funny look.

"And you all are leaving today, right?" he asked.

"After I print this water report."

Big Spoon contemplated something for several seconds.

"When I catch up to you once my shoes come in, maybe I could put some miles in with you, if that's all right."

I laughed. "What makes you think you'll catch up?"

The librarian shushed me again.

A second of silence lingered in the library's motionless air. I pressed the print button on the water report. Big Spoon was about to say something. But before he could, I leaned in and whispered, "I'll see you on the trail, Big Spoon."

CHAPTER 10

DEVIL'S SLIDE AND SHIN SPLINTS

After I left the library, a lady with short, frizzy hair and a long, flowing skirt gave the Tallyhos and me a ride in the bed of her truck a mile beyond Idyllwild to Humber Park. Bird—a petite woman who aspired to be a circus aerialist—rode with us too. She was a solo hiker from England I'd run into a few times since starting the trail. It was Purple Princess who'd told me that Bird would join the circus after the trail. She wore a tiny, compact backpack over her long-sleeved canvas button-down and matching pants. Her sandy hair fell just below her ears, and the tip of her nose was sharp like a beak. Bird intrigued me. I followed behind her as the four of us took to the steep and winding Devil's Slide Trail from Humber Park to reconnect to the PCT.

Devil's Slide presented a 1,500-foot gain in elevation within a brief span of two and a half miles before peaking at Saddle Junction, elevation 8,100 feet. Five days of food for the next ninety-mile stretch to Big Bear greatly weighed down my pack as I trekked uphill. Even though I'd had many days to tune my trail legs—a term tossed around in the hiking community—it hadn't become easier to hike up this tedious terrain. In fact, it would never get easier to hike up mountains of altitude on the PCT, even though I kept expecting it would.

Pandora and Saltlick took their time coming up Devil's Slide. I wanted to do the same. But Bird hiked at such a brisk pace, and I was so curious to learn more about this girl who dreamed of being in the circus, that I huffed and puffed my way behind her to keep up.

"What made you want to be an aerialist?" I asked as we walked farther toward the sky.

She seemed surprised that I knew this about her but answered in her stunning English accent, "I injured my ankle the year before in a game of netball, so I immediately sought out a sport I could do with only my upper body. I can't stand being immobile, you see." She started walking faster. "That's how I discovered aerials. I caught on rather quickly and fell madly in love. As I continued to work on acrobatic flying, my ankle healed, and

I planned my holiday on the PCT, a trip I've wanted to take for years. And because I didn't want to return to my job at the bank after this lovely hike, I applied to circus school, which I learned right after starting the trail that I got accepted into."

"Congratulations," I said. "That's incredible. You're going to be in the circus."

Bird sighed. "I do hope so."

Her appearance reminded me of a delicate gold-finch, but her movements were as dynamic as a hawk's. She never stumbled on a rock; she never swayed to one side of the trail or the other. She walked flawlessly, aesthetically, with purpose.

As we neared the summit of the difficult Devil's Slide, she told me rather intimately, "You know, you grow up and are told to get a job, get married, buy a house, have children." She breathed in the crisp mountain air. "But what if you don't want those things? What if you want something else? I'm thirty years old now. My parents think I've lost my way. They think circus school is a joke, and that I've missed my chance to be a successful wife and mother. I don't know, perhaps I have. Perhaps." Bird paused, looking out on the mountains. "But what they don't realize is that I have no desire for those things. I don't want what they think I should want."

"What do you want?" I asked.

We'd reached Saddle Junction, where a rock cliff protruded into the air. Bird and I stopped near it to view the spacious evergreen forest below and to marvel at standing among the surrounding 10,000-foot peaks, where patches of snow glistened in the sun. I stood in one spot. But Bird inched her way to the edge of the cliff, where a gentle breeze swirled up like a trapezist. She spread out her small yet muscular arms and lifted her head to the sky.

"I want to fly," she boldly declared. "I want to *fly*."

⊸⊱⊰⊷

Bird was gone the following morning when the Tallyhos and I started up. It was a downhill day—we would drop from 9,000 feet to 3,000 feet, from the pristine peaks back into the sooty desert, over the next fifteen miles. I set off strong from camp, moving swiftly through the fragrant pink flowers of pinkbract manzanitas, beneath the dangling pine cones of evergreens. My new boots, although not yet broken in and still a little stiff, felt wonderful. They gave my feet the room they needed to let my blisters finally callus over.

Indeed, I felt so good that I was nearly running down the path—a fantastic facet of the trail: how it could make you feel invincible and alive.

If only such liberation would last.

For, a few miles in, my victorious morale crumbled when after some unbalanced steps upon a stretch of loose scree, a shock of pain shot through my shin. I cried out, almost falling to the ground, so devastating was the blow. My fast pace slowed to an inch-by-inch shuffle as I instinctively applied all my weight to my left leg to take the pressure off my wounded right.

This was another facet of the trail: how it could bring you down fast and hard.

By the time the sun hung directly overhead, my shin felt like it was being split like a log with a dull axe. It throbbed without cessation with a terrible, blunt pain.

"What's wrong with you, Hands?" Saltlick asked when she and Pandora caught up to me for lunch. I was sitting against a rock, my pant leg rolled up, massaging my shin with my fingers when they arrived.

"Just a little sore," I lied, not wanting to admit I had developed a shin splint.

Which I knew this had to be. Several hikers currently suffered from them, being forced to wait in town until the injury healed. Repetitive stress on the shinbone proved to be the cause, putting anyone walking almost twenty miles a day, day after day after day, at risk. Rest was the only cure. Otherwise, the shin splint could augment into a stress fracture—a break in the bone bad enough to boot one off the trail for weeks.

But rest wasn't an option for me as I sat in the heart of this wasteland, the closest civilization being the road crossing at Interstate 10 fifteen miles ahead. I would have to push on, I determined after lunch. Saltlick and Pandora went on ahead while I mustered the mental strength to overcome what would be an agonizing span. With no one else around me, I stood, fastened my pack, and pressed my weight onto my right leg. Pain rang up and down my shin like the shout of a warning bell. I winced, drew in a deep breath, and then stepped forward. Why? I cried in my mind as I withdrew to a limp. Merely hours before, I had felt so strong. Now the pain was immeasurable. Why?

I had only four miles to go to reach camp, which the Tallyhos and I had decided to make at mile 200. Down, down, down fell the trail from the mountain, forcing my weight forward and crushing my fragile shin, tormenting me in a way that was worse than going uphill.

I tried to focus on the wind farm in the orange valley below instead of the adamant ache. Hundreds, if not thousands, of wind turbines spun round and round and round. Round and round and round by the wind that moved them to generate great energy.

Everything is connected, I thought as a lone pine materialized on the trail before me. I limped over to the tree and clasped my hand to its rough and rigid trunk. I closed my eyes, summoning the deep-rooted power enabling this tree to rise and thrive in this unforgiving land to rush up its bark and bleed into my hand all the way down to my damaged leg.

"God, heal me. God, heal me," I prayed as I clutched.

For the rest of the downward walk, I gasped rather than breathed as the nauseating pain persevered. I reached camp at sundown. The Tallyhos were eating dinner, their tents trembling in the wind that swirled from the solid base of San Jacinto Peak, 10,833 feet up. I released my pack onto the ground, and sand kicked up.

"What took you so long?" Pandora asked, and this time I told the truth about my shin.

Pandora and Saltlick left their food and helped me pitch my tent. Saltlick advised me to take four tablets of ibuprofen and get some rest.

"You might have to take a few days off if the pain persists," she said.

I swallowed the pills and then ate a handful of nuts, too worn out to cook. Then I crashed inside my tent, my injured leg elevated atop my pack. As I fell asleep, I thought about how the last thing I desired was to take a few days off the trail. This was my life now—the trail. And it was all about momentum. All about moving on—putting one foot in front of the other to get from one great and trying place to the next. It was about continuing. Enduring. Journeying on through the highs and lows to the ultimate destination. Which, I knew, I had not reached. No, I still had far to go. I couldn't stop now.

At dawn, I awoke, unzipped my mesh door, and carefully crept outside my tent into the blustery air. I stood, watching the wind turbines in the distance spiral with an electric fury that seemed to spark from the tail of the wind wrapping around me. I stepped forward on my right leg, and chills rushed down my spine. This was not the first time—nor would it be the last—that the fates of the trail filled me with awe. It's a miracle, I thought, bearing down on my shin. The debilitating pain was gone.

CHAPTER 11
CATCHING UP

That day, the wind slammed into us during our valley trek through the loose, deep sand to Ziggy and the Bear's. The elderly couple had served as the trail angels of Cabazon for years, having even bought a house near the trail by Interstate 10 for the sole purpose of housing hikers.

Thank God for that, I thought as I charged the wind, stronger than I was and stripping me of my energy.

Purple Princess and Donezo, whom the Tallyhos and I had caught up to earlier that morning, sought shelter from the gusts with us beneath the interstate land bridge at mile 210.

"This wind is waging war on us!" Purple Princess yelled, exasperated, his cheeks and thighs blood red with windburn. He pointed to the back of Donezo's bare calves, where the wind had blasted bits of sand into them like shrapnel. Saltlick pulled out her camouflage bandana and wiped her bloody nose while Pandora attempted unsuccessfully to smooth her wild and knotted hair. I swiped my tongue over my upper lip. The skin was dry, rough, and deeply split due to the unrelenting wind.

One mile later, we wearily arrived at the thin dirt path coiling off the trail to Ziggy and the Bear's. A row of blue Porta Potties colored the brown front yard at the end of the path, and a wooden sign pointed hikers to line up at the picket fence surrounding the back half of the house. We rang the bear-shaped iron bell outside the tall white gate. A wrinkled woman wearing red-rimmed glasses, lipstick, and a name tag that said Ziggy opened up, ushered us in, and made us wash our hands in the outdoor sink hooked to the clapboard house before we stepped any farther.

With our hands now clean, Ziggy led us behind the house to the backyard, where a herd of our weathered people huddled together out of the wind. Although this outdoor space was the only area where hikers were permitted to hang, it felt like being inside, what with the carpeted ground, high-ceilinged canopies, couches, and wooden shower shack. Before we were free to relax, though, Ziggy had us sign in on the piece of paper attached to the clipboard on the patio table. As we did so, she went over the house rules.

"No foul language. No using the bathroom without washing your hands. No washing your clothes in the sink; use the buckets we provide. No showers over five minutes. Call your mother this Sunday for Mother's Day."

I leaned over to Purple Princess and whispered, "I feel like I'm in time-out."

He snorted.

Ziggy glared.

Still, for all her sternness, this angel and her husband—who was out getting pizza for everyone—were charitable as they come for opening their home to hikers on this harsh and squally stretch.

After being released to roam, I delved into the four large hiker boxes on the patio—organized by clothes, shoes, food, and gear—nabbing an unopened Baby Ruth, a rare gem among all the pasta and oats. I then bought a cold can of orange soda from Ziggy for a dollar and found a seat in the shade on the red-and-green carpet.

Pandora and Saltlick paid Ziggy five dollars each to retrieve the resupply boxes they'd had mailed here. As they rummaged through their goods, the Bear—a big, bald man with a fierce look in his eyes—entered the backyard with the pizza. A Canadian girl named Gazelle sat next to me as we chowed down on the pepperoni and cheese. I hadn't met her until today. She was tall and thin with long red hair and beautiful porcelain skin. As we conversed, I learned that she'd started the PCT five days after I had and was pushing thirty-mile days in order to achieve the northern terminus at the Canadian border in a mere three months.

"That's insane," I said, since the majority of hikers, myself included, allotted five months to complete the trek.

"Comes at a cost, too," she said. "I pass pretty much everyone, so I'm not really making friends."

I admired her determination, but I also saw the hurtful compromise she was making as she observed those who had connected on the trail playfully interact.

"This trail wasn't meant to be hiked alone," she said. "But I'm not giving up on what I've set out to do."

The wind grew stronger after the Tallyhos and I left Ziggy and the Bear's. We pushed our way through the Mesa Wind Farm, the wind turbines spinning and whistling and humming us along all the way up San Gorgonio Pass, where the wind shifted violently to and fro like clashing ocean waves. This sheer terrain made my leg muscles burn as I flexed them harder than usual to steady myself in the wind. The other side of the pass lay ahead like a dream of golden hills. But the nightmare of the wind played on as we weaved down the switchbacks, having to lean into the mountainside so as not to be blown off the edge.

By mile 219, which we hit in the late afternoon, a junction gave way to a short side trail that shot into the Whitewater Preserve, a former trout farm turned Wildlands Conservancy on the Whitewater River, where the Tallyhos and I decided to sleep for the night. A vast beach of round, white stones surrounded the river running through the land. Striking green fields and tall, healthy sycamores overwhelmed my desert-accustomed eyes. The park ranger on duty walked out from the visitor center when he saw the three of us coming. He guided us to the clear pond stocked with rainbow trout and encouraged us to soak our feet there and even wade in if we wanted. Then he showed us to the best area to camp out of the wind—at the base of the hill below the bathrooms—saying that because we were PCT hikers, we didn't have to pay the nightly fee.

"But be sure to stake your tents in good tonight," he said. "The forecast calls for sixty-mile-per-hour winds."

Here we go again, I thought, recollecting my night at Laguna Campground.

Pandora, Saltlick, and I had to fight to raise our tents and light our stoves, because the wind just kept on and on. Purple Princess and Donezo arrived at dusk, and everyone helped everyone else secure each of our shelters with rocks. I dipped my feet into the pond before going to bed, watching the wind toss the surface of the water as if someone were throwing in rocks. It would have been incredible if anyone had been able to sleep that night. The wind seethed with the fury of God.

The next morning, dust covered me like a grave. It had blown into my tent throughout the night even though my rainfly was on. I brushed it off my face and hair, my eyes watering with the specks trapped inside. I realized as I dressed that the air outside was silent. I poked my head outside. The sycamores were still. The windstorm had passed.

The Tallyhos, Purple Princess, Donezo, and I left Whitewater Preserve together. As we did, I noticed a lone tent propped beneath a sycamore far down the field. Whoever was inside must have arrived during the night and not realized that greater protection from the wind existed down the hill.

Poor soul, I thought.

That morning, the trail ran atop a ridge of yellow grass that opened to views of silver peaks among which clouds rolled like visible breath. Later, at mile 226, the grade descended to Mission Creek, where everyone stopped and sprawled out on the warm river rocks for lunch. The rest of the day's hike required keen navigation through overgrown grass and a dry creek bed. I led the pack and saw a gopher snake swallow a bird, a grouse round up her hatchlings, two marmots chase each other, and a crow play with flight in the sunny breeze. I walked amid natural order—vibrant and true—and no matter how difficult the trek had been the day before, today it was magnificent, and all was most well.

At nightfall, we made camp on a hill above Mission Creek. The air was much colder than usual, and had it not been for the fire ban, we would have warmed ourselves with a campfire. Instead, Pandora wrapped her down sleeping bag around herself as she cooked a packet of couscous, and Saltlick, who only ever wore shorts, pulled on her thermals. Purple Princess and Donezo made dinner inside their tent. I dug out my fleece hat and gloves.

It soon turned miserably cold—a dramatic difference from the heat of the day. I was about to nestle into my tent when I heard footsteps stomping up the hill. Everyone turned to see who was coming at such a fast and heavy pace. First a full-brimmed hat appeared, followed by a bright-blue shirt.

It was Big Spoon.

"I thought you all were way ahead," Big Spoon cried, out of breath, when he realized he had caught up.

"Big Spoon!" I called, unable to contain my excitement. *He's here!* I thought warmly.

He picked a patch of dirt on the edge of the hill and set down his bulky pack. I noticed his new shoes: navy New Balances—and big. He grabbed his water bladder and gulped from the drinking hose. Then, despite the fire ban in Southern California, he said to us all, "I'm going down by the creek to make a fire. It's too cold out here not to. Feel free to join me if you'd like."

I watched from the top of the hill as Big Spoon assembled a fire pit in the shape of a semicircle out of the rocks he'd gathered by the creek. He rolled his shirt-sleeves up, exposing his forearm muscles as he carried the hefty rocks to the pit. Then he built a beautiful fire, starting with tiny twigs and gradually adding larger sticks and finally logs. Soon, a brilliant fire blazed on the bank by the freezing water. This drew everyone down. Big Spoon wandered a small way down the creek and returned dragging a long fallen limb. He placed it by the fire for seats. I sat as close as I could to the flames, not knowing until now how much I had missed being able to have a campfire.

It was illegal—and great.

Once Big Spoon had fostered the fire to his liking, he came over and sat next to me on the limb, a stick in his hand for poking the coals.

"I'm thinking of getting off the trail and skipping ahead to the cooler parts, like the Sierra," he said.

My heart dropped. "No!" I cried, realizing by my reaction that I had been hoping since our separation in Idyllwild that he and I would meet again.

Big Spoon jerked back, surprised by my passionate response.

"The desert is getting old," he said. "I'm not enjoying it anymore. My only motivation over the last two days was to catch up to you guys. I even hiked twenty-seven miles yesterday and camped alone in that crazy windstorm."

"Whoa," I said. "Where?"

"That place off the trail. Whitewater Preserve."

"That's where we camped last night too," I said, puzzled.

He poked the fire. "Huh. I didn't see anyone when I got in last night. It was so late that I just set up in that big field, figuring I was the only one."

"Oh," I said, the image of the lone tent by the sycamore coming back to me now. "I did see you this morning, alone by the tree."

"Yeah, that was me. So, I actually caught up to you last night."

"You did. And now that you're here, we can all hike together," I persuaded.

Big Spoon kept poking the fire, thinking out loud. "Before I started the PCT, my plan was to get a taste of each section—the desert, the Sierra, Oregon, Washington—then move on when I got my fill. I don't have the mind-set everyone else has of hiking the trail all the way through, every single mile. I'm here for exploration, for adventure. Not a hike from *A* to *Z*." He stood, added a log to the fire, and then returned to his seat. "You were right, though. About friendship out here. I didn't realize how crucial the camaraderie would be, how powerful it is in keeping you going. There's no point to any of this without it, I've learned." He repositioned the newly added log with his poking stick, causing the flames to burst up. "I guess I can go a little longer in the desert. Since I've caught up."

I could have leaped like the flames.

Instead, I remained seated as Big Spoon pulled a ruby stone from his pants pocket and handed it to me to see. "I found this earlier today by the creek," he said. "The desert isn't so bad, really."

The stone was small but dazzling, a handheld masterpiece of red crystals.

"You have good eyes," I said, returning his rock.

"I'm sure you do, too. We all see things at different times."

I was starting to see Big Spoon for whom he really was—a strong yet gentle soul, intelligent and hardworking, true to himself, and kind.

One by one, the hikers in our group filed back to their tents. But Big Spoon and I remained by the fire until it diminished to embers. Then we snuffed out the last of the glowing red ash with the rocks. When the fire was completely out, I walked up the hill ahead of Big Spoon, entered my tent—which didn't have its rainfly on—and watched from the mesh wall as he made a pallet on the cold ground with his sleeping pad and sleeping bag, even though it felt like a winter's night out there.

"See you in the morning, Hands," he whispered as he burrowed inside his bag.

"You too, Big Spoon," I whispered back.

I couldn't wait for the sun to rise.

CHAPTER 12

THE DREAM AND DESERT SNOW

That night, I had a beautiful dream. The ruby rock Big Spoon showed me by the fire must have triggered it. I was on the PCT alone, walking through mist and open meadows, when I saw something shining from the earth. I knelt to find the object, sifting the soft ground with my hand. What I discovered was something remarkable—a stunning crystal the size and weight of a chess pawn. I picked it up and examined it. The crystal emitted a dazzling white light that helped me see through the mist and made me feel secure. It had a perfect hole at the top to string a chain through so that it could be worn as a necklace.

I was trying to find this chain so I could put the crystal on it when the frigid morning air woke me. It was dawn. Black clouds smothered the sky, and a thin layer of white dust wisped across the roof of my tent. I looked beyond my transparent tent walls to find that it was lightly snowing. It's snowing in the desert, I thought, both amazed and concerned, instantly remembering that Big Spoon had cowboy camped in this bizarre and freezing weather.

I looked his way.

At some point during the night, he had wrapped himself like a mummy in his rainfly, which was now covered with snow.

We were at mile 235 in the San Bernardino National Forest; ahead of us was a climb into the coldness of 9,000 feet. I shivered as I dressed, slipping my pants and desert shirt over my thermals, followed by my down jacket, rain jacket, fleece hat, and gloves. The Tallyhos, too, put on every article of clothing they had. Purple Princess and Donezo remained in their sleeping bags.

"We're going to wait until it warms up before we head out," Donezo called from the tent to the rest of us as we packed up.

Big Spoon, who when he awoke got ready in a swift five minutes, told the couple out of concern that it might not get warmer for some time and that it looked like more snow was coming.

"Be careful you don't get trapped," he advised before tipping his hat at me and setting out.

Saltlick took to the trail next, followed by Pandora. I finished packing and started tramping a few minutes later as the surprising springtime snow grew to a freezing gush.

At first, the snow was beautiful—the way it draped over the curves of the mountains like a gleaming silk garment. But the higher I climbed, the harder it snowed, and the colder I became. The low temperatures provoked me to hike as fast as I could for the sake of staying warm. I passed Pandora and then Saltlick, eventually catching up to Big Spoon, who was looking all around at the beauty and taking his time up the slippery ridge with the use of his makeshift trekking poles—two pine sticks he had found in the forest.

"Incredible, isn't it? Who would've thought? Snow in the desert," he said when I pulled up behind him.

The land turned more powdery and pure the higher we hiked. Mountains emerged before us like wild angels. I was terribly cold but in awe, brimming with a wonderment that reminded me of my dream. I recounted it to Big Spoon as I stepped after him. He stopped when I'd finished. I stopped too. Large snowflakes fell over us and melted into our clothes. Big Spoon turned to face me, a peculiar look in his arresting blue eyes.

He unzipped his jacket, reached into the pen pocket of his shirt, and pulled something out. He stretched out his arm before me and opened his hand. What lay in his palm stole my breath.

"That's the crystal from my dream," I said, almost in disbelief.

"It's a Herkimer diamond." He placed it into my hand. "A quartz crystal mined in New York. My mom gave it to me not too long ago. When I was getting ready for the trail, something told me to bring it."

I held the Herkimer up to my eye, rotating it with my fingers like a kaleidoscope. Crude, translucent prisms made up its sharp, angular shape. It glowed on all sides as it let in and dispersed the bright whiteness of the snow. It was magnificent—the most beautiful stone I had ever seen. The only difference between it and the one in my dream was that instead of having a hole, this one had a delicate silver band soldered to it for a necklace to be strung through.

"Have you shown this to me before?" I asked Big Spoon, stunned by the sheer resemblance.

Big Spoon shook his head. "Never."

A moment of heavy silence weighed between us.

How odd, I thought. How very, very odd.

I handed the crystal back to him, and he returned it to his pocket.

Then we started again on the trail.

It snowed the rest of the morning. I wanted to keep moving to stay warm, but I had to stop at mile 240 to resupply on water at a spring inside a cave. Icicles adorned the damp, dark wall where the spring trickled out. Big Spoon and I stepped inside the confined hollow, careful to avoid the puddles of slush that had gathered on the rocky ground. I positioned my feet on two wobbly stones and then bent close to the spring, my empty water bladder cradled in my hands.

"Do you believe in God?" Big Spoon asked from behind me, his question echoing off the walls as the cold cave water dripped into my Platypus.

"Yeah," I said, focusing on the spring. "I really do. Do you?"

"Oh, yeah. I believe in God. It's hard not to when you really look around and see what's going on. Especially out here in nature. He's so...present."

"Yeah, truly," I agreed. "You know, it's been said He's everywhere at once, watching out for us, guiding us on."

"I believe that," said Big Spoon.

"Me, too." I hesitated for a moment. "What about destiny? Do you believe in that?" I asked.

"Big time," Big Spoon said, and then he paused to think. "But I also believe in the power to choose. Granted, we don't always make the right decisions. But I think destiny is the product of God's will and ours. I don't think we're ever forced to do one thing or the other so that our destiny plays out. But, like you said, we're guided that way. Then it comes down to us whether or not we go."

As I listened to his insightful words, my attention was pulled away from the spring. The water spilled over the opening to my bladder, and my gloves got wet, numbing my fingers and turning my hands stiff and slow as a rusty machine. My hands didn't thaw out until noon, when the sun faintly lifted above the bloated gray clouds. Each finger burned as if on fire as they slowly came back to life. I was alone now—Big Spoon had decided to eat breakfast at the spring, but I'd kept going after collecting my water because I was too cold to stand still.

The afternoon was warmer, but the snow kept on, transforming the trail and trees to a world of solid white. It was disorienting. Had it not been for the deep, sludgy footprints before me, it would have been easy to veer off the trail.

At dusk, the Tallyhos and Big Spoon caught up to me after I'd reluctantly halted in the icy air to make and eat a tortilla stuffed with peanut butter. Together, the four of us crossed a backcountry road bordered by large cages. A sign in front of the cages informed passersby that Hollywood owned them. Grizzlies slept and tigers paced behind the iron bars. Despite our shivering bodies, we gazed upon the animals for many minutes. How strange it was to see a tiger on the PCT. At the same time, it was fitting. From the very start, this day had been extraordinary.

A US Forest Service truck appeared on the road as we observed the lovely beasts. The ranger driving pulled off next to us and asked if we were okay.

"We're a little cold but otherwise fine," Pandora said.

"Something the matter?" Big Spoon asked.

"Just checking," the ranger said. "Two guys got off the trail at the service road you crossed a few miles back. The hydrologist on our crew happened to be there, and the guys asked him for a ride into Big Bear so they wouldn't have to hike in the snow. Our buddy who helped them said they looked pretty miserable."

"Purple Princess and Donezo," I said, smiling at the ingenuity of these fair-weather hikers.

The ranger went on, and so did we, arriving an hour later at the Arrastre Trail Camp at mile 256. Before anything else, Big Spoon cleared the snow out of the designated fire ring—a metal structure that signified that fires were allowed regardless of the ban—while Pandora, Saltlick, and I gathered stacks of the driest sticks we could find. Amazingly, Big Spoon started a fire with the wet wood, using toilet paper and pine needles to spark it. After setting up, the Tallyhos and I huddled on the log closest to the fire, absorbing its rich, glowing warmth as it became dark.

"It's twenty-eight degrees out," remarked Big Spoon, who sat on the log opposite us, employing the light of the fire to read the slender thermometer hanging from his pack.

"It's bedtime," Saltlick said, and just as we were about to retire to our tents, out of the darkness appeared Pine Stick—a witty old man with a white beard who walked with a single pine stick as if it were his wizard's staff.

I had met Pine Stick earlier that day as I passed him on the snowy ridge. Now, drenched from the snow, he plumped down next to Big Spoon, pulled off his soggy gloves, and extended his hands over the flames.

"Boy, oh, boy! Am I glad for this fire!" he said through clattering teeth.

Big Spoon threw some more sticks on it, and everyone remained outside a little longer as Pine Stick—a civil engineer from Washington—entertained us with his tales.

One story was about Cat Whacker—Pine Stick's son who was now ahead of him on the trail. Pine Stick narrated to us how Cat Whacker had received his trail name the first night on the PCT, when a ring-tailed cat had sneaked into camp and tried to steal Pine Stick's food. Consequently, the son grabbed Pine Stick's pine stick and whacked the raccoon-like pilferer over and over until the critter scampered away.

"So, I named him Cat Whacker," Pine Stick said, a lively air of amusement in his aged voice.

We laughed and laughed. It was the great kind of laughter, too—the kind that was deep and pure and effortless. The kind that even after the laughter ceased would radiate inside us like solar energy, harnessing enough heat to keep us warm through the cruel and bitter night.

CHAPTER 13
BIG BEAR

B ig Bear Lake was a rustic lakeside town in the San Bernardino Mountains where the Tallyhos, Big Spoon, and I sought sanctuary the next day—after our bout with the desert blizzard. It was Saturday afternoon, and I was depleted of all strength as I neared the end of a ten-mile slipfest through the deep, slick snow that made keeping a steady stride impossible. At mile 266, the trail crossed Highway 18 at a busy trailhead parking area, where the vehicles of day hikers occupied every spot. Big Spoon—whom I had hiked with since sunrise—and I reached the dirt lot together and plopped down in the dust at its perimeter to wait for Saltlick and Pandora before obtaining the short hitch into town.

Because the trail had dropped us to an elevation of about 6,800 feet, here the luscious sun had melted the snow. Leaning against my pack, I stretched out my legs (revealing my mud-soaked pants), and then spread open my arms (displaying my sweat-soiled sleeves), and tilted my ruddy face to the sun.

Big Spoon didn't make such a scene but sat cross-legged with his back slightly bent as he reviewed his map. I wasn't speaking to him because he'd made me mad. Several minutes before, after I'd opened my big mouth and asked if he and his girlfriend stayed in touch, he'd told me that he missed her.

"I try to call her when I'm in town, but with the time difference and her working, it's hard to connect. We're supposed to meet up in Lake Tahoe," he'd said, referring to the popular city located a few miles off the trail at mile 1,094. "But she doesn't have her plane ticket yet because it's too early to tell when I'll get there."

That was when I'd stopped talking to him, irrationally hurt by this as I was.

Now, as we sat there in the parking lot, he struck up a conversation. "Do *you* have a boyfriend?" he asked.

"No," I answered tersely, still facing the sun.

"That's hard to believe."

I laughed. "Uh, huh. Sure."

"No, really," Big Spoon guaranteed. "You're gorgeous, Hands."

My cheeks flushed. "Thank you," I said in a gentler tone.

"And you're not some phony, either," he went on. "I've watched how you interact with others and how they react to you. You draw them in with this—I don't know—brightness you have."

His flattery both elated and embarrassed me. I pulled up my legs and drew my arms around them.

"And for you to come out here alone shows you're extremely brave. It's crazy to me that no one has swept you up," Big Spoon said.

"Well, maybe I don't need to be swept up," I said, intending to end it there, but then something pushed me to divulge, "Or maybe the right person just hasn't come along."

"Maybe not," Big Spoon said, considering this, sounding almost hurt by my comment. "But how are you supposed to know who the right person is, anyway?"

Unsympathetically, I replied, "I already told you. Remember, right after the Third Gate Water Cache?" I turned to look at him. "You'll just know when you know."

Big Spoon shook his head. "Right. That's such a cop-out, though."

"I don't think so," I refuted. "You say you believe in soul mates. Doesn't it make sense that the soul would recognize its truest partner when the two came to cross paths?"

Big Spoon pondered this. "Well, I guess so," he finally concurred. "If you look at it that way."

"I don't want to cross any lines," I remarked, speaking daringly now, "but do you recognize even a hint of this in your girlfriend?"

He sighed. "I don't know. She's my buddy. And we've been together a year. Granted, we broke up once during that time. We get along great. But I've had this residual feeling that something's missing between us. When I came out here, we left things open ended. She even told me that if I met someone while I was away, then she'd be happy for me." He looked a bit distraught.

"Can I be honest with you?" I asked, softening my voice.

"Yes."

"That doesn't sound like love to me—your relationship with your girlfriend."

"What do you mean?" he asked, clearly wanting to hear my view.

"Well, I mean...two people who love each other and want to be together—in my opinion—should never be okay with one of them finding another. A person should do what it takes to be with the one he loves. Not leave it *open ended*."

Big Spoon nodded slowly. "You make a good point. When we meet up in Lake Tahoe, we're going to see how things are between us and go from there."

"That will be good," I said, and I meant it.

"Do you have your eye on anyone out here?" Big Spoon asked, changing the subject.

I was silent.

You. I have my eye on you, I thought sincerely.

But how could I tell him that?

"It's okay. You don't have to answer," he said after many seconds passed without an utterance from my lips.

How could he not know now that he was the one I saw?

⟞⟊⟝

That night, at the Motel 6 on Big Bear Boulevard, the Tallyhos, Big Spoon, and I split a room. We did this for the sake of saving money—each one of us had quit our jobs to hike the trail, so we had finite funds, forcing us to be thrifty with every cent.

Pandora and I shared one of the queen beds. Saltlick and Big Spoon shared the other.

In the morning, I rose before the rest, put on my freshly laundered clothes—still stained with dirt and sweat—and combed my wild, tangled hair that I'd done my best to wash in the motel shower the night before. It was Sunday. I caught the first shuttle outside the motel to attend the early service at Community Fellowship Big Bear—where the Motel 6 receptionist had recommended I go after I told her I hadn't been in civilization on a Sunday morning in a while and was looking to go to church.

A three-mile ride down the poppy-filled streets led to the little white church on Big Bear Lake. The calm blue water captivated me when I stepped off the shuttle—a liquid mirror that reflected the rising snowcaps peering in. A white glider soared over the lake in the sapphire sky as a lone man in his johnboat fished. I could have watched this scene for hours, but I adhered to my purpose for coming here and entered the church. Inside the holy halls, I instantly became aware of how badly I stank. Even though I had showered, my potent thru-hiker's whiff was getting harder to wash out.

Anxiously, I skipped to the coffee station in the corner of the chapel, where a plump woman smelling of lavender poured me a steaming cup.

"You must be a PCT hiker," she said, not backing away from my odorous self but drawing in close.

"I am," I said, and the woman waved over the other members, announcing, "She's hiking the PCT!"

Soon, I found myself surrounded by people of all stages of life, hugging me, congratulating me, and engaging with me about my trek.

No one seemed to mind my stench. They made me feel at home.

Back at the motel room—which smelled like a dirty locker room when I walked in—the Tallyhos and Big Spoon were gearing up for the trail. I squeezed over to my pile of groceries on the floor—the ones I'd bought yesterday—to do the same, finding a large, ripe orange that I had not purchased sitting atop my pack.

I held up the beautiful fruit and flashed them a curious expression.

"Big Spoon bought that for you while you were at church," Pandora said, ratting him out. "There's a fruit stand down the street."

I glanced over at Big Spoon, who was by the bed closest to the door, packing.

He smiled, not looking up.

"I mean, he got Saltlick and me one too, but probably only because he wanted to get one for you." Pandora continued to give him a hard time.

"Geez, you guys are so young." Saltlick shook her head.

I peeled and ate the orange, the juices running down my fingers.

"Thank you, Big Spoon," I said.

"You're very welcome."

I turned my attention to packing up, although at the moment, my eyes were fixed on him.

CHAPTER 14
A TRUE FIND

The next day, I hiked alone—ten miles through a thick pine forest, catching shiny glimpses here and there of Big Bear Lake through the trees. It was good to be alone. I'd started later that morning than the Tallyhos and Big Spoon for this sole purpose. Now I could soak in all of nature and reflect, realizing as I did how enamored I had become with Big Spoon.

The sun was high above me when I reached the Holcomb Creek crossing at mile 286. Big Spoon was there, sitting on a long, flat rock, using his pocket-sized magnifying glass and the sun to burn black, intricate letters and designs into one of his pine sticks.

The scene reminded me of the day before, when we were all waiting outside Motel 6 for a hitch back to the trail. Big Spoon had showed me a picture on his phone of one of his welded sculptures. It was a metal guard holding a scepter, the whole thing constructed out of the rusty car parts he said he saved from the beat-up Jeeps he liked to buy, fix, and resell.

"It's called 'Sentry,'" he said as I analyzed the details in the guard's stance and face that made him look as if he were really watching over.

I'd had no idea that Big Spoon was so artistic.

"My next idea for a sculpture is a big sleeping angel that I think would be cool to somehow place over the entranceway to a city. A symbol of both protection and peace," he said.

I thought that was beautiful.

At Holcomb Creek, Big Spoon set down his magnifying glass when he saw me. The hot, smoky smell from the woodburning wafted through the air.

"I've been waiting for you," he said, his voice confident and kind.

I removed my pack and sat next to him on the rock.

"Can I see?" I asked, referring to his pine stick.

"It's not finished yet," he said, showing it to me anyway.

The words Big Spoon were carved down the pine in simple lettering. Above the name was a warped spoon he said he'd messed up on and was trying to turn into a tree.

"It looks like a spoon to me," I said, setting the stick down and then kicking off my shoes and socks. I waded out into the shallow creek. Big Spoon stood and watched me from the grassy bank as I cupped my hands, dipped them into the cool water, and splashed my gritty face. He then unlaced his shoes, slipped off his socks, and waded in next to me.

"This feels so good," he said, using his hat like a bowl to pour water over his hair, which was streaked with the yellows of dappled light.

He looked at me, the clear water emphasizing his eyes, droplets running down his suntanned face.

I held his gaze. We stood there, close enough to touch each other if one of us were to reach out. I desired to reach out, but I didn't. Did he desire this too? He stared into my eyes, and all at once, I yearned with a fiery fury nearly too hot to bear for him to seize me and hold me. To pull me in so I could feel his body upon mine.

I dropped my eyes and walked away, back to the bank, because this was not right. He had someone else.

If it's meant to be, it will be, I consoled myself, putting my shoes back on. All the while, torment gripped me within.

He and I hiked together the rest of the day through fields of white talus that crunched underfoot. He told me many things, like how when he was growing up in New Jersey, his parents took him and his four older siblings to the Delaware Water Gap, a unique geological formation where Big Spoon had searched for and found basic fossils of shells and leaves.

"Those trips sparked my intrigue in the fossil hunting I do today," he said, revealing that he had a decent collection of petrified horse teeth and megalodon teeth, alligator bones and deer antlers—his favorite discovery to date being an ancient camel's tooth injected with a dazzling blue mineral he'd dived for and uncovered in Florida's Peace River.

"If we're only willing to look," he said, "there's always something to find."

I inquired more about him and learned that he was twenty-six, an ambitious young man who after college had worked for three years as a mechanical engineer at Picatinny Arsenal in Morris County, New Jersey. He'd made good money there but felt he was missing out on something—what, he could not say. So, going against the advice and judgment of his boss and coworkers, he'd quit his job and, after a few weeks of traveling down the East Coast in his truck, set up in St. Petersburg, Florida. There, he got certified to scuba dive in order to fossil hunt in the rivers and the sea. He picked up a job in the gun shop of the outfitters store, where he had received his certification. That's how he met his girlfriend. She worked in the kayaking department. And that's how he learned about the PCT—through his manager in the gun shop, who was a Triple Crowner, meaning that he'd successfully thru-hiked the three major long-distance trails in America—the Appalachian Trail, the Continental Divide Trail, and the Pacific Crest Trail.

"If I had to do one over again, it'd be the PCT," his manager, Jeremy, allegedly told him. "It had the best views of them all."

"From that point on, my interest was piqued," Big Spoon said as we hiked.

Being an explorer at heart who knew intuitively that Florida was not his final fate, he began meeting with Jeremy at the Cracker Barrel in the mornings before work to learn more about the trail.

"I never thought I'd want to try a thru-hike," he told me. "I'd rather make camp in a neat spot and check out that area for days. But," he confessed, "something powerful was drawing me to the trail. I swear something was pulling me here."

Thus, using the discounts he received from working at the outfitters, he started purchasing the backpacking gear he needed while conducting his own research during his work breaks by reading the discolored PCT guidebooks from the 1970s he'd found in the store's storage room.

"Against all odds, I decided just a few weeks before I came out here to really do this—hike the PCT," Big Spoon said as we approached camp at mile 293, where the Tallyhos had already set up.

"I quit my job at the outfitters, terminated my apartment lease, and drove my truck back up to Jersey to see my family before flying to San Diego."

He halted before entering the campsite and turned to face me.

"I wasn't looking for a girl," he said, taking me by surprise. "But that first day at Scout and Frodo's, I noticed you instantly. You stood out from the rest in a very unique way. Then our paths kept crossing on the trail, and I kind of couldn't believe what I was discovering. Hands, you're a true find."

≈++≈

Later that night after everyone had gone to bed, someone tapped on my tent. I opened the door and popped out my head.

"Big Spoon?"

"Come with me," he whispered.

I slipped my jacket and sandals on over my thermals, slid my headlamp over my head, and flashed it on.

In the darkness, Big Spoon led me up the trail in silence. I didn't question him but simply followed. A few minutes later, we arrived at the base of a mountainside, where a steep wash of fragmented rock had formed a rugged path.

"We're going up it," Big Spoon said, pointing to the wash.

I used my hands as I scrambled up, the soles of my feet feeling every rock jab through my flimsy shoes.

Two sitting stones were placed before a small stone
fire pit that Big Spoon had constructed at the top of the
wash. A tepee of sticks stuck up from the pit.

"When did you do this?" I asked, my heart swelling
with the ache of love.

"When you all went to sleep. It's not much."

We sat on the stones. He struck a match and held it
beneath the tinder. A stick caught fire—the flame like
a string of orange breath spreading to the other wood.
The fire popped. Soon, it blazed in the night like a diamond amid coal, its fine smoke snaking up to the stars,
the light of which bathed the black night.

"Big Spoon," I said carefully as he fed the fire a new
stick, "I think you're a find, too."

He smiled, keeping his eyes on the flames. "Thank
you for telling me that."

We remained at the top of the wash next to the
warming fire for hours, talking on and on and on about
everything we could think to say.

"I told my girlfriend about you," Big Spoon said
when my eyes had grown so heavy that I was squinting.

"What? When?" His unexpected disclosure woke me
up.

"In Big Bear. I called and let her know what was going on. I have a lot of thinking to do." His voice was very
serious.

"I guess I do too," I said, moved by the fact that we
were having this conversation.

"Good," he said. "Because I don't take things like this lightly. I'm very calculated about them."

"Me, too," I assured him. "I'm very guarded."

"That's good."

"Luckily, we have a long way left to go on the trail. There's no rush for anything."

"Okay," Big Spoon said, scooping up a handful of dirt and dousing the glowing embers that remained from the fire. "Okay."

The fire was completely out, save for the puffs of smoke spitting up from the dirt. Big Spoon dispersed the coals with his foot and then smothered them with the rocks he'd used to build the pit. I stood and brushed off the ash that had drifted onto my clothes. It would be daybreak soon. We walked down the wash back to our tents. But before we did, I realized something and looked up at Big Spoon's night-shaded face.

"What's your real name?" I asked.

This surprised him. "You don't know?"

I shook my head.

"Caleb. My name is Caleb."

Something stirred inside me. It was as if I had known it all along.

Later, I would learn it was a name that meant "bold."

CHAPTER 15
DIVING IN

At mile 308, the masses flocked to Deep Creek Hot Springs—a desert oasis in San Bernardino National Forest. It was the day after Big Spoon made the fire for me. I had hiked the fifteen miles from camp to the natural hot springs alone. The air was as arid as ash, the sun searing me through my clothes. I thought about my and Big Spoon's situation as I walked through the wretched heat, sweat dripping from my forehead, burning my eyes.

Are you blind? I asked myself, grasping the truth of the matter: that I had been on the trail for a mere three weeks and was falling in love with a stranger.

Fool. You're going to get hurt, I scoffed at myself.

After a full morning of this self-berating, the hot springs materialized before me like a distracting mirage—crystal water amid the coarse sand. I had never seen this many people in one place on the trail. According to my map, area locals could also access the springs from a trail on the other side of Deep Creek— the pristine stream that forked off from the Mojave River. I descended the skinny side trail to this retreat, remembering the other thing my map had disclosed— clothing optional.

The hikers wore underwear, revealing their callused skin and funny tan lines. But the locals strutted the sandy beach and lounged in the steaming water naked, exposing everything—shameless and free.

I wanted to strip naked, too—to also be so free. But there were just too many people around. So, I leaned my pack against a boulder and pulled off my white shirt, settling on bathing in my sports bra and shorts.

Some locals had dragged a keg of Bud Lite to the beach for everyone to enjoy. I filled one of my water bottles with the warm beer and then went over to Saltlick and Pandora, who were eating lunch on the sand.

"Big Spoon's somewhere around here," Pandora said, as if she knew I'd been wondering where he was. She and Saltlick both had wet hair—they'd already been dipping in the springs.

"How's the water?" I asked, taking the focus off Big Spoon.

"Life changing," Saltlick said. "What are you waiting for?"

"Me," said Big Spoon, who seemed to appear magically before our group, a big grin on his bearded face.

He was wearing his blue shirt and black boxers, his long, pale legs on display.

"Ow! Ow!" Pandora catcalled as he unbuttoned his shirt and threw it on the beach, revealing his sculpted stomach.

Big Spoon blushed. "You coming, Hands?"

"Yes."

Fool, fool, fool, echoed inside my head.

With my water bottle of beer in hand, I joined Big Spoon for a swim in the creek, which had been divided by rocks into several pools. The main pool was cold, long, and deep. We swam to the other end to get to what some locals said was the hottest of the three springs. Boulders surrounded the water like beautiful gates, and waterfalls trickled down from the cracks. We climbed up a slippery rock to access the hot spring, where steam rolled off the surface as scalding water from the earth sprang into it from underneath. I stuck my toe in and then sank down neck deep, sitting on the stone bottom and leaning against a lichen-covered rock, soaking in the bliss of this all-encompassing heat.

Big Spoon slipped in more slowly, letting his body adjust to the high temperature. His thigh touched mine when he was all the way in. Neither of us pulled away.

I sipped the beer and then passed it to him. He took a swig and then passed it back. We spent the next several hours in the water, hopping from spring to spring, diving into the main pool when the heat swirling between us became too much to bear.

Back on the beach, we lay out in the sand to let the sun dry our shriveled skin. I was about to fall asleep when Saltlick and Pandora came over and said they wanted to put in another five miles before the day was done.

"Come on, lovebirds, it's time to go," Saltlick commanded like a mother.

The hike that evening cut through the burnt-orange mountainside high above Deep Creek. The sun hung right in front of us, and although it was hard to see ahead, the very bright glow illuminated our next steps exactly.

At mile 313, we came upon the Mojave River Forks Dam—a dry dam built for flood control, spilling like a concrete slide into the daffodil-colored earth below. We crept to the end of the massive dam and looked beyond into a barren land of a thousand power lines. It was like standing on the edge of an abandoned world. Then the four of us sat on the convex ground between the colossal concrete walls and called out like crows—"Caw-caw! Caw-caw!"—again and again for the echo.

When the sun went down, the wind picked up. Saltlick and Pandora took this as their cue to seek out a campsite a little way down from the dam. Big Spoon and I remained where we were, watching the pink-and-purple sky change into the starry night as we sat next to each other. And that was all.

With the stars fully out, we rejoined the Tallyhos, having to take off our shoes to cross the warm creek and access camp.

In the morning, after everyone had packed up, Big Spoon pulled me aside by the clear, shallow creek and said he had done his thinking.

"In the next town, I'm making the call to my girlfriend to end things between us for good."

"Are you sure?" I asked, feeling nervous.

Big Spoon didn't hesitate. "I'm sure."

The day consisted of a twenty-two-mile hike along the alluring Silverwood Lake. In the morning, I stuck with Saltlick and Pandora, whom it seemed I hadn't spoken to in weeks.

I tried not to mention him, but after walking for several miles through the fantastic wildflowers in full bloom with only him on my mind, I had to ask them, "What do you think of Big Spoon?"

Pandora answered first. "He's solid."

"Yeah? You think?"

"Oh, yeah. As solid as they come."

"Saltlick?"

"He's a good guy," she admitted. "But I'd be careful. He has a girlfriend. And heartbreak's a bitch."

At mile 328, we stopped for lunch at the Cleghorn Picnic Area. Big Spoon was already there, skipping rocks on the bank near a duck and drake floating side by side in the water. We took advantage of the available amenities—pit toilets and trash cans—and then gathered together at the picnic table by the dazzling lake to share an odd feast of trail food—granola, chocolate, red beans, and rice.

Afterward, Big Spoon and I hiked together for the rest of the day to camp at mile 335. At one point, he stretched out his arms to the open trail and cried, "Life is starting over for me in the best possible way!"

I laughed. "How do you know?"

"I just do. Don't you? It's like it slapped me in the face."

"I'm scared," I confessed.

"Don't be," he said. "Trust me."

"Can I?"

Big Spoon didn't answer my question. He simply said, "You'll see."

CHAPTER 16
HIKER HUNGER

I ndigo clouds whirled above us the next morning as we broke down camp. A cold breeze ran through the long grass, leaping up and nipping me on the face. It looked like another snowstorm was coming in. Fortunately, Cajon Pass was only seven miles away. Cut between the San Bernardino and San Gabriel Mountains, the highway pass was known for its McDonald's right off the trail.

By now, my hiker hunger bit at me nonstop. No matter how much I ate, within minutes I was always hungry for more. This relentless appetite was the result of walking all day with a pack over difficult terrain. All day long, I burned calories. Even when I lay down to sleep, my body continued to burn calories at a high rate, making me feel like I was continually on empty.

The Tallyhos and Big Spoon had contracted hiker hunger, too. The condition dominated our daily conversation. As we hiked, we'd ask each other questions like, "What's your favorite food your mom makes?" Or "If you were on death row, what would you choose for your last meal?"

Saltlick wanted crab. Pandora craved lasagna. Big Spoon desired Chinese dumplings. My mouth watered at the thought of prime rib.

"Today is a glorious day," Pandora proclaimed as we huddled together over our mushy morning oatmeal. "For today we reach the Golden Arches."

"Tallyho!" I shouted.

"Tallyho!" echoed Pandora, Saltlick, and Big Spoon.

It started to rain as we reached Highway 138, where the curved, monumental *M* reigned like the sun in the stormy sky. Next to the highway ran railroad tracks on which yellow Union Pacific trains chugged. We walked a quarter mile down the side of the busy road, forced to dodge the long line of semitrucks waiting to fill up at the gas station in the same plaza as the McDonald's.

Inside the fast-food restaurant, a mixture of musty hikers and people in business suits stood in line at the counter. The clock on the wall announced that it was 10:30 a.m.—the cutoff time for breakfast.

"Is it too late to order a sausage biscuit?" Pandora asked, desperation in her voice.

The Hispanic cashier showed compassion. "We make you the last one," she said.

"Could I get one too?" Big Spoon asked.

The cashier sighed. "Yes, we can make exception. Hikers," she muttered under her breath.

Along with the biscuit, Pandora also ordered two double cheeseburgers, an order of chicken nuggets, and fries. Saltlick went with the Big Mac, ordering one after the other, followed by coffee and pie. Big Spoon and I split a total of four trays filled with chicken nuggets, cheeseburgers, cherry pies, milkshakes, coffee, and Coke. It was like greasy manna from the sky. We ate at a red booth in the corner, and for the first time in days, I felt full.

The rain plunged down in sheets as we sat back in the booth to let our food settle. The hikers at the surrounding tables said they planned to get a room at the Best Western down the road to wait out the storm. This sounded great, but it presented a dilemma for Big Spoon and me because we had resupply packages at the post office in Wrightwood—our next town stop twenty-six miles away. Today was Thursday. We needed to reach Wrightwood by Friday afternoon, because the post office was closed on the weekends. Therefore, by staying at the Best Western instead of putting in the rest of the day's miles, we wouldn't make Wrightwood in time to get our boxes, meaning we'd have to stay in town through the weekend to pick them up Monday, which would create an undesired setback.

But the storm was getting very bad, and no one wanted to get back on the trail.

"I know," Big Spoon said, his logistical lightbulb flashing on. "Hands and I can hitch a ride to Wrightwood today, get our packages, and then hitch back to the Best Western for the night."

It was a good plan. Now we had to find someone willing to drive us twenty-six miles.

As Big Spoon and I buckled our backpacks over our wet rain jackets to go stand by the highway with our hoods and thumbs up, two young women walked inside and announced, serendipitously, that they were giving rides to Wrightwood to any hiker in need.

"It's like magic," I said, turning to Big Spoon.

"It's something," he said.

During the twenty-minute drive, as we passed tan boulders and green groves of Joshua trees, Big Spoon and I learned that the women were thru-hikers, too—Luxury and Innuendo.

"We're yoga instructors from Alaska," said Innuendo, who was clothed in tight spandex.

"And we started the PCT together," Luxury added, waving her hands in the air, showing her manicured nails.

They went on to say they'd only recently rented the Honda we were in because Luxury had suffered a nasty bone contusion to her knee that had forced her off the trail.

"I didn't want to go back to Alaska, though, because I'd planned for months to spend the whole summer out here. So, Innuendo, the good friend that she is, stepped off with me. And now we're following the herd, trying to help out where we can."

"So, you're trail angels now," I said.

"We're just trying to spread the love," said Innuendo.

They dropped us off at the Wrightwood post office, saying they'd return in a few minutes to transport us to the Best Western.

"Luxury wants to find a Starbucks," Innuendo said, rolling her eyes. "We'll be back."

Inside, the tiny stone building was packed. Big Spoon and I waited in line for several minutes and then, with our boxes in hand, scooted past the crowd and returned outside, where we bunched beneath the building's awning to wait out of the rain for our drivers. The air was turning colder with each icy raindrop, and I shivered like a leaf in the wind. Big Spoon grabbed my bare hands to gauge how cold they were. Then he took off his jacket and slipped it over me.

At the Best Western, hikers roamed the outdoor halls, carrying loads of dirty laundry to the washer and dryer on the second floor and then sprinting to the patio downstairs in sports bras and boxers to claim a spot in the bubbling hot tub. Big Spoon and I split a ground-floor room with the Tallyhos. When we arrived, Pandora was dancing to a song she was singing while washing her spoon in the bathroom sink. Saltlick was relaxing on one of the beds, eating a gas-station burrito and watching the weather channel, which showed a foot of snow high up on the trail.

We combined our laundry, put it in a pile by the washer and dryer behind the other rancid loads, and made for the hot tub, where we spent a good portion of the night soaking in the grimy—although to us luxurious—water as the freezing rain came down. Many others I hadn't met before crammed in with us—like Firecracker, Big Fish, and Baby Eater. Nervously, I asked how Baby Eater had gotten his name. He said he'd accepted a challenge in Big Bear to eat a seven-pound burrito as big as a swaddled babe.

"Well, I ate it—every bite," he said, patting his stomach. "And it earned me my title on the trail."

The storm only worsened. With the lights out in our room, Pandora and Saltlick crawled into one bed. Big Spoon and I slipped into the other. I stayed on my side for several minutes. Don't do it, I thought. Don't do it. But, having such deep desire, I rolled near him and, with great caution, placed my head on his bare chest. It was warm and strong. He put his arms around me and rested his chin on my head. It was as if we had performed this ritual for years.

It was as if a hunger I didn't even know I had was being perfectly fed.

CHAPTER 17

KEEP YOUR EYES OPEN

Big Spoon called his girlfriend the next morning. She didn't pick up.

"I'll have to try her later," he said to me in the hotel lobby, disappointment in his voice.

"Are you sad at all?" I asked, referring to his looming breakup.

"No."

"Are you sure?"

He looked at me deeply. "In my mind, it's done."

After checking out at noon, our group hiked thirteen miles through Angeles National Forest to a campsite on a hill that looked out on the San Gabriel Mountains. It had snowed twelve inches in the mountains the day before—a rare event for Southern California in May. Pandora and Saltlick were ahead. I hiked with Big

Spoon along the open ridge, a series of snow-covered peaks beyond. It was a cold day, but the sun was out. The snowcaps captured and emitted the golden light like a lamp.

Big Spoon checked his phone constantly.

"I actually have service here," he said when we summited an 8,000-foot peak. "I'm trying her again."

"Here?" I asked. "On the trail?"

"Here," he said. "I don't like to draw things out."

"Well, me either. Good luck."

I went on ahead while he paused on the peak to place the call. As I walked through the fresh, deep snow that concealed the trail like whiteout, I thought of the first time I saw Big Spoon. It was the day I'd arrived in San Diego. He was at Scout and Frodo's, and—looking back on it now—I remembered him standing tall and quiet in the corner of the backyard, observing everything, as if he were watching over.

My phone rang, interrupting my contemplation.

"I know I could've caught up to you to tell you this," Big Spoon said when I answered. I was surprised the reception reached this far. "But I couldn't wait."

I stopped ankle deep in the snow. My heart raced.

"I explained our situation to her," he said.

I held my breath, feeling sick, as if I were to blame for another's heartbreak.

"And you'll never guess what she did."

"Oh, no. What?" I blurted out.

"Laughed," he said.

"What?"

"She laughed. She said, in her eyes, we weren't really together anymore. She said she knew we were, in a way, saying good-bye when I left for the trail."

I didn't know what to say.

"So, you know what that means?" The sound of his breathing came harsh over the phone as he hiked.

"I have no idea."

"Claire, it means that when I catch up to you, I'm going to give you a big kiss."

It was the first time in days someone had called me by my real name.

Big Spoon caught up to me several minutes later. We took off our packs where we were and used them as seats upon the frosty crest. The cliff over which we dangled our feet looked out upon massive mountains glowing in the sun. Big Spoon took my hand and held it tight.

"You know how you can see things sometimes that aren't really there?"

"I think so," I said, the tension rising.

"Well, on my walk to you just now, I saw a red rock in the shape of a heart. This might sound hard to believe, but as I passed it, it looked like it had a face that was smiling. It only looked like that for a second, though, before it turned back into a rock."

"Maybe it's a sign," I said.

"I think so. Life's fascinating." He looked out. "How you can't see ahead, but you can see back. It's like I'm seeing how all the events in my life were signs leading me here. How all the decisions I made and the steps I took brought me to my destiny."

"What is your destiny?" I asked.

"You know. I swear, from the moment I saw you, I felt this connection between us. I just needed time to process everything. Now I see," he said. "Where have you been all my life?" He looked at me when he said this.

I answered, "I've been walking to this point, just like you."

Big Spoon smiled. "Good thing you didn't get lost."

Then he kissed me on the ridge beneath the beaming sun.

———

The next morning, I stayed behind to write in my journal—leaning against an evergreen at camp—to get everything that had happened out, a release of the heavy truth that Big Spoon and I were on a new journey together now, with the great unknown before us.

Once on the trail again, I felt lighter and hiked harder than ever before, as if a new, more powerful, more vivacious self had slipped over my weathered being. Wrightwood was thirteen miles ahead at mile 369. I was alone, hiking up a steep and snowy path, unconcerned about my freezing feet in my eagerness to meet back up with my unforeseen companion. Fog blanketed the air, making it hard to see. It evoked my memory of a few days before, when Big Spoon had been ahead of me and left a message at the side of the trail out of rocks that read "Hands." However, because I was walking with my head down—with what I called "trail vision"—I'd passed the message without seeing it.

Big Spoon had asked me later that day if I'd found his note.

"What note?"

"Be sure to keep your eyes open so you don't miss anything," he'd said after he told me.

Now, at the top of the demanding hill, I stopped to examine my surroundings. It was quiet out, as if the snow had snuffed all sound. The snow was everywhere—draping the pines like robes and lying atop the earth like tangible clouds. The ground was solid white save for something small and dark permeating my peripherals. I walked over to the oddity and was elated when I discovered what it was: another message—this time made up of pine needles and sticks. It read "J'aime Claire."

A little farther on, I found Big Spoon crouching in the snow in a tangled thicket, guarding himself from the wind.

"What are you doing?" I asked, amused.

"Waiting for you," he said as he crawled out of the brush.

I laughed. "If you're not catching up to me, you're waiting on me, it seems." He had his red bandana wrapped around his neck. "It's freezing out. How long have you been here?"

"Maybe two hours. Did you get my note?"

"Yes. Thank you." My soul swelled with love. "What have you been doing all this time?"

"Oh, I've been keeping busy."

"Doing what?"

"Well, I wrote a poem."

"You did? I love poetry. Can I hear it?"

He was standing before me now and pulled a folded piece of paper from his pants pocket.

"It's not finished," he said.

"That's okay."

He cleared his throat. "It's called 'What's Not Seen.'" Then he read aloud, mixing his lyrics with the wind:

For those with eyes that see what's not seen.
That explore what is beyond.
That dare to take a step off the path
of convention
shall be given a journey of limitless length
where treasures abound
of greatness and glory.
For things exist out there, just waiting to be found,
touched, held, enjoyed.
For whether they are sights, smells, or sounds,

all it takes is a tiny discovery to make
your efforts
profound.
For in each square inch of this universe, a microcosm
of life
thrives on its own.
Things live and die, strive and survive, all a part of
it all,
a fraction of the pie.
So take a close look, and look close indeed,
for you might be surprised at what you might see.
For when you go where they haven't and explore what
they won't,
you, too, will see
what's not seen.

━╬╪━

Smoke danced from the chimneys of every Wrightwood cabin. The whole town smelled of the richness of firewood. Minutes before we'd arrived, Big Spoon and I had received a hitch at the road crossing called Inspiration Point from a bear of a man in faded overalls and his dainty, well-dressed wife, who said they owned several rental properties downtown. They offered to rent us a room at their cabin, Bear with Us, for twenty-five dollars a night. I called the Tallyhos, who were already in town, to gauge their plans.

On the phone, Pandora said she and Saltlick were staying with a woman they had contacted from the Trail Angel Directory posted at the hardware store. "But, sorry, Hands!" Pandora said. "There's not enough room for you guys. We asked."

I wondered. Was the bond Big Spoon and I had developed creating a rift between the Tallyhos and me?

As a result of that conversation, Big Spoon and I took the couple up on their offer to stay the night at their cabin. They swung us by, gave us the tour, took our cash, told us the front door was always unlocked, and left. Big Spoon and I didn't even take off our backpacks before racing to the Grizzly Café a few blocks down, where according to our burly landlord, "They got the best damn burger in town."

Deer mounts and wicker snowshoes decorated the country restaurant. Big Spoon and I sat in a booth by the window and ordered two burgers with fries—a beer and the house salad to share. I smelled so terrible that I excused myself while we waited for our food and went into the bathroom, where I scrubbed my armpits with hot water from the sink. Then I rinsed the dirt off my face, plucked the blackness out of my fingernails, and retied my bandana around my knotted hair. This was, after all, my first date with Big Spoon out in society.

It was dark out when we left the restaurant and walked down Angeles Crest Highway, which ran through the town, to grocery shop at Jensen's Finest Foods. The old-man cashier laughed as we checked out, because together we must have bought forty Snickers bars.

Inside the cabin, a collection of bear paintings and trinkets hid the walls, tables, shelves, and fireplace mantle. A hiker named Piggy—short and round—was lying on the couch watching TV as Big Spoon and I ambled around the living room, viewing the various souvenirs, playfully analyzing each one as if we were in a museum.

"Could you guys keep it down?" Piggy snapped. "I'm nursing a possible meniscus tear here. I've been held up in this town for a week. The downstairs room is mine. You're upstairs."

The bear paraphernalia cluttered its way up the stairs to our charming little room. I showered and then sank into bed, where Big Spoon held me throughout the night. In the morning, as the sun streamed through the cracks in our bedroom blinds, he leaned in to me and whispered in my ear, "Let's elope."

I was waking up now, and everything was coming into focus.

"Yes," I said. "Let's."

CHAPTER 18

THE TRAIL TALKS

That day, we hiked to the top of Mount Baden-Powell—the tallest peak on the PCT in Southern California, booming up to 9,399 feet. Icy winds darted into us on the eight-mile climb through the snow. The Tallyhos were a few miles ahead because they'd returned to the trail earlier that morning. Big Spoon and I had waited until noon to start. As we progressed up the mountainside—Big Spoon behind me—we continued our conversation about marriage.

"I wasn't kidding when I said let's elope," Big Spoon said.

"I wasn't kidding when I agreed."

"That's crazy."

"What?"

"You really do know when you know. It's like a knowl-edge deeper than knowledge."

"Yeah, truly," I said, having experienced this same stupendous awareness. "But marriage is no joke."

"I know," Big Spoon said. "It's forever."

"And there's a lot we still don't know about each other."

"Well, what do you want to know?"

I thought up a question. "Do you want kids?"

"Four. You?"

I smiled. "I was thinking three. But four sounds nice." The next question arose. "Do you want a joint or separate bank account?"

"Joint, without a doubt. You know, because I see it like we'll be one once we're married—our own unit. And none of this prenuptial-agreement crap, either. There are no terms and conditions to the commitment I'm going to make to you."

"Good," I said. "I feel the same way. You sound to be very loyal." This point was important to me to bring up because when I was a young girl my parents divorced—a devastating event that had left me determined to marry a man only if I believed with all of my heart, mind, and soul that our marriage would last until death did us part.

"Fiercely," Big Spoon said. "And in every way, too. You'll have to take my word on it for now, but when I vow to do something, I see it through. And there's many things I've vowed. Like continuing to do the things I love and living the life *I* choose. I don't ever want you or me to settle again into some role we're doing just because. We've got meaningful things to do—you'll write books, and I'll make my art based on our experiences, which we will never let run dry. Also, I want to start my own company someday. I don't know what it'll be just yet—maybe something in metalwork or product design. But I can feel it—I have something big to contribute to this world. And I know I will, because something I'm learning out here is that we have the power to make our greatest dreams come true. We just have to be purposeful, every day, in seeking them as the divine winds guide us on."

We approached the peak of Baden-Powell, where fresh snow hid the tracks of those who had walked before us.

"I think we can do that," I said, overjoyed by this deep and wonderful phenomenon taking place between Big Spoon and me.

"I know we can," Big Spoon said. "I love you." He looked into my eyes. "We're getting married."

⚜

At mile 445, we reached the Acton KOA, one of hundreds of Kampgrounds of America. It was Thursday. Gray weather had devoured the last four days, during which the trail had challenged us with cold climbs while forcing us to dodge the poodle-dog bush—known for its potent leaves of poison. Thus, everyone herded to this commercial campground in the rural valley with its hot showers and mowed field—our temporary sanctuary where we gathered and caught up on the latest trail news.

For the trail talked. Gossip blazed down it like a wildfire started with a single match. Especially when it came to romance.

All of this prefaces several miles back to the night before Big Spoon and I caught up with the Tallyhos. We were at the Cooper Canyon Campground in Angeles National Forest, where we ran into Malibu and Endless—the gregarious guys known on the trail for their big mouths. The duo sat at a picnic table, bantering back and forth in witty ways, when Big Spoon and I took a seat next to them to make dinner. Currently, they were discussing Mr. and Mrs. Egg—the couple they'd been hiking with, trail-named so because of their Easter egg–colored shirts—and how the two had known each other only six weeks before getting married.

"What...you don't think that's enough time to know?" Big Spoon said, smiling at me.

"No way," replied Endless, a firefighter from Boston with sky-blue eyes and an amusingly heavy accent. "Six weeks to seal the deal with someone for the rest of your life is crazy. Beautiful if it works, man. But crazy." He was trail-named, I had learned days before when we first crossed paths, for being as fun and relaxed as an endless summer's day.

"I don't know," said Big Spoon. "I know a couple on the trail who decided to get married after only knowing each other two weeks. And I know they're going to make it."

"Two weeks?" exclaimed Malibu, a paramedic from Seattle with a bushy red beard and a surfer-dude accent. "Do tell, Spoon. Who are these fools?"

"Yeah, yeah, spill," Endless begged, practically foaming at the mouth like a dog waiting for scraps. Out here, so far away from the world we once knew, any information was like a great feast.

I shot a look at Big Spoon. Was he really going to tell?

"Actually, it's Hands and me. We're getting married."

Their expressions turned blank.

My cheeks heated up, and I didn't know what to say. He really told, I thought. This is really happening.

"Whoa...congrats," Endless offered, breaking the awkward silence. "You guys look good together."

"Yeah, dudes, whoa. This means you'll have to change your name to Little Spoon," Malibu said to me, and I nodded, playing along.

"Where will you have the ceremony?" Endless asked, looking back and forth from Big Spoon to me.

"Don't know yet," answered Big Spoon. "We haven't figured that out."

"What about the big day? When's that?" asked Malibu.

"Don't know that either," Big Spoon said, "but hopefully sooner than later."

From that point on, the hasty engagement of Big Spoon and Hands turned into the raging talk of the trail. Hikers who passed us either stared our way and then turned their heads to whisper, or they blatantly shouted out, "Congratulations, Spoons!" At first, the Tallyhos had shrugged it off as a very funny joke, a trail rumor they highly discredited, to the point that on the night before we reached the KOA, I had to sit them down at camp to tell them that this was real—that Big Spoon and I were getting married.

Saltlick shook her head. "Divorces are expensive," she said, deeply concerned.

Pandora kept quiet.

I asked her later if she thought I was making a mistake.

"You shouldn't care what I think," she said kindly. "You know in your heart what's right for you."

By the time we entered the KOA that misty morning, Big Spoon and I were a legend. Even the nonhiker campers knew our tale.

"The proof is in the pudding. I'll believe it when you're actually married," Malibu said playfully once Big Spoon and I had paid for a spot and were setting up camp in the field.

Endless was in the background, humming "Here Comes the Bride."

Big Spoon looked at me with knowing eyes. But this time he kept quiet. For there was something we now knew that we couldn't tell. It was a secret not yet ready for the trail.

CHAPTER 19
MILE 445

"A day on the trail is like a month in real life."
That's what hikers would say. It referred to the connection one made with one another on the trail. The connection that was so instant, so raw, and so true that after hiking together for only a few days, strangers felt as if they had known each other for years.

Which was the case for Big Spoon and me. In a mere two weeks—from mile 235 where Big Spoon had caught up to me at Mission Creek to mile 445 at the KOA—we had spent our waking and sleeping hours together, showing each other our naked souls as we hiked through the hard yet stunning snow, desert, and mountains, our certainty that we were meant to be solidifying as we stepped.

It made sense too, this rapid determination of ours to be permanent partners. Because where we were was not the typical dating arena of the so-called real world, where two people would meet but perhaps not go on a first date until many days or even weeks later, meeting up afterward (if the date went well) once or twice a week for two or so hours at a time due to scheduling conflicts with work or school or what have you, thus trying new things together and getting to know each other slowly, over a year or two or more, possibly knowing quite soon they were meant for each other, but waiting to follow through with a lifelong commitment to the other until having shared the various experiences of life that truly expose one's soul.

But on the trail, you could get all of that with someone in a few days. And Big Spoon and I had. During our two-week courtship, we shared telling moments, such as having to problem solve on this challenging path and deal with the stresses that came with living off the great and merciless land. We interacted with each other one second after the next, where in a world without showers, makeup, fresh laundry, and deodorant, we witnessed each other's daily urge to use the bathroom, nagging hunger for food, and constant thirst for precious water. Furthermore, as we walked together, we dug deep into intimate discussions and conversations about life, our beliefs, our goals, and expectations. We recounted every moment we could recall of our history—family, favorite pastimes, hardships, and more. We discussed finances and our mutual hope to live frugal but fulfilling lives. We talked about God and Jesus and the Holy Spirit, and the mysterious way of our Heavenly Father's good and higher plan. The miles passed by, and we continued to consider everything we could think to consider, voicing it to the other like a great and endless story, learning profoundly and effortlessly who the other was as we lived immersed in the utter truth and beauty of the wild.

"The PCT is a filter," Big Spoon would say over and over again as we hiked, always with a tone of wonder.

He meant that the trail attracted to it kindred spirits: lovers of the outdoors, explorers of a determined kind, those willing to face challenges and risk, and those open to the unimaginable possibilities of the unknown.

"No wonder we click like we do!" he'd exclaim.

Thus, with our shared experiences and rich knowledge of each other now wedged within our minds, hearts, and the tread of our boots, we resolved to get married, to complete what fate had begun, to not wait but act now, sealing our souls as one—forever.

But how? How could two hikers get married on the trail?

The answer came to us right before the KOA. It was Thursday, May 21. One mile before we reached the campground, something urged Big Spoon to halt. He crouched in a sandy gully that blocked the wind. I ducked in next to him. He pulled out his phone. "Aha!" he cried.

An abnormally strong Internet connection existed in this remote spot.

"I'm going to do a little research," he said.

I peered over his shoulder as he opened Google and searched for information on what it took to get married in the state of California.

"A valid ID and a marriage license," Big Spoon read.

"Not a blood test, too?" I asked.

"Nope, no blood test. They make it easy."

Next, he searched for the nearest place to obtain a marriage license. The first thing that popped up on his handheld screen was the Los Angeles County Clerk Office in Lancaster—a city thirty miles north of the KOA.

Big Spoon clicked on the website for the county clerk.

"Looks like they do marriage licenses, and—wait... whoa," he interrupted himself after reading on and realizing something big. "What day is it? Thursday, right?"

"Yeah, I think so. Why?"

He checked the date on his phone to confirm it.

"Look. They do wedding ceremonies here, too. On Fridays only."

Chills ran down my spine. "Tomorrow's Friday," I said, the whole of it now sinking in.

Big Spoon echoed, "Tomorrow's Friday." And we looked at each other as if we had discovered a life-changing truth.

Had Big Spoon not stopped and performed this research when he did, there's no telling if we would have found out about Lancaster, for the KOA's cell service was weak, and there was no Internet connection there.

After making camp in the foggy field, we returned to the camp store (where we had paid for our spot) to strategize a hitch to the county clerk's office for Friday. We needed to do this ahead of time, because Lancaster was an uncommon destination for hikers—most hitched from the KOA to the town of Acton six miles away. Furthermore, since the KOA resided on an isolated canyon road, traffic in this area was unpredictable and light.

"We could get a taxi," I suggested.

"Or ask the cashier to drive us," countered Big Spoon.

Then the bulletin board hanging on the wall by the entrance caught my eye. I went up to it and found several colorful notes all signed by the same person.

"Can drive hikers to post office/grocery store in Acton!—Trail Angel Marie," the notes said, followed by a phone number.

I waved Big Spoon over.

"Let's call her," he said.

We stepped out onto the gravel parking lot, where my phone had one bar of service. As I dialed the trail angel's number, a green Subaru pulled in.

"Thanks again, Marie!" called the hikers who piled out of the backseat.

Big Spoon and I ran up to the car. The woman in the driver's seat wore a light-blue sweatshirt and paint-splotched jeans. She had dark-red hair streaked with strands of gray and tawny eyes that glistened like watercolors as we told her our story and then asked if she'd drive us to Lancaster in the morning.

Marie jumped out of the car and flung open her arms.

"This is incredible!" she cried, embracing us. "I've seen hikers do a lot of things but never get married on the trail. And you say you just met, too! I'll be here tomorrow at seven o'clock sharp."

That night, the clouds parted like a stage curtain to display the silver stars. I sat in the field with Big Spoon as the other hikers fastened themselves inside their tents. Together, we watched the sky and were quiet. I contemplated the whirlwind day. Merely hours before, after speaking with Marie, we'd called our parents to tell them the news. Tears were shed, but they took it mysteriously well. My dad had given Big Spoon his blessing.

"It's because they trust us," Big Spoon said after the nail-biting calls. "They believe us when we say we're doing the right thing."

It occurred to me as I sat on the starlit field that since Big Spoon and I weren't being secretive about our coming union, we weren't actually eloping.

"No, we're not eloping," Big Spoon said when I mentioned this to him. "You and I are getting married."

"What will we do afterward?" I asked, realizing I hadn't considered what was to come after we said I do.

"What do you want to do?" Big Spoon asked.

I didn't have to think.

"Continue on the trail. Until we make it to the end. That's what I want."

"Okay," Big Spoon said. "Okay. But first..." he paused and took my hand. Now it was as if the stars were watching us, their eyes of light casting down. "Will you marry me?"

⇒⊣⊢⇐

I readied myself in the bathhouse at sunrise, using the mirror over the paint-chipped sink. Never once had I imagined I'd look this way for my wedding. The skin on my nose was red and peeling. My lips were chapped and blotted with dried blood. My hair was hopeless. It had grown to be so wildly uncontrollable that it broke several teeth of my comb as I raked through it. I gave up, tied my turquoise bandana around it—my "something blue"—and let my hair drape in knots down my back.

My armpits stank. The smell soaked through my hiking shirt, which used to be white but was now eternally discolored from sweat. I wore nylon pants. I slipped my feet into muddy boots.

Today's the day, I thought, taking one last look in the mirror. May 22. Exactly one month after I'd started the PCT.

With my backpack already loaded, I met Big Spoon and Pandora in the parking lot. Pandora was coming with us as our witness. I had asked her the day before if she would.

"Yes, I'd be honored to," she had said.

I had asked Saltlick, too. But she'd declined, saying, "I want to get an early start on the trail."

That had hurt my feelings, but I understood Saltlick's opposition to the giant decision Big Spoon and I were making in such a short span of time. Besides, I wasn't focused on her disapproval now as I approached Big Spoon, who stood tall in his robin's-egg shirt and full-brimmed hat that highlighted the ruggedness in his face.

"You look beautiful," he said when I stopped before him.

"And you look very handsome."

"How do you feel?" he asked.

"Ready. You?"

"Oh, I'm ready."

Marie pulled in and popped the trunk. We set our packs inside.

As we did so, she stepped out of the car. "These are for you," she said, smiling radiantly as she handed me a bouquet of pink spray roses with a red ribbon wrapped around the stems. "And this one's for you, dear." She gave a single rose to Pandora. "I picked them up on my way after it dawned on me that you couldn't have a wedding without flowers."

"Thank you," I said, touched by the trail angel's gesture. "They're perfect."

I tilted my head toward Big Spoon and picked out one of the roses. "May I?" I asked Marie. She nodded in understanding, and I snapped the bright bud off the stem. Then I reached into the trunk and undid the safety pin on the outside of my pack—the one I used for hanging wet socks to dry—and made a boutonniere, which I pinned to Big Spoon's shirt.

The sweet scent of the roses saturated the car on the highway drive to Lancaster. As we inched through the city's morning traffic, we learned that Marie was a painter whose primary subject was the wild horses in the area.

"It's their power," she said, "that fascinates me and draws me to them. In a world where we aim to tie these beasts up and mold them to our will, I can't help but be moved by the ones that break away, holding nothing back but charging the open earth as unbridled as the wind. It's the most beautiful thing I've ever seen. Wild horses running." She looked at Big Spoon and me through the rearview mirror. "You two are making a wild-horse move."

The county clerk's office was closed when we arrived. It wouldn't open until eight, another thirty minutes.

The parking lot was empty, and Marie was gone. She'd left after expressing her deepest regrets for not being able to wait to take us back to the KOA.

"If I didn't have to drive my seventeen-year-old to film school in Hollywood, I wouldn't dare leave," she'd said.

We thanked her for her help and told her not to worry. "After the ceremony, a ride will come," Big Spoon guaranteed. "That's just how it works out here."

It was an incredibly sunny day, the first in a while. We sat on the bright curb before the small, cream-colored building.

"This is great, you guys. You're such a beautiful couple," Pandora said again and again, her joyfulness sincere.

A large black woman unlocked the doors and waved us in.

Inside, Big Spoon and I filled out our marriage license at a computer against the back wall. I watched over Big Spoon's shoulder as he typed out my new name: *Claire Henley Miller.*

All was most well with my soul.

Meanwhile, several people filed in. Once we'd finished at the computer, we waited in the congested line at the front counter to pay. It cost $131 for the combination of the marriage license and the wedding ceremony. A slim black woman with blue-streaked hair, wearing dangling gold earrings and a fitted pink dress, checked us out. Her nameplate read Nadine.

"Okay, now, go wait by that wooden door down there at the end," she said, sliding us our receipt. "Your ceremony will start shortly."

"Dear God, thank You for all You've given us and for bringing us this far. Please, be with us both now—on this very special day—and forevermore. We love You, and we look to You to guide us in this life," Big Spoon prayed in a huddle of Pandora and me as we stood, heads bowed, by the door.

"Amen," Pandora and I said when Big Spoon finished his prayer.

The door opened.

To my surprise, Nadine—who had slipped on a long, black judge's robe—welcomed us inside the chapel. It looked like the inside of a cardboard box: bare, windowless, compact. A handful of plastic chairs faced the front, where a wooden podium adorned by the seal of the County of Los Angeles stood. The room was silent. Nadine stepped behind the podium and opened a navy folder upon it. She motioned Big Spoon and me to join her. We placed our packs on the chairs next to Pandora. I handed her my roses. Big Spoon took off his hat.

He clutched my hands before the seal.

"Caleb Miller," Nadine read from her folder, "do you take this woman to be your wedded wife, to live together in marriage? Do you promise to love her, comfort her, honor and keep her, for better or worse, for richer or poorer, in sickness and health, for as long as you both shall live?"

"Yes," Big Spoon loudly proclaimed, tightening his grip on my hands.

Nadine recited the same text for me.

"Yes," I said, my eyes locked into Big Spoon's.

"Do you have rings to exchange?" she asked.

We didn't. Everything between us had happened so fast. We hadn't had time to acquire rings.

However, we did have tokens to swap representing our commitment to love and stay true to each other until death did us part. Mine for Big Spoon was a rock of many colors I'd found several days before near Silverwood Lake. It was shaped like a small spearhead and had glossy white quartz sticking out at the end. I had kept it because it was beautiful.

"A solid rock to symbolize the solid marriage we're entering into," I said, giving Big Spoon the stone.

He folded it in his right hand and then reached into his shirt pocket with his left. I gaped at what he presented me. The Herkimer diamond—the crystal I'd dreamed about the first night it had snowed in the desert. In my dream, I'd searched without success for the chain so I could wear the pendant as a necklace. Now, in the chapel, my eyes widened. Big Spoon had strung the Herkimer onto a fine piece of twine. I lowered my head, and he looped it around my neck.

Oh, my God, I marveled to myself as the weight of the crystal settled against my chest. My dream has come true.

"By the power vested in me by the State of California, I pronounce you husband and wife. You may kiss your bride," Nadine said, closing her folder.

Big Spoon drew close and cupped his hand behind my head. Holding nothing back, we met each other's lips. Something like wind swept through me. It was the most powerful kiss of my life.

⇥⇤

Pandora wiped her eyes and then signed the line on our marriage license that called for the witness.

I'm married now, I thought. *Married.*

My life changed forever at mile 445.

Back outside, to our surprise, we found Marie parked in her car, waiting.

"Turned out my daughter had a stomach bug and decided to skip school," she said as we hopped in. "Where would the newlyweds like to go?"

We had planned to hit the trail after the ceremony. But, in the spirit of celebration, Big Spoon said with a brilliant smile, "How about we get some food!"

The clock on the console read 10:00 a.m. For the sake of time, Marie drove us through a Jack in the Box, where Big Spoon ordered bacon double cheeseburgers, curly fries, and large Cokes for all. As we ate in the car, it occurred to us to use this opportunity to run some needed errands. So, we stopped at the bank to restock on cash from the ATM, resupplied on food at a normal-priced grocery store in the city, and swung by the post office in Acton, where I happily spent seventeen dollars to mail home my tent.

"This is the greatest thing I've seen since being a trail angel," Marie said as we said our good-byes in the KOA parking lot. "You two break the mold. It's inspiring. Really. Keep living your unbridled lives."

She kissed our cheeks, ushered a fresh group of hikers into her car, and pulled away. Marie—the lovely trail angel who drove us to our wedding.

It was early afternoon. Pandora, Big Spoon, and I stuffed our groceries into our packs at a picnic table. I strapped my roses on top of mine so they could be seen as I hiked. Then the three of us took to the trail.

It was a stunning stroll through the Vasquez Rocks. The white, flowing stone ripped high into the sky like waves.

"We're married," Big Spoon stopped me to say as we walked in the shade cast by the rocks' grandeur. It was as if he was only now realizing it for what it really was. "We're married," he said again. "You're my wife." His eyes were full of love.

"And you're my husband," I said, knowing as I did that this would forever be the truth.

At mile 455, Agua Dulce appeared—a quaint desert town of dirt roads, orange rock, and cacti. Dusk fell as we followed the trail into downtown, where both locals and hikers were out enjoying the pleasant night. Our plan had been to push through the town without stopping in an effort to catch back up to Saltlick. But now that we were mixed in with the lively scene, we desired to stay—at least for dinner—before putting in a few more miles.

Pandora ordered a round of margaritas for our booth at Maria Bonita. The Mexican restaurant was loud and colorful and great. It was our wedding reception, where we ate good food, drank good drink, and relished the merriment of this profoundly uniting moment in my and Big Spoon's lives.

Midway through the meal, a waiter brought out an additional round of margaritas that we hadn't ordered.

"From them, over there," he said, gesturing to the nicely dressed couple on the other side of the restaurant waving at us.

"How could they have known it's our wedding day?" I asked, giddy and bemused.

Big Spoon went to thank them. When he returned, he reported that their names were Greg and Katie, a married couple from the area who'd seen us walk in with our backpacks.

"They told me that they've lived here for years but only recently learned what the PCT is all about, and they wanted to do something nice for us when they saw we were hikers." Big Spoon said. "I told them that Hands and I just got married, so their gift was special in more ways than one. That got them pretty excited. They said they'd drop by our table on their way out."

"We wanted to congratulate you!" said Katie, a bright-eyed blonde in sleek leather pants and snakeskin heels, when she and Greg appeared.

"And we're curious what your parents think," joked Greg, a kind-souled man wearing a handlebar mustache, cowboy hat, and dark jeans.

"They're happy for us," Big Spoon said. "We spoke with them not long ago."

"So, where are you staying tonight?" Katie asked.

"After this, we're hiking beyond town to camp," I said.

"But it's dark out," Greg said.

"And cold!" cried Katie.

They looked at us as if we were nuts.

"Oh, we'll be fine," Pandora said. "This is how we live."

"Well, okay then," Greg said. "Best of luck to you all in every way."

"And congratulations again!" Katie called as they walked off.

Pandora leaned in. "I bet they'll come back and offer us a place to stay."

"You think?" I asked.

"Oh, yeah. You saw how concerned they looked when we said we were sleeping on the ground." And just as she said this, the couple returned.

"Katie and I were just talking," Greg said. "And while it's nothing glamorous, we have a motor home outside our house that has a pullout couch and queen bed if you want to stay there tonight instead."

"The only catch is...we have peacocks," Katie said. "They get pretty loud at night. But we'd love to have you all. Why don't you think it over while you finish your food? We'll be waiting at the bar."

"What did I say?" Pandora said, looking rather pleased, once they'd left for the second time.

"I vote we go with them and meet up with Saltlick tomorrow," Big Spoon said,

and Pandora and I concurred.

The couple lived on a hill off Tumbleweed Lane. Katie gave us the tour while Greg prepared the motor home and turned on the hot water. Outside, the silhouettes of mountains curved on the horizon. Cherry trees grew between the cacti in their dusty yard. A chicken coop where chickens and peacocks reigned resided next to the flower garden. The home was simple and clean on the inside, replete with hardwood floors, granite counters, and photographs of family.

"This is our first time to host hikers," Katie said. "Now that both our kids are out of the house, we like the idea of opening it to those on the trail."

She set her large leather purse on the dining-room table and rummaged through it. "I ended up stepping across the street to the convenience store while you all finished up at the restaurant. I don't even know if this is what you like when you're backpacking, but here you go. Please, take and enjoy." She handed us a variety of goodies from her bag: Gatorade, chocolate, trail mix. She had even bought and transported three bright bananas without them getting bruised.

"Thank you," Pandora said, clutching her banana like gold.

"That's so very thoughtful," I said, almost moved to tears.

"Truly," said Big Spoon. "It's generosity like yours and Greg's that blows me away the most out here."

The motor home slept us beautifully. Pandora sank into the couch behind the steering wheel, and Big Spoon and I took the bedroom in the back. We were alone now for the first time as husband and wife. We slipped into the bathroom to shower. The cylinder stall was so small that our bodies never ceased to touch as the hot water washed us. Back in the bedroom, Big Spoon closed the door.

"We get a bed on our wedding night," I whispered of the wonderful and unexpected gift.

He pulled back the covers and laid me down. The peacocks squawked outside the whole time. I cried at the end. I clung to Big Spoon's stalwart back and just cried.

"It's okay, Claire. It's okay," he said into my ear. "Today was a big day."

"We got married today," I said, my tears splashing into the sheets. "We got married, and everything went so perfectly—with such grace and flow—as if a Divine Hand played it along." I took a deep breath. "I love you, Caleb. You must know that's why I'm crying."

"I know," Big Spoon said. "I know." He kissed me on the forehead. "It's you and me now. You and me. I will love you the rest of my days."

With those words, we fell asleep. It was a night of warmth and peace as we slept soundly, wrapped in each other's hold, our bodies so close that our heartbeats touched, as if we were no longer two...but one.

CHAPTER 20
DESTINY

K atie and Greg made us breakfast the next morning. Katie brewed coffee and sliced kiwis while
Greg cooked bacon and scrambled the eggs laid by their
own chickens. We dined at the table in the kitchen, sipping down two pots of coffee and eating every crumb
while answering the couple's questions about the joys
and trials of the trail.

"Be safe out there!" Katie cried after she hugged
Pandora, Big Spoon, and me good-bye beneath the
cherry tree in the front yard. "I'll remember you all
forever."

We piled into Greg's work truck, and he drove us
back to the trail.

On my first day of marriage, I hiked twenty-one
miles. The stretch landed us at Casa de Luna—the

home of trail angels Tony and Shyanne Smith, where hikers had flocked over the past sixteen years to party. The three of us arrived at sunset, after a plumber had transported us there in his van from the trail crossing at San Francisquito Valley Road. It had been a short ride through the twisting desert hills. A metal crescent moon marked the angels' home. It swung in the breeze from the oak over the Porta Potties. Rock 'n' roll roared from the outdoor speakers, soaking the small neighborhood with sound. At least sixty hikers were there, dressed in the Hawaiian shirts the Smiths provided, eating taco salad and drinking beer on the tattered couches out front.

Among the hikers was Saltlick. She was conversing with the Oregon brothers when Pandora, Big Spoon, and I walked over to say hi.

"You made it," she said, not mentioning the wedding.

"Is it true?" Sticks—the middle brother—shouted above the music.

"It's true," Big Spoon replied.

"Have you guys lost it?" Pogo, the youngest, cried in jest.

"Nah, man. They followed their gut." Shades, the eldest, stuck up for us.

Big Spoon and I set our packs by the industrial trash cans behind the couches and then slid into line at the food table. A stainless-steel pot, so big I could have squatted inside it, steamed with chili next to an assortment of chips, lettuce, and cheese. Tony oversaw things as we went through, swaying to the music with a ladle in his hand, his long, silver hair bouncing against his back. As we topped our mountainous taco salads with sour cream and hot sauce, he asked, "What brings you young bloods to the trail?"

"Marriage," Big Spoon said, his voice exact.

Tony took a closer look. "Wait a hot second. You aren't the couple that met and got hitched out here, are you?"

We nodded.

"I'll be damned. I heard you'd be coming through. It's all everyone's talking about, you know. Shyanne! Come here, baby," Tony yelled. "The newlyweds are at the House of the Moon."

"Is it true, sweethearts? Do your poor parents know?" Shyanne said in a deep, raspy voice when she met us at the table. She pinched a lit cigarette between her fleshy fingers.

"It's all true," Big Spoon said. "We got married yesterday."

She sucked from her cigarette and spit the smoke out as if this news distressed her.

Tony laughed. "Never in my sixteen years as a trail angel have I heard such a thing. And I've heard some shit, trust me." He pointed the ladle at us. "What you did will either be great, or it will be terrible."

His words struck me. Not until now had I considered that my hasty marriage to Big Spoon could result in something bad.

I gulped.

Big Spoon looked him in the eye.

"Oh, it's going to be great," my husband said.

That night, I could tell something was off between the Tallyhos and me. We lounged at opposite ends of the yard and didn't speak except when Pandora came over to inform us that she and Saltlick were traveling on in the morning.

"She wants to get out of here early to beat the crowd," Pandora said. "I don't know what you guys are doing, but I'm going with her. She's my hiking partner, after all."

We're all hiking partners, I wanted to say. What about no Tallyho left behind?

But I merely nodded. For now I knew the painful truth: that my marital bond to Big Spoon had divorced me from the Tallyhos.

"Happy trails," I wished my looming long-lost friend.

When the stars bled into the black sky, Big Spoon and I made camp in the manzanita forest behind Tony and Shyanne's home. We chose a private spot within the snaking trees—the red, intertwining enchantment. Fortunately, Big Spoon didn't subscribe to the modern mentality of ultralight backpacking, which forced its followers to compromise on comfort in order to minimize pack weight. Instead, he believed in having what he wanted on the trail, even if that meant he'd have to haul a heavier pack. For example, he was the only hiker I'd met on the PCT who carried a double-padded sleeping pad and extra-large sleeping bag, which—he was always proud to divulge—could keep him warm in temperatures down to zero degrees.

"I work like a mule, but I sleep like a king," he'd tell me when I'd make fun of his gear.

In fact, his things were so big and deluxe that he couldn't fit them all inside his pack and had to strap several items to the outside. One such item was his tent. Unlike the majority of solo hikers—myself included—who strictly stuck to the confines of a one-person tent for the sake of lugging less, Big Spoon challenged convention by towing a two-person tent because he desired the extra legroom.

And now I applauded him for his hefty home. Because now that we were married, we had a place at night into which we could both fit. Not to mention, I no longer had to carry a tent.

We finished staking the shelter between the dark, twisting roots and burrowed inside. I zipped up in my sleeping bag and nestled next to Big Spoon. The hikers in the front yard clinked beer bottles as they mingled in the mix of the blaring music. They had started to dance when Big Spoon and I had decided to call it a night. I wondered if I was missing out. Although, truthfully, I had no desire or energy to partake in the festivities. Getting married and still having to make my daily miles drained me.

In the morning, the Tallyhos went on. Big Spoon and I stayed at Casa de Luna to have a day of solid rest:

my first zero on the trail since I'd started the PCT nearly 480 miles back.

I awakened disturbed, sat up in the tent, and stared straight ahead. The sun had risen hours ago. Things were sinking in. I married a man I just met, I thought. It suddenly upset me. What the hell was I thinking? Why didn't I wait until after the trail?

"What's wrong?" Big Spoon asked after his eyes opened.

"What were we thinking?" I said, desperation in my voice.

"About what? About getting married?" He shot up beside me.

"Yes. It changes everything. We don't even know each other." I was becoming hysterical.

Big Spoon drew a deep breath. "Now, just hold on a second," he said in a soothing tone. "What you're thinking is normal. But don't let your mind deceive you. We do know each other," he assured. "We did what we did when we did it exactly because we know in our souls who the other is. Listen to me. Let me tell you a story."

He seized my hand and told a mesmerizing tale.

"Two years ago, while I was still living in Jersey, I came across an online ad for free coal. Well, one of my good friends owns a coal stove that he uses in the winter to heat his home. So, I called the number on the ad and scheduled a time to pick it up that day for my friend. When I arrived at the address I was given, I met a guy a little older than me. He said his dad had lived there—a mad scientist, apparently, who had died from chemical exposure. The son said he was trying to get rid of his dad's hoard of things. He led me to the basement, which was swamped with tarnished beakers, test tubes, and an astounding amount of coal—*fifteen hundred pounds*—that was stacked in the back for the taking."

Big Spoon paused.

"You're probably wondering what this has to do with anything, but bear with me. See, because I didn't mention that the son was an otherworldly sort. He had those far-seeing eyes, you know, and a mystical air about him that I swear I could feel like wind. So anyway, as I loaded the coal into my truck, he asked me what I did for a living. I told him I worked for the Department of Defense. He jolted back. Then he stopped me, stared me in the eyes, and said, 'You don't belong there. There's a dark energy there. But I see a white light that surrounds you. It's the whitest light I've ever seen surrounding another soul.'"

I shivered and reached with my free hand for the Herkimer diamond around my neck, remembering the bright white light released by the crystal in my dream.

"I thought the son was crazy," Big Spoon went on. "At that time, I'd never once considered leaving my job, which others would have killed to have." He squeezed my hand. "But then, about a month after I got the coal, it hit me that the son was right. The DoD wasn't where

I belonged. It didn't quench my desire to create and explore. And not until I realized this did I see for the first time that I could quit my job and pursue what I love. Which is what I'm getting at. See, because if I hadn't met the son when I did, then I wouldn't have quit my job when I did. And if I hadn't quit my job when I did, then I wouldn't have moved to Florida and learned about the PCT when I did. And if I hadn't learned about the PCT when I did, then I wouldn't be on it right now, and I wouldn't have met you, and we wouldn't have gotten married." He spoke with tremendous confidence. "Do you see, Claire? Everything happens when it happens for a reason. So have peace. Because you and me, we happened when we did for a reason. Our marriage happened when it did for a reason. I promise you. Everything is as it's meant to be."

⇥⇤

We left Casa de Luna the following dawn, after a full day of indulging in stillness. Shyanne drove us back to the trailhead. But before she did, she lined us up in front of the Casa de Luna banner plastered beside the front door. Tony took out the camera, and just as he snapped the shot, Shyanne turned her back to us, dropped her jeans, and mooned us with her flabby white behind.

"And that's how Casa de Luna got its name, kids," she said, her cigarette flopping in her mouth as she zipped back up.

Big Spoon looked horrified. "I never want to see anything like that again," he said as we took to the trail.

Over the next three days, we were alone together as we wandered through the Mojave. "Our honeymoon," I joked. For this was the hardest drag yet: the land all around was a stark red haze of heat.

I missed the Tallyhos and wondered if I'd ever see them again. The cracked ground beneath my feet sizzled *no, no, no.*

However, I was profoundly thankful to be with Big Spoon. His words had been true. Once my flash of doubt about our marriage fled, a sense of serenity settled within me that said everything was as it was meant to be.

This peace stayed even as we trudged through the hellish heat, where the wind turbines didn't spin, the cattle swayed with hanging tongues, and every Joshua tree reached with prayerful limbs to the fuming sun. I felt like a wilted grape by the time we exited the trail at mile 558 to regain civilization in Tehachapi.

It was evening. A woman was waiting in a silver Suburban at the trailhead when we emerged from the desert.

"Big Spoon and Hands?" she rolled down her window and asked.

"Yes."

"Thought so. I'm an acquaintance of Tony and Shyanne. Spoke to them a few days ago, and they said you'd be getting here by today. Glad I didn't miss you. I'm Trish. The undercover trail angel in these parts."

She was stout and muscular with crystal-blue eyes and a fullness in her voice.

"You're invited to stay at my house tonight if you'd like. Otherwise, I can take you to the airport, where they let hikers sleep in the lobby. But it'd be a pity to do that. I have something special for you at my home."

She was jovial and looked harmless, so we got into her car.

"What do you mean by undercover trail angel?" I asked as she drove us to her house.

She cleared her throat. "My husband would kill me if he knew I did this. He thinks hikers are dirty scoundrels. But I know better. You all are gems. So, because he travels a lot for work, I take you in when he's gone. Been doing it for years." She grunted. "He's never caught on."

Big Spoon lifted his nose and sniffed when we stepped inside her home. "What is that?" he asked. The richness wafting through the rooms made my mouth water.

"In honor of your marriage, I prepared you a meal. Please, put your backpacks here in my daughter's old room. Then meet me in the dining room down the hall."

Minutes later, we joined Trish at her white wooden table, where steaming plates of prime rib, vegetables, and rolls with melted butter were spread out before us. There was even a strawberry cake topped with figurines of a bride and groom. Trish removed three crystal flutes from her china cabinet and filled them with champagne.

"Cheers to the happy couple," our undercover trail angel said, raising her glass.

"Cheers to destiny," said Big Spoon after everyone had taken a sip.

CHAPTER 21

THE LAST DESERT STRETCH

B ig Spoon and I had been in the desert for thirty-six days. For thirty-six days, we had fought through the sand, snow, and wind. Our noses were blistered from the sun. Our feet were stained black from the dirt. Our eyes were weary from seeing the same desolate land for hundreds and hundreds of miles.

It was time for a change.

Fortunately, the forthcoming stretch marked our last in the desert on the PCT. It was Friday. The greatest battle of the vast and grueling world we had come through loomed ahead: 144 miles through the merciless Mojave—our longest slog yet between towns and the most dangerous, too, because of the deadly heat and scarce water.

It was a bright-blue morning at the Willow Spring Trailhead when trail angel Trish dropped us off. Seven days of food and five liters of water weighed me down. Big Spoon and I had readied our packs an hour before at Trish's after she drove us grocery shopping. In her living room, I was intimidated to find that I could hardly seal my pack. Big Spoon struggled to cinch and strap his together, too. When he did, the main compartment bulged out like a pregnant belly.

"This must weigh sixty pounds," he said, looking miserable as he heaved his backpack on.

Now, as I stepped up the loose sand beneath the naked sun, my pack tormented my every muscle. It felt like cruel punishment—like carting a bag of bricks up mountains. Eight miles in, the trail spit us out on State Route 158—a strip of highway cut through the brown, barren crags. We crossed its busy pavement, onto which the high noon sun beat ruthlessly, to reconnect to the trail. On the other side, a water cache slumped like melted wax next to a burned patch of cacti.

Many of the one-gallon jugs were empty, and none were full. Big Spoon and I grabbed one each—the liquid inside as warm as bathwater. Seventeen miles menaced from here until our next water source, meaning we'd be walking across dry earth until the next day. Big Spoon examined the thermometer dangling from his pack. "It's a hundred and six degrees out," he said, wiping the sweat from his forehead with his red bandana.

To be safe, we topped back off at five liters each—enough water meant to last us twenty miles.

But over the next five miles, we climbed. From 4,000 feet above sea level up to 6,000 feet, our bodies worked like machines to stabilize our monstrous baggage while we pushed on. By midafternoon, I was spent. Sweat poured from my skin like blood from open wounds. My breaths came heavy, making my throat dreadfully dry. Big Spoon faced this same fatigue. When we summited the crest that looked out on the pale, hot doom, he said, "I have to stop. I don't feel a hundred percent. I need rest."

A single sliver of shade shot from a boulder on the ridge. We dropped our packs in the middle of the trail, plopped down, and reclined against the rock with our legs extended over the path. Within minutes, we fell asleep. Not until hours later, when the shadows were long and the air was cool, did we wake to a group of hikers tiptoeing over us.

Big Spoon checked his water before we started up again.

"Oh, no," he said.

"What?"

"I drank three liters since we left the water cache."

"Oh, no," I echoed his previous concern. "In only five miles? That's twelve miles' worth of water."

"I know," he said. "I know. I have two liters left."

I checked my supply.

"I have a little less than four."

We had twelve miles to go until we'd reach the next source.

"I'll give you a liter," I said.

"Are you sure?"

"Yes, of course. But we have to make what we have last until tomorrow."

That night, at mile 578, we cowboy camped beneath the waxing moon. We did this to ensure a quick cleanup in the morning in order to get an early start toward the water six miles away. Big Spoon fell asleep as soon as he'd bunched up inside his sleeping bag. I stayed awake, looking up at the sky. Sleeping without the walls of a tent around me sparked a much different feeling, a heightened awareness. Now, I was exposed to all the beasts and elements of the wild. The tent seemed to keep me safe, the flimsy nylon separating me from the brutal world beyond. But without this shelter, I became part of this world—the creeping spiders and swirling sand and howling coyotes. While I dominated the space inside the tent, I became a mere speck in the wilderness as I lay on the open ground. It was eerie, in a way, to be so uncovered. At the same time, it was great. Because now I wasn't just in the wild. I was wild, too.

The sunrise brushed us awake. We deflated and rolled up our sleeping pads and crammed our sleeping bags inside their sacks. I had one liter of water left. Big Spoon had a half. If we left now, we would reach Golden

Oaks Spring before the vile midmorning sun burned through. I had to use the bathroom before we left, so I shuffled down the sandy hill that led to a dry creek bed to squat. On my way back up, I noticed a glossy red rock glinting from the ground. I picked it up and showed it to Big Spoon back at our site. He studied it much longer than I'd anticipated he would, flipping it over with his fingers and bringing it up to his eye.

"Do you know what this is?" he asked, his tone spilling with excitement.

"A rock," I dryly said, focused on getting to the water.

"This isn't just a rock. It's an arrowhead flake. Claire, you made a good find." He examined the area. "It makes sense you found it here, too. Native tribes used to dwell near creeks or rivers on a hill, like here, so they could have access to water while being able to keep watch. I bet that thousands of years ago, that dry creek down there flourished." He pointed out the grooves in the flake. "See the unique makeup, how it looks like someone used a tool to chip this off a larger stone?"

I nodded.

Big Spoon continued, "This type of stone is called chert. It's the material Natives used to knap arrowheads with natural resources such as antlers."

"How do you know all of this?" I asked, enthralled.

"Artifacts are akin to fossils," he said, smiling. "And they fascinate me just as much, if not more, because an actual human once made and used them. I haven't told you this yet, but before coming out here, I did some re-search and found that the trail went through several areas where Native tribes once thrived." His eyes were begging me for something. "So, I prayed to find a complete arrowhead at some point along the trail." The heat had begun to rise. "I know we need to get to the water," he said, "but can we stay here a little longer so I can look around?"

Over the next two hours, we probed the pebbly hill-side and the dry creek bed below. I was thrilled to join the hunt, although our limited water supply continued to concern me. Big Spoon finished the last of his off as he searched. I'd hardly sipped mine, and I was thirsty. By the time the sun had sucked up the early morn-ing breeze, we had reaped two overflowing handfuls of flakes—yellows, pinks, whites, and blacks. All were beautiful, but none were whole arrowheads. I looked for one minute more. The sun-charred ground seared my fingers as I brushed away the sand. My throat was as dry and dusty as the ground. It was time to go.

"Ten more minutes!" Big Spoon called from down the hill as I meandered up to my pack. He was in his element, a treasure hunter at heart whose impassioned quest fueled him. I took a sip of water that soaked my cracked tongue with healing moisture. I wanted more. Don't do it, I thought. Don't do it. The spring was over a two-hour walk away. And now the sun was spitefully out, whipping my flesh through my clothes with its rays.

Save your water.

But I couldn't. I had to drink. I desired to drink. I *needed* to drink. I raised my water bottle to my lips. And I gulped. Until every drop was gone.

Big Spoon paraded up to me minutes later, his palm outstretched victoriously.

"It's not an arrowhead," he said as I studied the black triangular stone he presented. "But I think I found a spearhead. Do you feel its weight? And it's all in one piece."

I held the ancient weapon in my hand. It was heavy and well crafted. The tip was still sharp.

"It's made of obsidian," Big Spoon said, "a kind of igneous rock that looks like black glass."

"I bet it cuts like glass, too," I said, swiping my thumb along its serrated edge.

He stowed it in his pack. "And it's a once-in-a-lifetime find."

As we left, glory emblazoned his eyes. In fact, finding the spearhead boosted Big Spoon's morale so much that I don't think he felt his lack of water over the next six miles. On the contrary, I panted with stricken steps. My head felt heavy, and my body felt light. The land spun and turned blurry before me. I was dizzy, but I kept telling Big Spoon that I was fine. Then, four miles in, I had to stop.

"I'm so thirsty," I croaked, taking an abrupt seat on the trail, my dehydrated state now apparent.

Big Spoon looked worried. "This is my fault," he said. "I'll never let this happen again. Here, if you stay with the packs, I'll run for the water and bring it back to you."

No one was around, and I felt very weak. I didn't want to be left out here alone like this. Deep down, I knew the water was close. Thus, my second self kicked in—the self of instinct that surfaces in times of survival. I stood and tightened the straps around my hips. "Let's get to the water," I said, gritting my teeth.

I don't remember the next two miles, only that I hiked them furiously—as if I were fighting my way out of the clutches of death. When we reached Golden Oaks Spring at mile 584, I wondered if it was a mirage. Terrific trees reigned over the earth, casting a whole field of shade. The crystalline spring streamed out of the mountainside and dripped into a metal horse trough. I stood in awe, watching as a congregation of hikers—not one of whom I had seen over the last few days—lined up to fill their bottles straight from the trickling source.

Then, snapping to, I saw Big Spoon leaning over the trough, using his pump to filter the horses' water into his plastic bladder. In doing this, he avoided the line and got water sooner. I joined him at the trough, and he instantly forced the hose connected to his bladder into my mouth.

"Drink," he said as he continued to filter the water.

I guzzled it down like a ravaged wolf.

We filled our bladders and bottles to the brim, drank them down, and then filled them again before eating lunch and then taking naps beneath the golden oaks. Every hiker there did the same. For hours, we sprawled in the shade like tired old dogs. Because it was so relentlessly hot during the day, the common strategy among our peers had become to hike at night, when the climate was dramatically cooler. Big Spoon and I decided to continue in this way, too. We got going again at dusk, walking as the nearly full moon rose to light the blackened terrain with just enough of a glow for us to see our way.

At mile 602 the next day, we caught up to the Oregon brothers. They were looking over the water report, slouched in line from oldest to youngest against a crumbled retaining wall at Robin Bird Spring. We sat with them to strategize. According to the report, after Robin Bird Spring, Landers Meadows Spring at mile 609 served as the last reliable water source for forty-three miles.

"A forty-three-mile waterless stretch," I whispered in disbelief.

The gravity of this daunted me. Big Spoon and I were hiking an average of twenty miles a day. In this heat, we typically consumed one liter of water every four miles. Therefore, a forty-three-mile waterless stretch meant that we would need to carry at least ten liters of water, if not eleven, for two full days of hiking. A liter of water weighed over two pounds. Ten liters of water weighed over twenty. Even if we had the capacity to carry ten liters of water (which we didn't—both Big Spoon and I had capacity for only seven), it would have been absolutely wretched to lug that added weight.

"What's the game plan?" Big Spoon asked the brothers.

"We're hiking to Landers Meadows today to camel up at the spring. Then we're busting out thirty miles tomorrow to Yellow Jacket Spring," said Shades, his orange polarized sunglasses hiding his eyes.

(In hiker vernacular, to camel up meant to hydrate as much as your body allowed while at a water source in order to carry less water between sources.)

"Wait...what's Yellow Jacket Spring?" I asked.

Sticks—the brother who hiked with two sturdy pine sticks—answered, "It's about a mile off the trail. The water report says you can dig a hole in the grass there, and sometimes water comes out."

"Sometimes?" I asked.

The brother, Pogo, bobbed his head up and down like a pogo stick in confirmation.

I looked at the water report and located Yellow Jacket Spring, which as Shades had advised was located thirty miles north from Landers Meadows.

"That's still a long carry between sources," I said. "Thirty miles. And what if no water comes out when we dig?"

"We'll have to trust that it will," Big Spoon said. "What else can we do at this point?"

It would have made for a thrilling story if he and I had had to walk as far as we expected through the desiccated desert without resupplying on water. But because several unadvertised water caches were stocked along the way, we'd never voyaged more than twenty miles before coming upon a source. Nevertheless, after parting ways with the brothers, we night hiked from Landers Meadows on the trail's highway of scorpions and black widows. It wasn't until the next day that we veered down the dirt road to Yellow Jacket Spring. We had filled up on water a mere ten miles before from a cache but were curious to see if the water would flow from the ground. We ripped a hole in the tall grass with Big Spoon's trowel. Nothing happened at first. Then came a gurgle, and the dark water bubbled out.

"The trail takes away, and the trail provides," Big Spoon said and then splashed his face.

That night, at mile 651, we camped at Walker Pass Campground—the finish line of the alleged forty-three-mile waterless stretch. The brothers were there, along with Sketch—the Japanese artist who kept a spellbinding sketchpad of drawings inspired by the trail. Sketch built a fire at his site, around which everyone gathered as the full moon rose to meet the stars. The flickering light from the flames skittishly brightened the grease, sweat, and dirt on everyone's hair, cheeks, and clothes.

We vented about the waterless stretch—its unnerving peril—and it became clear that after miles and miles of toil, these moments of camaraderie made the hardships of the trail worthwhile.

The camaraderie continued a few days later on Friday, June 5, when Big Spoon and I strolled in to Kennedy Meadows at mile 702. Known as the gateway to the Sierra, Kennedy Meadows was a town of dirt with roughly two hundred inhabitants. It existed at an elevation of 6,427 feet and was a famous milestone of the PCT: the one that stamped in our weathered soles the completion of the desert.

Big Spoon and I were walking up to the general store, where hikers could sleep in the dusty side lot, when we saw a pack of our people celebrating on the big back deck. As we got closer, we heard clapping. It was quiet at first, and then it grew louder and louder, like a musical crescendo. We scanned the grounds to see for whom they were cheering. But we were the only ones coming up. Then it struck us. The hikers—those we had labored with and laughed with over the last forty-four days—were putting their hands together for us.

Big Spoon grabbed my hand and raised it to the sky. We had won the battle of the desert.

Now the war of the high country stared us in the face.

CHAPTER 22

ALTITUDE SICKNESS IN THE HIGH SIERRA

It was late afternoon when the rain came. Big Spoon and I had just finished setting up our tent next to the general store when the big, cold drops dashed down. The clouds from which they streamed were black and loud, warlike. It had been weeks since my dry, cracked skin had been touched by rain. Several hikers sprinted for the communal tepee down the hill from our tent. But we stood out in the storm to let the shots of sweet water soak us to our bones.

The lush green peaks of Sequoia National Forest rose before us into the clouds. Soon we'd enter their heights, but first, we'd take care of some things. Eating burgers on the general store's back deck, doing laundry inside, and showering with actual soap in the wooden shack up the hill marked our priorities. We also needed to buy bear canisters—the sixty-five-dollar cylindrical hunks of plastic designed to block bears from breaking into a camper's food. Every hiker was required to carry the awkward item in the Sierra. Thus, as the rain poured down—darkening the dirt lot into slick mud and washing away the Porta Potty smells—I went to the general store and made the pricy purchase.

Back outside, I set the canisters down and weighed myself on the scale on the front porch. Surprisingly, I had gained six pounds since leaving home.

"Muscle weight," the hiker drinking a beer in the rocking chair next to me said when I asked if the scale was right. "Guys tend to lose it. Girls tend to gain it."

This was certainly the case for me. After six weeks of continuous hiking, my torso had morphed into something like stone. My back was hard as a wooden board. My thighs and calves bulged with muscles of steel.

Although I was physically stronger, that evening, a debilitating migraine crept into my skull. The abrupt climate change from a low and arid land to moisture in the high mountains had triggered it. This was an affliction I had battled all my life: migraines. They started as a prick in the head, like the peck of a bird trying to break out of its shell. Then the pain slowly increased, causing subtle smells to fume like gas, faint sounds to blare like sirens, and the softest light to pierce my eyes like the naked sun.

At its worst, a migraine seemed to bash my head like a sledgehammer. Dizziness and nausea arrived as the bully's ugly hecklers. The only defense I'd ever found effective was a very still rest in a dark and silent place.

Therefore, I went to bed that evening without dinner. I didn't wake until dawn when the rain had cleared, making way for the cobalt sky. My migraine had also passed, and I was starving. I remembered that the day before, I'd overheard the cashier at the general store tell a group about the local who swung by every morning at seven to drive hikers to the diner down the road. Dressed in shorts and light jackets, Big Spoon and I therefore waited with the ravenous pack in front of the store. Among the crowd were the Tallyhos. They had arrived at Kennedy Meadows right before Big Spoon and me and had been sorting through resupply boxes at a picnic table when we got in. It was wonderful to see them again—like reuniting with long-lost friends. But the tension between us because of my marriage remained taut. Now, as we waited for the local, none of us spoke. In fact, everyone was silent as the anticipation built. "He's not coming," someone called out. Several left. But most continued to wait, and at fifteen past the hour, the local pulled up in his beat-up blue truck. He got out and waved us over with his stick-thin arms. The pack rushed toward our chariot.

Grumpy Bear's Restaurant was a log shack in the middle of nowhere that served eggs, bacon, and all-you-could-eat pancakes for breakfast. Big Spoon and I sat at the corner table with the Tallyhos. Saltlick didn't speak but gazed up at the antler chandelier illuminated by white Christmas lights. Pandora focused her attention on the restaurant dog—a frisky Chihuahua named Pixie. She was holding the tiny thing in her lap and taking a sip of coffee when the waitress brought out our plates stacked high with pancakes. As she set the dishes before us, one of them slipped out of her hand and slammed onto the table. The harsh sound startled Pixie, and she yelped as if someone wearing steel-toed boots had stomped on her delicate paw. This in turn startled Pandora, who screamed and jumped up, spilling Pixie and her coffee on the floor.

Pixie whimpered off, and the buzzing restaurant silenced. Every head turned to glare at Pandora, whose cheeks were rushing red. The waitress looked annoyed. Then, beautifully and unexpectedly, Saltlick burst into laughter. Her fixed face contorted with her grand amusement. She threw back her head and roared.

This sparked me to laugh, too. Big Spoon joined in next. And, once her shock had subsided, Pandora howled in with the hilarity, and the four of us laughed and laughed until we were bent over, scrounging for air, tears dripping off our chins.

And just like that, the tension between us shattered.

I couldn't have known then that would be the last time I'd see the Tallyhos on the trail. After Pandora's little scene, we divulged all that had happened since we'd parted ways at Casa de Luna. It was as if nothing between us had changed. However, back at the general store, after we said our good-byes and the Tallyhos strode off into the mountains, I cried. Big Spoon and I would stay at Kennedy Meadows another day to rest and regroup, but it was time for the Tallyhos to move on.

"They were my first partners on the PCT," I said to Big Spoon, who came to put his arm around me as I watched them walk away. "My companions. My team. My Tallyhos. That means something, you know. I love those girls."

"They love you, too," Big Spoon said, his voice gentle and pure.

But that was the way of the trail. No matter your closeness to another, you had to follow the unique path this single trail set for you if you wanted to reach your destination. It was hard. But it was the way. The trail taught you to love. And it taught you to let go.

———

The next morning, Big Spoon and I set foot into the High Sierra. Glassy obsidian adorned our path. It was a sunny day. Three miles in, we came upon the South Fork Kern River. The water snaked down an orange and narrow riverbed. We slipped off our shoes, rolled up our pants, and waded into a shallow pool. It was clear and cold—a gift after the parched desert land.

A few hours later, we stopped for the day at Monache Meadow. Located at mile 717 at an elevation of 7,864 feet, this wide-open space could have passed for paradise the way the meadow spread between the colorful mountains with the glittery river running through. It was bright and alive, beckoning us to join it. We crossed the steel bridge arcing over the Kern and picked a place on the plump grass for our tent. A drake and duck floated in the river next to our site. Beyond them, on the underside of the bridge, dozens of swallows swept in and out of their nests made of tightly clumped mud. As the sun slipped down, lighting up the clouds above the mountains like rubies atop a crown, Big Spoon and I took our dinner and sat beneath the bridge to watch the swooping swallows.

The methodical birds flew in and out of their homes with either food or building material, and I realized that this perpetual pattern was the whole purpose of their lives. It prompted me to ask, "What do you think is the purpose of *our* lives, Caleb?"

Big Spoon thought a minute, staring out on the shining clouds. Then he scanned the shadowy meadow, turned an ear to the rustling river, rubbed some soil between his fingers, and smelled the brisk mountain air. "Experience," he finally said. "Our purpose, I think, is to experience."

He went on to say that life was like a library.

"Because in a library," he explained, "we can dive into all sorts of books to explore thousands and thousands of stories. The same goes for life. I think we're meant to dive into one experience after another to see what we can find. Like these swallows beneath this bridge." He pointed to each white-bellied bird. "I wonder how many people actually come down here to watch them. But look at how amazing they are, how flawlessly they fly into the tiny holes of the nests they built with their beaks." He paused. The harmonious caws of the aerodynamic creatures increased. "It would be a shame to go into a library and not pick up a single book," he said. "And it would be a real shame to go through life and not seek out experiences—our stories to live and then tell."

The last curve of the sun lapsed behind the mountains. The stars started to appear. I like that, I thought. The idea of life as a library, where endless stories waited for us to slip inside.

And we get to choose what our stories will be, I marveled.

Instead of going to bed, Big Spoon and I stayed sitting out until the Milky Way bleached the black sky.

And then I realized: The important thing is to choose.

⇥⊣⊢⇤

Over the next several days, we traveled at an average elevation of 10,000 feet. I felt the intense difference of hiking in high altitude. My head bobbed on my shoulders like a balloon. But my body felt as heavy as bricks, and I was constantly short of breath.

The Sierra slowed us down. We went from crushing at least twenty miles a day in the desert to being lucky if we finished fifteen in the lofty peaks. This wasn't a bad thing, though, because there was so much to see. Like the auburn marmots sunbathing on boulders, the black squirrels scampering between fallen limbs, and the yellow deer leaping angelically through the royal fields. We were in the Golden Trout Wilderness of Sequoia National Park. Trees were everywhere. Among them ruled the bristlecone pine—bent by time yet firm, gnarled with ancient power—the oldest tree in the world.

It was educational to walk with Big Spoon, because he saw things in a different light. He found fantastical faces in the hollow logs and warped rocks all around us. He stopped to touch the textured bark of the different trees and to smell each flower. He often stepped off the trail itself to see what lived beyond our walkway's boundaries.

One time when he did this, he climbed up a large stack of loose scree. I watched from below, and when he made it to the top, he passionately waved me to come up. A stunning view of Sierra crests met me at the top. They went on and on forever in stone yellows and forest greens. A cool wind whirled up from the canyon below, and just as Big Spoon and I sat to take it all in, a fighter jet zoomed in, and a sonic boom rang out. We jumped up, and the silver jet nosedived before us into the canyon, diving farther and farther toward the ground while performing a series of brilliant spins. Then, in the moment before it would have hit bottom, it flipped back up and scaled the dark walls, its wings slicing through the wind, until it burst back into the open sky and whooshed away like a shooting star.

We wouldn't have seen this aerial show had we remained on the tree-covered trail. Big Spoon had a knack for finding other worlds within our very own.

At mile 742 in the early evening, we came upon a junction with a side trail that dived down Mulkey Pass. We were low on food and needed to resupply in the next town, Lone Pine. Based on our maps, the short side trail ended at a horse camp in Horseshoe Meadows. From there, Lone Pine was twenty-four miles down a mountain road.

"Hard weekday hitch," read the words scribbled in black ink on the sign marking the junction.

I asked Big Spoon what day it was.

"Tuesday," he said after counting in his head.

"Damn," I said. "A weekday."

This didn't faze Big Spoon, though. With cool confidence, he said, "Don't worry. We've been provided for this far. I know we'll get a hitch."

No one was around when we completed the two-mile side trail. We marched out of the mountains toward Horseshoe Meadows Road, praying aloud for God to send us a ride. The sun was setting as we stepped onto the abandoned road. "Someone will come," Big Spoon said.

Then, as if his words had held magical summoning powers, a silver Honda rolled into view. Our thumbs shot up, and the car stopped in front of us. The woman driving didn't even ask where we were going. She simply unlocked her doors and let us in.

Yet another example of the divine providence that never failed us on the trail.

The mighty peaks of the Sierra overshadowed the anthill town of Lone Pine. Mount Whitney soared at the forefront—the tallest mountain in the lower forty-eight booming in the sky at over 14,000 feet. After our godsend of a ride let us out, we rented a room at the Whitney Portal Hostel on the main—and only—drag. Then we walked across the street to a steak restaurant called Totem. This made us laugh. After three weeks of marriage, only now were we sitting alone together at a table.

The next day, we savored town life by strolling the street, perusing the shops, and sucking on fresh oranges. Lone Pine thrived at an elevation of 3,700 feet. The sun in the valley scorched our skin, but navy clouds rumbled over the mountains up high. That afternoon, when it started to lightly rain, we huddled inside the local barbershop, where a big man named Bear took a straight razor to Big Spoon's scruffy blond beard. I read a magazine in a seat against the wall while Big Spoon sat with his head back in the leather barber chair decked with turquoise studs. Bear lathered Big Spoon's cheeks, chin, and neck with shaving cream and then slowly scraped away.

"I feel like a new man," Big Spoon said outside the shop, stroking his smooth face.

"You look like one, too," I said, a little taken aback. This was the first time I'd ever seen my husband clean-shaven.

An old man named Fred drove us back up to the trail the next morning. He was a retired air force pilot who charged fifty dollars a ride to shuttle hikers from Lone Pine to the peaks. We found his number posted in our hostel lobby and decided to pay the fee instead of work for the lengthy hitch when another couple, Shaggy and Baloo, agreed to pitch in with us. On the steep way up, Fred gave us a tour in his van through the Alabama Hills—the unique geological formation of crumbled granite rock where hundreds of westerns had been filmed. The shuttle ended at Cottonwood Pass, situated in the thin and chilly air at 9,920 feet. In a mere thirty minutes, we had gained over 6,000 feet in elevation. I felt the difference. My head started to throb, and my stomach turned queasy. This air was hard to breathe.

Nevertheless, Big Spoon and I pushed forward a few miles to Chicken Spring Lake—our first alpine lake of the Sierra.

Sun-bleached talus encased the rippling water that sparkled like chandeliers. To get there, we'd clambered to an elevation of 11,276 feet. It was early afternoon, and I dreaded taking another step, for I now had a full-blown migraine, and all motion was making me ill. So, I sat while Big Spoon pitched our tent on the white-stone beach. He blew up my sleeping pad and spread my sleeping bag across it. I crawled inside and lay down. Please God, I begged to myself, let me fall asleep.

But my migraine only got stronger, forming waves of nausea that crashed into me. Before long, I couldn't take it anymore and rushed out of the tent, sprinted to the nearest boulder, and bent over behind it. My whole body tingled as if I'd just stepped out of freezing water. The vomit rocked in my gut and then rose to my throat. I retched. And I retched. Meanwhile, my migraine screamed and scratched against my skull like a demon desiring release. I kept vomiting, and bitter, brown bile spilled out. Painful dry heaves followed that forced tears from my eyes. My throat burned, and I was out of breath, but my body scraped for more. Then a metallic taste wetted my tongue, and with my final heave, blood fell, coloring my vile vomit at my feet with velvety drops of red.

When it was over, I collapsed against the boulder and gasped for air. I felt like an emptied river. Big Spoon ran up to me with water. He had been walking the bank by the lake when he'd heard my violent gags.

"I'm carrying you back down to a lower elevation," he said, holding the water bottle to my lips. "You have altitude sickness. That's serious."

"Please, no," I wept after sipping what I could. "My head's killing me. It's awful to move. Please. I just want to go to sleep."

Big Spoon looked up at the sky and smelled the air. "A storm's coming in," he said and thought a moment more. "I guess we can stay," he allowed, "but you have to drink the rest of this water. And if you throw up again, we're going down."

Had we known of the fatal risks altitude sickness could cast upon its captives, we would have descended the mountain immediately, regardless of my incapacitating migraine and the coming rain. As it was, we stayed at the lake. I melted into my sleeping bag as the clouds growled and then slavered down heavy rain. Big Spoon sat up over me, making sure I was okay. Before I fell asleep, he swiped his thumb over my forehead in the sign of the cross.

"My mom did this to comfort me as a boy when she tucked me in at night," he said of the sweet symbol. "Oh, and I have something else that might make you feel better, too." He dug into his pants pocket and then held his closed fist before me. "Here," he said, opening his hand. "I found this on the bank. It was right there in plain sight, as if someone had purposely left it for me to find."

Enough light remained outside to see. I feebly sat up, and Big Spoon placed the treasure in my hand. It was a silver heart about a quarter-inch thick the size of a silver dollar. "It looks old," I said, examining the fancy filigree that scrolled out from the heart's inscription. I read the engraving aloud: "For someone special."

"Pretty neat, huh?" Big Spoon said. "I want you to have it."

"Thank you," I said, moved by his beautiful find. "But this is for you. You're the someone special this belongs to." I returned the token to him and lay back down. "I love you, Caleb. Thank you for taking care of me," I said, closing my eyes.

It rained into the morning. When I awoke, a light pain lingered in my forehead, but the nausea was gone. I readied for the rainy day ahead, working with Big Spoon by my side. As I did, I reminded myself that we were on a journey. And journeys were hard. But they were full of grace, marked with meaning and gifts that made us stronger and got us closer to the place where we belonged while opening our eyes to one spectacular thing after the next—like Big Spoon's heart—so long as we didn't give up.

I reminded myself that in a matter of days, I would acclimate to the High Sierra.

CHAPTER 23

TRIAL ON MOUNT WHITNEY

Something I'd greatly looked forward to on this journey was summiting Mount Whitney. The PCT didn't scale up and over the tallest mountain in the contiguous United States, but since it weaved right by it, most hikers took a day to step off the trail and bag the famous climb.

Big Spoon and I approached the base of this serrated crag two days after my spell of altitude sickness. I felt much better now. My body had adapted to the thin air, and I was eager to ascend the 14,505-foot-high summit. Observing it from the bottom, I could already feel in my bones the glory of standing atop that record peak.

The evening stayed gray as Big Spoon and I made camp by Guitar Lake. Shaped like an acoustic guitar, the lake rippled four miles off the PCT and marked the westward entrance to Whitney's rocky grades. On the hike up to this portal, it hailed. It was June. Yet the frozen rain spilled down like crystal beads, nipping our hatted heads.

"All that snow up there is new," the ranger had said as he passed us, stomping down in the opposite direction. He wore a red rain jacket and heavy high-top boots. "If you're planning to summit, be extremely careful," he warned, pointing to the jagged, jutting stone now blanketed in white.

Blobs of tents surrounded us at the lake. We were at an elevation of 11,200 feet; before us was a five-mile scramble up sharp switchbacks through the dense scree. The hikers we spoke with all planned to make the climb the next morning. But I desired a sunrise ascent, which entailed reaching the top before the sun to watch it awaken this supreme land.

Big Spoon went along with the idea. Thus, after stuffing ourselves with pasta in the cold drizzle, we immediately went to bed. Big Spoon set an alarm on his digital watch that woke us at one in the morning, six hours later. Now, instead of the rain, big, blinking stars reigned in the luscious black sky. It was cold. My breaths came out of my mouth like clouds.

"Thirty-six degrees," Big Spoon said, shining his headlamp on his thermometer. "And it'll only be colder up top."

We put on all of our layers, refitted our headlamps to our heads, and filled our packs with enough food and water for the climb.

Slippery snow smothered the slender trail to the summit. Because it was summertime, and because the Sierra had accumulated a mere 6 percent of its average snowfall that year, Big Spoon and I weren't prepared with crampons and ice axes like we should have been for this trek. We kicked our threadbare boots into the slushy snow for footing. We stabbed our trekking poles into the icy ground.

It was hard to see. The two dots of light from our headlamps hardly touched the surrounding black abyss. Only one other group traveled behind us as the trail launched up the thin, vertical ridge. The farther we progressed, the more we crept along the edges of cliffs, skirting drop-offs like black holes around every rock-faced bend.

Halfway there, something rumbled in our midst. Big Spoon froze and listened. I halted behind him, startled by the noise that crackled down like rubble after an explosion.

"Rock slide," Big Spoon said. "I bet the change in pressure from the snow on the scree caused it." He looked up the slope to the snow-covered rocks. "That's frightening. We have to be on our A game."

We journeyed on. Two miles from the summit, the snow was up to our shins. I followed Big Spoon, who stepped into the deep holes of footprints from those who had tramped here the day before. As he moved, he used his trekking poles to prod the ground beneath the brittle snow. The time I failed to do this, I slipped on a covered patch of ice and teetered like a toddler on the exposed rim. My heart stopped. Below me was nothing but darkness—for miles. Big Spoon clutched my arm.

"You all right?" he asked as I regained my balance.

"Yes," I said, the word trembling off my tongue.

The terrain only intensified. At roughly 13,500 feet above sea level, the path drastically narrowed to the width of one shoe. Here, there was no room for error. The saw-toothed slope flew up on our right. On our left, we edged a shadowy void of doom. I was scared. What the hell are we doing out here? I thought again and again, my heart pacing and mind racing like a bee trapped in a jar.

"Keep calm," Big Spoon said over and over. "Keep your mind calm."

I tried to listen to this advice as I copied his strategic steps on a fifty-foot stretch that felt like imminent death. I moved painfully slow, my knees sinking into the snow as I leaned my body into the mountain so as not to hang over the cliff. It was like walking on a tightrope without a net to catch me if I fell.

On the other side of that deadly strip, my legs shook like sewing machines. We stood on wider ground now and shone our headlamps to the dusky pitch ahead.

With one mile left to climb, our lights revealed even steeper, more treacherous terrain.

"I'm a risk-taker," Big Spoon said, turning to face me. "But this isn't worth the risk. With the snow, darkness, and lack of proper gear, we'd be foolish to keep trying for the top. When the horse is dead, dismount, my dad always says. We need to turn back."

"Thank God," I said, exhaling. "Okay." Inside, though, my heart sank at failing to make it all the way.

On our way down, we came upon the group behind us and found them turning around, too.

"The wise adventurer knows when to call it a day," one of the bearded members said on the descent.

The sun rose as Big Spoon and I regained the base. The pale-pink sky illuminated the rising stone now reflecting from Guitar Lake. Back at the tent, I watched hiker after hiker start the ascent. The sun would melt the snow soon, and the people would pack it down, making the tricky sections of the trail easier to traverse.

"We were too ambitious to do a sunrise ascent," I told Big Spoon as our herd dashed by, fueling me with envy and disappointment. "I really wanted to make the top." I sighed. "And we failed."

"We weren't too ambitious," Big Spoon said. "And we didn't fail. It's just, there come times when we must push on, and there come times when we must choose a different route. We needed to choose a different route this time, is all. Mount Whitney's not going anywhere."

Yet even with his reassuring words, I felt like a failure. I despised giving up on things that I had set out to do. I was a go-getter by nature, one who followed through with my declared task. Yes, I knew it was right that we'd turned back. Whitney could have killed us. But, *oh...* how I ached to reach that peak and touch the very sky.

As Mount Whitney became busier with foot traffic, Big Spoon and I walked around the lake. It was a bright and beautiful day. We watched rainbow trout hatchlings chase each other's tails through the alpine water. The fish swam in a dazzling dance and didn't seem to care if they couldn't catch up to the rest of their school.

Not everything had to be a victory, after all.

CHAPTER 24

THE HONEYSPOONERS

Nearly four weeks had passed since Big Spoon's and my civil marriage ceremony in Lancaster. The trail community now referred to us as the HoneySpooners. When we met new hikers in the wild, jaws dropped. "No way!" they'd cry. "You're the ones who got married. Everyone's talking about it. You guys are insane!"

While Big Spoon and I didn't intend for our marriage to become the talk of the trail, we did aim to find rings to symbolize our unending commitment to each other. In each town we hiked into, we'd search the shops for wedding bands but always left, quite literally, empty-handed.

"The right rings will show themselves to us at the right time," I would say.

Big Spoon would nod accordingly but reply, "I really want a ring."

Thus, the quest for our bands continued the day after we attempted Mount Whitney. Our world shone blue in King's Canyon National Park, where gray mountains congregated like great, wise kings. Big Spoon and I had lunch by an icy alpine lake and then made our way up Forester Pass, the highest point on the PCT at 13,200 feet. The sun mixed wonderfully with the brisk mountain air as we spiraled up severe switchbacks cut within the loose scree. At the top, views of diamond-cut lakes and silver-lit peaks demanded our deepest awe. Snowmelt cascaded down the granite grades as we stood unblinking upon the pass, trying to take it all in: beauty in the raw.

On the other side of Forester, we camped in the valley by a gurgling stream. The days were at their longest, with light lasting until hiker midnight. In the warmth of the sun, we stripped off our clothes and waded in the water, balancing barefoot on slick black rocks as we washed our dirty skin.

A buzzing army of mosquitos took our naked vulnerability as an opportune time to attack. They swarmed us in the frigid water and battled for our blood. Big Spoon and I swatted and swirled like clumsy dancers as we tried to rinse off. The mosquitos dodged our efforts, clung to our bare bodies, and feasted. In a second attempt at defense, we sprinted out of the stream and suited up in pants, jackets, and bug head nets. But the mosquitos prevailed. They slipped under our collars and bit us on our throats. We slapped them dead and then tied bandanas around our necks so that we could cook dinner in the grass in peace. But, alas, when the nasty little menaces pierced through the bright-patterned cotton, we surrendered. I shoveled my mashed potatoes into my mouth and then rinsed out our pots as if I were in a race. Big Spoon rushed to lock up our food and store the bear canisters several feet from our site. Together, we fled for the tent and zipped up tight. The horde hummed over our mesh refuge ominously until the sun went down.

The next day, at mile 789, we broke off from the PCT to reconnect to society by hiking eight miles up and over Kearsarge Pass. With its vistas of sapphire crests and pensive alpine pools, this was the goddess of passages through the Sierra. The splendor of this stretch was so diverting, in fact, that I didn't once scratch my fresh, inflamed mosquito bites.

At dusk, we reached the campground on the other side of the pass. The last van that shuttled hikers out of the remote mountains to the town of Bishop sixty miles away had just left. A cloud of gravel dust dawdled in the air from where it had driven off before we could wave it down. The parking lot was empty.

"We'll have to wait until the van comes back in the morning to get a ride to town," Big Spoon said, reading the sign next to the pit toilets that listed the shuttle's schedule.

My stomach growled. All I had left to eat was a bag of peanuts. "So be it," I said.

We were scanning the area for a campsite when a different van pulled into the lot, and a crew of hikers popped out.

"Howdy," Big Spoon greeted them, ditching the task of finding a site and going up to the driver. "Are you going back down the mountain, by chance?"

"Where you need to go?" the driver asked. He had spiky black hair and giant ear gauges.

"My wife and I are on the PCT and need to resupply in Bishop."

Hearing Big Spoon call me his wife caught me off guard. I wasn't used to being referred to like this—*wife*—and it struck me deeper than ever before that I was no longer a solo being wandering this world alone but rather a fixed companion facing the challenges and joys of this life with my loving mate. I was Big Spoon's wife now. And he was my husband. The two of us had joined to walk this world as one. How mysterious it was, I thought, to find my very life in him.

"Yeah, okay. I have to go through Bishop anyway. I'll take you," the driver said as the hikers he'd brought up dispersed.

Bishop flashed with hotel vacancy signs and the neon lights of loud pubs. With a population of four thousand, it was the largest town in Inyo County and a mecca for rock climbing and tourism. Our driver let us out in the heart of downtown, where silhouettes of the Sierra towered above saloons. We ate a late fast-food dinner and then walked down Main Street beneath the glowing streetlamps to Hostel California. I'd read about this place in my guidebook and was hooked when I saw that it gave PCT hikers a discount.

Bicycles smothered the entrance to the festive lodge, which stood out with lime-green and sky-blue walls. Inside, posters of famous rock climbers hung in the living room above the old-fashioned TV, and dusty novels were strewn about. People rummaged through the communal kitchen for snacks and beer as the manager at the front desk—who wore that classic stoned look of squinty eyes and an elevated smile—checked us in for twenty dollars each.

The manager led us out the back, through the patio, and up the balcony stairs to our coed room comprising six queen-sized bunks. Some hikers were lazing on the patio couches—cigarettes on their lips, their heads swaying to the turned-up tunes—as we mounted the squeaky stairs. I didn't know any of them, but they seemed to know us. Someone yelled out, "Hey! It's the HoneySpooners! Those crazy fools are still together!"

And everybody howled.

━◄┼┼►━

Diesel trucks and eighteen-wheelers screamed by as Big Spoon and I pedaled the hostel's bikes down Main Street, the smell of fresh Danish from the historic

Schat's Bakery leading our way. It was the morning after our sweltering night's stay in a room crammed with ten others. As we ate hearty ham croissants and hot apple turnovers in the open air of the bakery's front porch, the Bishop Trading Post next door caught my eye.

"Maybe it has rings," I said to Big Spoon, whose mouth was full of dough.

"Maybe," Big Spoon said, a few flaky crumbs fluttering out.

A black Great Dane was sprawled out on the cool cement floor of the trading post. Big Spoon and I strolled through the shop, admiring the sundries—like arrowheads, bull skulls, and black-and-white prints of the Sierra.

"Looking for anything in particular?" the soft-spoken salesman with platinum hair and white eyelashes asked. He was sitting at a table in the middle of the store, Phillips screwdriver in hand, tinkering with a clock.

"We are," Big Spoon and I said.

The salesman stood to help us, revealing his stature as the Great Dane of men. "And what might that be?" he gently asked.

We told him our story—how we'd married on the trail and had been searching for rings ever since.

His pale-blue eyes presented a look of intrigue. "I have just what you need," he said.

He went behind the glass counter near the cash register, unlocked it, and pulled out a velvet display tray of handcrafted rings.

"These were made in New Mexico. And these were made right here in Bishop. Here, try this one on. It's sterling silver and turquoise." The salesman handed me the polished band inlaid with vibrant blue stones. "A local artist made it. He says turquoise is his favorite gem to work with because it 'calls on the green of the earth and blue of the sky to bring greater awareness of all things necessary for the progression of life.'"

I slid it on.

"It fits. Caleb, look!" I showed him my ringed finger.

"It's beautiful on you," he said, gazing at my left hand.

The salesman wore a winning smile. "I can always guess a ring size."

Next, it was Big Spoon's turn to pick a ring. The salesman selected a nickel-plated band that had been shaped out of a quarter. "Quite a unique piece. Light yet lasting," he assured, placing the white metallic circle into Big Spoon's palm.

Big Spoon brought it up to his eye and rotated it. "In God We Trust," he read aloud. "It's a Florida quarter, too," he said, slipping it on with ease.

"I feel more married now," I said as Big Spoon and I exited the store. Combined, the rings cost eighty-two dollars—after the 15 percent discount the salesman gave us for being newlyweds. I would continue to wear the Herkimer diamond around my neck. But I was glad for our rings. They emblazoned our tanned fingers in a mesmerizing way—the shining symbols of our continuous link.

We spent the rest of the day beneath the swishing trees of Bishop City Park. I read a musty-paged book on the meaning of life that I'd found in the hostel while Big Spoon carved designs into a stick with his knife. In the late afternoon, a Hispanic woman with long black hair and dark-brown eyes walked over with her son and sat at the same picnic table as us.

"Are you two hiking the PCT?" she asked, her face beaming with curiosity.

"We are," I said, winking at the boy, who gawked at us in our hiker garb as if we were aliens.

The woman's face brightened even more.

"Show her our rings," Big Spoon urged.

We set our hands so the woman could see our wedding bands and then told her our tale.

Her cheeks bloomed with a growing smile. "Oh, how I understand!" she shrieked when we finished. "Have others given you much reproach? Oh, I understand. I was eighteen when I met my husband. I just knew he was the one. He was thirty-two. My friends and family said I was mad—*reckless*—making the biggest mistake of my life." She looked lovingly at her son. "But I knew the truth. He was the one I loved. And love knows no bounds." She paused, as if slipping back into this profound time in her life. "We've been married twenty-three years and have three beautiful sons," she said. "I tell my love today, if you ever leave me, I will never marry again. Because he is the love of my life. I understand you two. I do. You must live your life—*your very life*. You must follow *your* very heart."

━━┽┾━━

Later that evening, Big Spoon and I biked to the high school rodeo we'd learned of from the flyers around town. It was at the Tri County Fairgrounds off Sierra Street. We sat high in the bleachers, which shook each time the cowboy-hatted crowd cheered. The air smelled of popcorn and cattle. The rodeo boomed with galloping horses. They were mighty beasts with mighty hearts under someone else's control. I desired their freedom. I desired for them to roam the mountains and run as they were made to—far and unbound. I looked at my turquoise ring and then at my husband. He, too, fixated on the harnessed horses. Did he desire the same thing for these beautiful steeds?

We're all mighty beasts with mighty hearts, I thought, striving to live our unrestrained lives.

"Live your life—*your very life*," the Hispanic woman had said. As I watched each horse adhere to its reins, I realized that I was free. By marrying Big Spoon like I did, I had followed the woman's advice. It was wild. But it was my very life.

CHAPTER 25

A TRIGGERING FALL

It was the morning of June 22. I rolled over in my sleeping bag and kissed Big Spoon on his bearded cheek. "Happy birthday, Caleb," I said as his eyes flickered open.

We had camped at mile 832 by Middle Fork Kings River. At an elevation of over 9,000 feet, the river was so cold that it shocked me awake when I crawled from the tent and splashed some water on my face. The morning air felt like ice. Big Spoon built a small fire in the stone pit, using our coals from last night's blaze to ignite it. I spun around the flames like a marshmallow on a stick to allow heat on all sides. As I did, I caught sight of a doe grazing in the sunny grass across the river. She ate slowly, lifting her head and pricking back her ears every few seconds, displaying her golden grace. The creature's peaceful beauty made me long for something in my soul.

But what? I wondered as I sat on a stump, switching out my sandals for my tattered boots. After two months of being on the trail, it seemed that each mile was more demanding than the last. I'd thought it would be the opposite. I'd thought I'd be so accustomed to this lifestyle by now that I'd breeze through the rest of the PCT. But no. The steep passes of the Sierra mocked my wishful endurance. Every day, Big Spoon and I summited soaring peaks like a never-ending staircase that drained my body and exhausted my mind. Like my boots, I was starting to get worn out.

As I tied my frayed laces, I noticed a chunk of rubber sole flapping from my left heel like a loose tooth. I ripped it off and slipped it into my shirt pocket, intending to glue it back on in the next town. Then I swept my thumb over where the grip had been. The bald tread felt slick as gums.

It took me longer than usual to pack up. Big Spoon waited patiently by the undulating embers, looking over his exquisitely detailed National Geographic map. We were in the John Muir Wilderness. Before us loomed Muir Pass—a six-mile clamber up a rugged crag. Not a single cloud clotted the azure sky. The pristine day called us to join it. But I lingered by the fire's smoky ash, dreading to embark on the 3,000-foot climb.

"What would you be doing today if you weren't on the trail?" I asked Big Spoon, delaying the inevitable schlep.

He was using his foot to separate the coals we had just doused with water.

"Tradition has it that I go on a birthday hike," he said. "Usually to Delaware Water Gap with my brother and friends. Then we go to Hotdog Johnny's. It's a roadside stand on Route 46. Their dogs are decent, and you can walk down to the Pequest River to eat them."

"Sounds wonderful," I said, imagining myself there.

Big Spoon scattered the final coal. "It's a good time."

When we finally hit the trail, I lagged far behind. The scenery was spectacular. Towering cliffs, textured talus, and tiny purple petals popping from the rocky ground painted my winding way. Large, black tadpoles with long, bent legs lay on the dirt bottoms of every creek. A mother grouse and her chicks toddled down the muddy banks. I walked through a lively land of dreams. But something concrete was building within, blocking my happy escape into this picturesque day.

One mile from the top of the pass, a charging creek blocked the trail. The high-speed runoff from the melting snow fueled its roaring laughter. By this point, I had forded many creeks in the Sierra, but none as loud and intimidating as the one before me now. I inched closer to the white water and saw Big Spoon standing on the other side. Knowing I wouldn't hear him if he yelled, he pointed to the precarious path of gray stones he had taken to cross the swiftness. I examined the route and then stuck a trekking pole into the creek. The current flung against it, and my pole kicked up.

I took a deep breath, dug both poles into the rocky bed, and leaped onto the first stone. It wobbled back and forth like a seesaw, so I quickly jumped to the next. My abrupt movement made my pack shift on my back, throwing me off balance. Again, I hurried forward, this time to a rock that jutted out from the creek at a slant. That's when the unexpected happened. My boot with the ripped sole slipped on the slanted rock. I lost my balance completely and fell backward. The world turned silent as snow. Then I crashed into the creek, slamming into the hard bottom, my elbow catching my fall.

Pain zapped through my bones. The water was so cold it felt like daggers digging into my skin. As I staggered to regain my stance, I saw Big Spoon strip off his backpack. He was about to jump in after me when I raised a trekking pole to let him know I was safe. Then I wrestled my way through the waist-deep rushing water.

Big Spoon grabbed my wrist and pulled me up as soon as I was close enough to dry land. Water gushed off my person and pack onto the stony ground. Other than being a little shaken up, I thought I was fine. But then Big Spoon gripped me in his arms, and my face suddenly contorted. My eyes bunched up, and tears fell. Big Spoon unstrapped my soaking pack and set it to the side of the trail. He held me even closer as I cried and shivered like a wet cat.

"Did that scare you?" he sweetly asked.

I buried my face in his shirt. "I hit the wall," I said, my words muffled. "All I did was fall in the creek. But really, I hit the wall. I'm tired of the trail." I understood this as I said it. "I'm so tired."

And I was. I'd just realized. Colliding into the creek had knocked this awareness into me. I'd been living in the wilderness for sixty days. For sixty days I'd slept on the ground, gone unwashed, walked up mountain after mountain, and traversed treacherous creeks galore. And I was tired. I longed to be the grazing doe basking in the sun without a daily destination to reach.

Big Spoon sat me down on a smooth rock. My sopping boots dripped into the stone as I continued to cry into him.

"What we're doing is extremely hard," he consoled. "You're not alone in how you feel. I've been really tired at times, too. Fed up, actually." He paused. I looked into his eyes and saw something weighing there.

"Go on," I said.

"It's just...well..." He struggled to find the words. "Something to remember is that, you see, this trail doesn't own us. We can get off it at any time." He exhaled heavily, as if he had released a taxing truth.

This upset me even more. Why walk for hundreds of miles, why journey for days on end, only to get off the trail before that journey was done? Why work so hard for something, only to quit? I thought. At the same time, I knew Big Spoon was right. The trail was starting to take its toll. Over the past few sunrises when I'd awoken, I'd groaned at the thought of hiking all day.

This realization ripped me deep inside, and I cried harder. I cried because I wasn't a quitter, but for the first time since starting the trail, I wanted to step off. I cried because the trail had become my life—it was what I knew now—but my passion for it was slipping away.

"I'm...so sorry...to cry...on your birthday," I eventually offered through my sobs.

My hysteria made Big Spoon laugh. He tried to contain it, but it spilled out of his being like light. Here we were in the middle of the Sierra—the golden stone encasing us like heaven—while I was as wet as a dishrag, my elbow swelling up, wailing like a child in pain and apologizing seriously about it.

"You can cry on my birthday," Big Spoon said, laughing some more. His merriment dashed into me like a refreshing breeze. Soon, I was laughing too. As we looked out on the large land we were traveling, together we laughed and laughed.

At the top of Muir Pass, I rummaged through my bear canister for Big Spoon's present: my last Snickers bar. My elbow ached, my eyes were puffy, and my hair was still wet. But I was calm now, restored after a good cry. Big Spoon and I took a seat against the stacked stone of the John Muir Hut. Erected in 1931 by the Sierra Club and the US Forest Service, the Muir Hut honored the spirit of the nineteenth-century conservationist and writer whose passion had enveloped the Sierra. I huddled close to Big Spoon and handed him the chocolate bar, followed by the letter I'd written him in secret the night before. A mountaintop wind made the edges of the journal paper flap back and forth as Big Spoon unfolded it and silently read.

"My passion for life has never been so profound now that you and I journey through it together," I said in the letter. "This is a tremendous journey I want to complete with you. A journey of merit, hard work, and joy. A journey worth fighting for to the end to reap its great rewards. No matter the trials of some stretches."

CHAPTER 26

SO MUCH ALL AT ONCE

B ig Spoon and I would continue on our journey, but
we needed to take a break. Thus, with the Fourth
of July approaching, we planned to get off the trail at
Tuolumne Meadows, ride a bus two hundred miles west
to San Francisco, and spend a few days out of the mountains by the sea.

We thought it a solid scheme for some respite from
the trail. But first we had to get there.

At mile 879, sixty-four miles from Tuolumne, Big
Spoon and I met a man named Squirrel on Edison Lake.
Squirrel looked like a squirrel: fidgety and thin, his lit-
tle face bunched up to his nose. It was early morning.
The night before, we had camped next to the parched
lake in anticipation of Squirrel's picking us up. He fer-
ried us a mile in his rusty green johnboat to Scarlet
Valley Resort—a major destination for PCT and John

Muir Trail hikers, as it was one of the few accessible areas in the Sierra where hikers could resupply and eat a hot meal.

During the ride, Squirrel raised his voice above the sound of the motor to tell us that Edison Lake had been constructed in 1954 for water storage and hydroelectric power generation. He said the reservoir had been completed on the seventy-fifth anniversary of the invention of electric light and was therefore named after Thomas Edison.

"In all my years of ferrying folks back and forth, I never seen it so low," he said, shaking his coarse-haired head. "This drought better end. Otherwise, this time next year, people will be walking across here. And I'll be out of a job."

He went on to say that the lake had shrunk by two-thirds since the start of California's drought four years ago. The earth the water had once covered was orange and cracked like dry skin. Change is constant, I thought as I faced forward, the wind on the remaining water kicking back my hair.

Squirrel docked on the land extending from the lake. Coyote tracks padded the thirsty bank. The ferry should have brought us right to the resort. But because the lake no longer stretched that far, Squirrel shuttled us a half mile farther in a commercial van.

Scarlet Valley wasn't so much a resort as it was a campground with a general store and an overpriced restaurant. It cost forty-two dollars for the two burgers, fries, and puny piece of apple pie that Big Spoon and I demolished for lunch. And that didn't include the tip we left for our flighty waitress, who skipped around in a skimpy top that exposed her floppy breasts.

We left early the next morning after a sleepless night, thanks to the rowdy hikers who'd stayed up late drinking beer and belching out discourteous horselaughs. I was glad to leave. Other than the unopened box of Clif Bars that Big Spoon acquired from the metal trunk of a hiker box, Scarlet Valley had let me down.

We reached Red's Meadow Campground two days later. At mile 907, Red's Meadow was steps off the trail and offered showers, laundry facilities, a general store, and designated lots for RVs and tents. The night we stayed there, a mischievous black bear sniffed his way into camp. Big Spoon and I were walking back from the showers when we spotted the round, heavy creature creeping in. We paused on the path mere feet from our site. The bear proceeded toward the red cooler that had been left out beside the RV straight ahead. It lifted the lid with its long, black claw, looked around, and then dug in.

"Hey, buddy!" Big Spoon called to the man slouched asleep in his camp chair. "A bear's stealing your food!"

"A what?" the man asked drowsily.

"A bear!" Big Spoon elongated the words. "Quick! Behind you, at your cooler."

The man shot out of his chair. "Shit!" he cried upon sighting the thief. He grabbed the nearest weapon—a cast-iron skillet—and bolted for the bear, now neck deep in an icy box of fish.

The daughter, who had been Hula-Hooping by the creek, ran to her mother beneath the awning as the man raised the skillet above his head and yelled at the bear to get. The harmless beast jumped back from the cooler and fled. It tore for dear life through the field toward the forest, its head hanging low after getting caught.

The next morning, after taking the bus from Red's Meadow to the ski-resort town of Mammoth Lakes, Big Spoon and I attempted to go to church. We rode the open-air trolley from the bustling town center to the end of the line. Walking a half mile more led us to the white-shingled chapel the old camp host at Red's Meadow had recommended. The parking lot was vacant.

"It is Sunday, right?" I asked.

We opened the creaky door. The inside smelled like formaldehyde—a compound that could have been sprayed to preserve the ancient members of the congregation, whom I could count on one hand.

They sat silently in the stuffy sanctuary like skeletons. The walls were windowless and blank. Big Spoon and I looked at each other warily before taking a seat in the pew closest to the exit. The balding pastor patted the hunched backs of his time-worn members and then sauntered our way. He held a mason jar at his hip in which gray liquid sloshed.

Poison, I thought as he shook our hands. His fingers were freakishly cold. His complexion was as dull as a ghost's.

"It's a rare treat to see such youthful souls in this here house of God," the pastor said, emphasizing the words *youthful* and *house of God*.

"We're on the PCT, just passing through," Big Spoon said, being polite. I could tell he wanted no part of this conversation.

The pastor sipped from the mason jar. "Say, I've got a new grill at home I've been meaning to test out. Why don't you two come over after the service for supper? I'll grill lamb. *Lamb,*" he stressed. "What hungry hiker doesn't like *lamb?*"

I shot a look at Big Spoon, who shot one back at me.

"Thank you very much," I said, searching for words. "But we have several errands we need to run today before we get back on the trail."

"But I'm having *lamb,*" the pastor persisted. "I'll drive you to my home myself and then take you on your errands. I've never met a young person who didn't just love *lamb.*" He gulped from his drink and then gazed at Big Spoon and me as if to hypnotize us into coming.

Are we the lambs he wants to grill? I couldn't help but wonder.

Eyeing the man, Big Spoon flatly and firmly said, "No."

The pastor spit out a laugh. "Suit yourselves," he sneered before finishing off his drink and slithering between the pews to the pulpit. When he bowed his head to pray, Big Spoon tapped my thigh and tilted his head toward the exit.

"And may God's wrath reach those who continue to not listen!" the pastor bellowed in prayer as we stood, tiptoed out of the sanctuary, and ran like hell.

⊷⊶

The sky thundered and threw lightning spears into the Ansel Adams Wilderness. The wind swept the pollen off the pines, creating clouds of yellow dust, as the rain pelted into Thousand Island Lake, making its small, rocky isles look like black ocean waves. We were at mile 922, trekking up the slick, dark stone at an elevation of 10,000 feet. Although it was early afternoon, several hikers had stopped in the storm to set up their tents at the side of the trail for shelter. The clouds clashed, and I wondered if Big Spoon and I should do the same—or just keep going.

"All we're getting out here is wet," Big Spoon called above the rolling thunder when I voiced this thought. "There is a risk. But I say we keep going."

So, we walked on, which at the end of the day—come hell or high rain—was all we could really do: continue.

Even with the tormenting mosquitoes. They ate us alive on this stretch, those bloodthirsty terrors. In fact, they were so bad that I deemed them the devil's spawn: vicious and incessant, out in the world to bring us down.

Every person we passed had been afflicted. They, like us, wore pants, long sleeves, and mosquito head nets in an effort to shield against the vexatious bites of this dive-bombing brigade.

"I pity the soul who doesn't have a head net," Big Spoon would say each time we charged through a sinister swarm.

We had come through a lot. By the time we reached Tuolumne Meadows, also known as the gateway to Yosemite National Park, Big Spoon and I were ready for our vacation. Which was odd, seeing as we had quit our jobs and spent the last ten weeks on the PCT. Yet, while the PCT was a break from the professed "real world," it was not a vacation. Vacations meant rest and relaxation. But the PCT was work. Enjoyable work and rewarding work, but work all the same—tough labor that demanded our blood, sweat, blisters, and tears: our new nine-to-five in the great outdoors.

Therefore, we couldn't wait to start the four-hour bus ride from Yosemite Valley to San Francisco that I had read about in my guidebook. We would get out of the mountains for a few days and go visit the ocean. Fortunately, Big Spoon's cousin Autumn lived in the Bay Area and offered to let us stay at her house when Big Spoon contacted her with our plan.

It was a bulletproof plan, too. Or so we thought. For when we hiked into Tuolumne that Tuesday afternoon and learned from the general-store clerk that the bus we needed didn't run on weekdays, we were stuck.

Big Spoon and I picked a fly-infested picnic table in front of the store to sit at and think. Several minutes went by. The green tea I had bought was now empty, and a storm was coming in.

"Either we try to hitch to San Francisco, or we forget the whole thing and keep going on the trail," Big Spoon said, inspecting the indigo clouds.

"I don't want to forget the whole thing," I whined. "I want our holiday."

"So do I," Big Spoon said.

It thundered.

"That's a really long hitch, though," I complained.

"Two hundred miles."

"Is it possible?"

"What do you think?" Big Spoon said in an annoyed tone, answering my question with his.

Several minutes later, we were standing on the side of Highway 120, our packs leaning against our shins as our thumbs waved high before the Yosemite tourists wheeling by.

There was a key strategy to hitchhiking that Big Spoon and I were well aware of by now: the girl always stood up front. That way, the driver saw the female first, likely perceiving her as a helpless stray to stop for and help, rather than seeing the male first, who no matter how nicely groomed appeared more like a maniacal threat than a man on foot in need of a lift.

Therefore, I stood in front of Big Spoon as the dark clouds thickened, my sweaty bandana pulled off and greasy hair let down. I wasn't ashamed that I was—for lack of a better phrase—working what my mama gave me to get a free ride. After all, it worked every time.

About thirty cars passed before a massive motor home stopped in the middle of the two-lane road. The Latino driver rolled down the passenger side window, leaned toward us, and asked, "Where to?"

"San Francisco," I said, batting my eyes, praying my stench would miss the driver's nose.

Cars piled up behind the motor home as the driver thought this over.

"Eh," he bobbled his head from side to side, debating with himself. "I can give you ride, but only so far. Just beyond the park is where I stop. Come on if you can find seats. We have a full house."

He called something in Spanish, and a curvy woman in tight, zebra-printed pants opened the RV entry door. Big Spoon and I climbed in. The four women and three teenagers inside stared at us with rich curiosity in their chocolate eyes. The women helped us situate our packs on the floor and then pointed to the kitchen booth. The girl and two boys sitting there scooted into each other as we shuffled past the women on the leather couch and slid in to take our seats.

When the driver started up again, the woman in zebra pants reached into the cooler at her feet and passed two cans of dripping, cold Coke to Big Spoon and me. Except for the teenagers, who were mostly quiet, the family spoke little English. But the mothers and grandmother communicated well enough to keep offering us food. Even when we politely declined, saying the ride alone was plenty, the grandmother hobbled to the refrigerator, whipped out some white bread and a homemade spread, and in her grandmotherly way coerced us to eat what she called "*mi sándwich de queso especial.*"

"Those were incredible," Big Spoon and I said in praise as we licked the cheese off our fingers.

"*Uno mas?*" the grandmother asked, a proud smile on her face.

She didn't wait for our answer before making us another.

Two hours later, after a winding mountainside drive in bumper-to-bumper traffic, the driver stopped for the evening at a campground off the highway.

"God bless!" the woman in zebra pants cried as Big Spoon and I refastened our packs in the parking lot. Her name, we'd learned during the hitch, was Penelope. And although I couldn't tell if she understood a word we'd said, she acted fascinated when we'd described our journey.

With our packs secured, Penelope hugged us like a mother.

"God bless!" she called again, waving good-bye passionately as we returned to the highway to thumb another lift.

"Time for round two," Big Spoon said.

I got into my ready position.

We were 150 miles east of San Francisco now. No cars passed by for minutes at a time. The dark clouds had cleared, and it was humid in the valley. Beads of sweat rolled off my chin as we waited. Then a red car appeared on the horizon. Our thumbs burst up. As the car came closer, it braked.

"You may come with me," the East Indian man with smooth walnut skin said after pulling off on the side of the road. "Though I will be stopping soon."

Because any bit of advancement helped, we leaped into his car.

"My name is Vivaan," the man told us on the ride, and we asked him where he was from.

"New Delhi, but I have lived in New York the last eight years, working in finance." His accent was as thick as his black beard, and he spoke as fast as he drove. "But now, praise Brahma, I am finally traveling around this beautiful country. That is what I aimed to do, you see, when I first came to America. Not become complacent like I did in my soul-sucking career."

Vivaan's shrill voice made the term *soul-sucking* ring like a clock alarm. He went on to say he'd quit his job two months before and had been on the road ever since.

"In fact, earlier today I was hiking in Yosemite and had to hitchhike back to my car. A nice elderly couple gave me a ride. So, when I saw you two just now on the side of the road, I thought to myself, 'This must be a test of karma.'"

"We're very grateful for your help," said Big Spoon, who was sitting up front.

"I do know it is dangerous to pick up strangers. Yes, I do know this," Vivaan continued, eyeing me in the rearview mirror. "But this life is dangerous, no? And if you do not get in on the danger, then you are not really living, I believe. Just do not slit my throat," he said with a laugh. "Now, where are you two going?"

Big Spoon told him about our goal of getting to San Francisco.

"Ah, I see. I am staying at the motel here in Groveland tonight," Vivaan said as we entered the town. "But tomorrow morning, I am driving to San Fran. If you split the cost of gas with me, I will drive you there also."

Big Spoon glanced my way, and I nodded.

"You have a deal," he said.

Our driver gave us a time and place to meet.

Groveland was a one-horse town of old saloons and western buildings where tourists who didn't want to pay the price of staying in Yosemite slept. Big Spoon and I stayed at the same place as Vivaan—the Main Street Motel. Except there were no rooms available, so the receptionist—who was visibly high on something—accommodated us with one of the eight-person tents staked in the motel's yard.

"Your room will be tent number five," she said, leaning against the wall behind her desk and staring at something—who knows what—beyond Big Spoon and me. She wore pajama bottoms and a sheer shirt that didn't quite cover her flab. Her hair was as tangled and unwashed as mine. "The tent has an air mattress inside, and the bathrooms are right across the lot," she said, pointing out the window. "Comes to twenty-five dollars."

"Where the hell are we?" I asked Big Spoon later that night as I rolled around on the partially deflated air mattress, trying to get comfy. With the darkness came the stray dogs, which roamed around our spacious tent, sniffing and howling.

"I have no idea, but this place creeps me out," Big Spoon said, his knife tucked beneath the pillow he had made out of his spare clothes.

"Thank God we have a ride to the city tomorrow," I said.

"Yeah, thank God."

⇒╫╪⇐

Over the next five days, we slept on the pullout couch in Autumn's Oakland cottage. The high school guidance counselor lived with her wife, Mia, and their two-year-old twins in a bright neighborhood where roses and lemon trees grew in every yard. She let us borrow her car during our stay, and Big Spoon and I took off with this freedom down the open road.

One day, in the drenching fog of dawn, we traveled across the Golden Gate Bridge—the burnt-orange wonder of cables spanning almost two miles over the Golden

Gate Strait. The bridge connected us to Highway 1, where we rolled for hours with the windows down along the Pacific coast.

Fruit stands lined the highway, and the air smelled like salt. At noon, we stopped in the elegant coastal city of Half Moon Bay. I bought some fresh strawberries from the corner market, and Big Spoon and I ate them as we strolled from the town square to the beach. Here, white cliffs rose from the sand like something out of a poem. We kicked off our shoes and walked upon the gritty shore, which massaged our callused soles. At one point, I stopped to look out on the Pacific Ocean—it seemed to go on forever. The wind coming off the water was strong. The dark waves slammed into the shore and struck me deep inside.

From the mountains to the sea, I thought, looking out. We've roamed from the mountains to the sea.

And we were still going.

><del>+ +</del>——

The Fourth of July smoked with fireworks over the foggy city. That night, Big Spoon and I met up with a college friend of mine, who lived in the area, to watch them. Her name was Hope, and because she worked on the forty-fourth floor of the Transamerica Pyramid—the tallest skyscraper in San Francisco at 853 feet—she invited us to view the light show from these corporate heights.

Shoulders touched on the hot and crowded subway ride from Hope's Berkeley apartment to the city. A security guard at the Transamerica checked our IDs before allowing us to ascend on the elevator. Hope's roommate, Jules, came with us, and we were the only ones on the forty-fourth floor. In a sleek conference room overlooking the bay, we sipped the sparkling wine and sucked on the dark chocolate Hope and Jules had supplied. It was grand. The only misfortune was that the fog smothered the night sky. So, when the fireworks went off, we couldn't see them—we could only hear their thundering pops and catch their shimmery reflections in the water far below.

We departed in the morning on an Amtrak train. Autumn and Mia, as well as Autumn's dad (Caleb's uncle George, who also lived in Oakland), had surprised us with the tickets, allowing us a hitch-free trip back to Yosemite.

"It's amazing the kindness you receive when you have a pack on your back," Big Spoon said as we boarded the train in Jack London Square.

Since leaving Tuolumne, not a day had passed that someone hadn't offered us a hand.

"Truly," I said, feeling rested and ready to return to the trail.

Or so I thought.

We sat on the top floor of the double-decker by a window on the west side in order to see the bay. So much had happened—all at once, it seemed. Now, the view of teal water gradually turned to that of pure stone.

Our break was over. Back to the trail we roamed.

CHAPTER 27
TO THE LEES

Sonora Pass couldn't have been more beautiful. The overcast morning made the pale-green meadows pop. The mountains flaunted the colors of wild horses. Coats of red dashed into hides of tan dashed into flowing manes of black. It was brisk out; the hollows of the higher peaks still cradled snow. The wind blew as I walked up the pass, along the ridge rising in elevation to over 10,000 feet. A hawk overhead glided in the wind, its strong yellow wings spread wide.

I needed this walk. By now, Big Spoon and I had traveled over a thousand miles. This was a major feat that should have invigorated me with a powerful drive. But the last four days through the white-cliffed climbs of Yosemite Wilderness had depleted my stamina. I was weary. Burned out. During the eighty miles after our trip to San Francisco, my thoughts had revolved around life beyond the trail.

Then came Sonora Pass. It seemed to work this way: the trail would start to demand too much, making me feel like its slave. My steps would lose purpose then, and I would merely toil to meet my daily miles. A single memory offered hope. It was the memory of reading my guidebook several months before, when I first began preparing for the PCT.

"If you feel like quitting, wait a week," I said, reciting the guidebook's words as I hiked. "Something amazing always follows your most difficult days."

The truth of this embraced me as I sailed up Sonora's edge into the painted land. Chickarees screamed out from the pines as I made my way by, warning their fellow wildlife of my presence. I was ahead of Big Spoon, who had stopped at the foot of the pass to give me a few minutes' lead. I'd asked him to do this because I wanted to hike alone, not knowing who or what was ahead. I wanted the wilderness all to myself for a time to remind me of why I was here.

"For life," I told Big Spoon when he met me at the top. "I'm here for life." I fixated on the one violet flower springing up from the pebbled ground.

Big Spoon looked out on the sweeping beauty and nodded.

"This last stretch was exhausting," I went on. "It really drained my desire to keep going. I can't tell you how many times I thought over the last four days that *I want this thing to end.*" I sat next to the flower, my pack clinging to my back. "But where we are now is revival. The majesty of this place is beyond words. You don't get this outside of the wild. It makes me remember why I came to do this hike in the first place."

Big Spoon crouched next to me. "Why?"

I took a deep breath of the cold air. "My life before this was deadly. Spending day after day confined to my tiny gray cubicle. It didn't even have windows. It didn't even let in real light." I shuddered, remembering my cell. "I was suffocating in there—like a flame covered up. Little by little, I was shrinking away as the customers I catered to demanded more and more." I paused, considering my past life. "And it was all by *my* choice. Crazy. I was allowing my life to waste away." I thought on this for a moment. "But I came out here to *save* it. To live and drink life to the lees. Do you know that poem? The lees are the wine sediments at the bottom of the barrel. They're considered the waste. But I never want to waste another drop of life again. I want to drink life all the way down to the sediments at the bottom of the barrel. That's why I'm here."

Big Spoon put his hand on my back. "I understand you," he said.

"I don't know what's ahead. The trail may only get harder." I focused on the little flower that had somehow bloomed above the crumbled soil of this gusty peak. "But

I do know this." The wind suddenly picked up. "A beautiful life comes to those who stick on the narrow path."

≫⊰⊱≪

Bridgeport was an old town. The Mono County Courthouse—a wooden-slat structure painted in heavy coats of white—had held its ground since 1880. A red telephone booth stood outside the downtown saloon. The White Lady was still the talk of the town: the one who'd hanged herself in her wedding dress in room 16 of the Bridgeport Inn after her fiancé had suddenly died.

A thirty-mile hitch from Sonora Pass down Highway 108 and US 395 landed Big Spoon and me in Bridgeport's core. With ten minutes to spare, we ran to the post office before it closed to ship our bear canisters home, as we had completed the section in the Sierra that demanded we haul these heavy cans.

The postmaster held a crying baby at her hip and was clearly ready to lock up.

"Know a decent place we could grab a bite to eat?" Big Spoon asked, raising his voice over that of the baby's after paying the cost of shipping.

"What you see here is what you get," the postmaster said, swaying from side to side to calm her wailing child.

"Do you have any recommendations?" Big Spoon asked, his hunger hindering him from perceiving the woman's desire to leave.

She looked at the clock and answered, "We're closed."
We therefore walked down Main Street until we came upon the Burger Barn, a fast-food stand with outdoor seating where a mass of locals flocked. The burgers were greasy and good. I polished mine off with a chocolate milkshake while Big Spoon went with the onion rings. We split a plate of fries. When we inquired about cheap lodging, the busboy, who was at least sixty years old, advised us as he cleared our plates to stay at the Black Rock Hotel.

"It's just across the street," he said, the mustard stains on his white apron as flashy as a vacancy sign. "Cheapest place in town."

On the outside, the hotel stood like a dilapidated barn still decorated in Fourth of July wreaths. Rusty hinges squeaked when we opened the door. As we entered the lace-curtained lobby, our feet sank into the red shag carpet that looked like a pool of blood. No one was at the front desk. The lobby let in just enough light to illuminate the dusty portraits hanging from the wallpapered walls. The faces in the sepia-toned photographs stared at us with sharp, black eyes.

"Gone for the day," said the sign at the front desk. "To rent room, go to sports bar next door. Pay Sherry. $70/night. Checkout 10:30 a.m.—Janice."

"What do you think?" Big Spoon asked as I sat in an old rocking chair as delicate as toothpicks.

"I don't think anyone's here," I said, afraid to rock backward.

"It's a little strange. But there's no camping here. And our other options cost twice as much."

"And we'll only be here a night."

"So, we'll get a room here, then?" Big Spoon asked.

I glanced at the portraits, locking eyes with a wrinkled lady whose face looked as cold as snow. "I guess," I said and gulped.

Our room seemed fine at first. The bed took up most of the space, and our backpacks took up the rest. The bathroom appeared clean, and the linens were washed. But in the tub, mold crawled up the shower curtain and down into the drain. This didn't distress me as much as the colony of ants I discovered crawling up the nightstand after I got out of the shower and into bed. Big Spoon was showering when I found the ants—he was wearing his camp shoes as he washed because the tub was too grimy to stand in barefoot.

"These ants are worse than the ones we deal with camping," I called.

"I feel like I'm showering in the slime of a thousand slugs," he replied.

We called Sherry at the sports bar, followed by the hotel owner, Janice, to ask for a different room. But neither picked up.

I slept with one eye open.

The next morning, as Big Spoon and I packed up, a thunderous knock came at the door. Checkout wasn't for another hour, but when Big Spoon opened up, a wrinkled woman with black hair and sharp eyes—like the one in the old-fashioned portrait—yelled at us to leave.

The woman was Janice. She stormed into the room and continued to scream. When she saw that we were hikers, her rage flared even more, like a fire doused in kerosene. She walked over to the bed and squashed an ant with her long-nailed finger.

"How dare you let mites into my hotel," she said, her eyes cutting us like broken glass.

"The ants were here before us," Big Spoon argued. "And what's going on? The sign in the lobby says check-out's at ten-thirty."

In her anger, Janice managed to say that we shouldn't have stayed in this room, that a guest was coming any minute who had reserved this very space.

"And now you filthy hikers have tracked in bugs!" she roared.

"Good riddance!" I said after Big Spoon and I had buckled our packs and hustled out of the demented Black Rock Hotel.

In fact, we were in such a rush to get out of Bridgeport that when we went to the grocery store down the street, we stayed only long enough to buy the bare necessities for the next seventy-five miles.

Thus, over the next several days through the Toiyabe Wilderness and El Dorado National Forest, Big Spoon and I had to ration our food into pitiful portions that never satisfied our hunger. Not having as much to eat on the trail as we normally did irritated us like an un-relenting itch we couldn't reach to scratch. On our sec-ond-to-last day before making the next town, we were practically mad.

"Do you know what I want more than anything in the world?" I said to Big Spoon, who was a step ahead of me as we climbed up Carson Pass. At mile 1,075, all I'd eaten that day was half a Snickers bar and a spoonful of peanut butter.

"What?" Big Spoon said.

"A big, fat, gooey chocolate chip cookie. Homemade. And hot."

"I want fried Oreos from the Jersey Shore," Big Spoon said.

"Are those any good?"

"You've never had fried Oreos?"

"No."

Big Spoon shook his head. "Have you lived?"

We progressed up the pass like snails, not reach-ing the top until late afternoon. Here, the trail crossed Highway 88, where a trailhead parking area and infor-mation center extended from the road. Big Spoon and I staggered up to the information center, where a woman wearing a green uniform was just locking the door.

Famished, Big Spoon didn't even say hello but im-mediately asked, "Is there a vending machine inside?"

"Are you PCT hikers?" she asked, her white, silky hair reflecting the sun. The name tag on her vest said Sue.

"Yes," Big Spoon said.

"And we're hungry," I declared.

Sue unlocked the door.

"Say no more, my darlings. Take your packs off and sit down at that picnic table there. Thank goodness you came when you did. I was just about to close."

We followed her every instruction as she disappeared inside the information center.

"Do you like hot dogs?" she called. "They were grilled two hours ago, but they should be—"

"We'll eat anything," interrupted Big Spoon, his eyes as wild as a ravenous dog's.

Sue came back outside. "We just love to feed you hikers," she said, her arms loaded with buns, mustard, pickle relish, and a Tupperware container of dogs.

We helped her set the delicacies on the splintery table. Big Spoon untied the bag of buns and plunged in his hands. I opened the container to the hot dogs. The smell of smoked meat swirled through the air. A pool of saliva swelled on my tongue.

"Do you mind if we have two each?" Big Spoon asked as he squirted mustard on his bun.

"Have them all!" Sue said, amused by our fervor to eat.

We feasted until our stomachs bulged out like balloons and not a crumb remained on the table.

"Good-bye! And thank you again!" we called to our angel Sue as she walked to her car. She had finished closing up, and we thought she was leaving. But instead, she'd gone to her car only to get something out. Then she walked back over to Big Spoon and me.

"Do you like chocolate chip cookies? I made them this morning," she said, unfolding the paper towel in her hand to display two golden cookies shining like rare gems. The chocolate chips had melted, and Sue said the sweets were still warm from sitting in the sun. I looked at Big Spoon with something like awe. My exact wish had come true.

"This is living," I said and then licked the chocolate off my fingers, paying no mind to my dirty nails.

Sue had left, but Big Spoon and I stayed awhile longer to savor this blessed moment.

"This *is* living," Big Spoon said.

He placed his last sweet morsel on his tongue before we returned to the trail.

CHAPTER 28
LUXURY IN LAKE TAHOE

Casino signs danced with light on the streets of Lake Tahoe. On Friday afternoon, Big Spoon and I had entered this loud and glitzy land after hitching fourteen miles from Echo Lake, the recreational glacial pool at mile 1,094, not far from the highway. Men in suede cowboy hats escorted women in high heels down the sidewalks. Shopping bags swung from the arms of almost everyone. The few hikers we saw roaming about looked like vagabonds in the midst of all the glam.

"I guess we look like vagabonds, too," I said to Big Spoon on our hot walk past alpaca fur shops and fine-art galleries to the bus stop.

"We look normal," Big Spoon said in his direct way.

Beyond tourism, Lake Tahoe was famous for its alpine lake—the largest in North America—gleaming for twenty-two miles with the emerald tints of the Caribbean Sea. Big Spoon and I decided to splurge and rent a car to travel around the lake with ease. We'd devised this plan merely minutes earlier as we loitered in the McDonald's on Lake Tahoe Boulevard. Loitering, like hitchhiking, was another art to this journey we had mastered. Finding a fast-food restaurant in town was like striking gold. Not only was the food cheap and the service quick, but hikers could hang out in the dining area for hours if they were smart.

The strategy was simple: never order a full meal at once. For example, Big Spoon and I would order burgers first, fries a few minutes later, followed by a second round of burgers, and then, finally, milkshakes. This bought us plenty of time to wash our arms and faces in the bathroom sink, charge our cell phones at the outlets against the wall, and sit to figure out town logistics— like where we would stay and how we would get there.

At Lake Tahoe's McDonald's, Big Spoon and I resolved to take a zero in this exciting town to see what it was all about. A quick bus ride into Stateline, Nevada led us to a busy Budget dealership, where the lady at the front desk handed us keys to a Kia Soul—a compact cube on wheels that was the striking yellow of a bee.

Freedom was ours as we cruised around the ocean-like lake beneath the waning sun. Several miles into the drive, Big Spoon pulled off on the side of CA 89 behind a long line of cars. We crossed the hectic highway to the crowded parking lot, where a one-mile path coiled down to Emerald Bay.

An evergreen forest blocked the view of the National Natural Landmark on the paved walk down. At the bottom, the path opened to a pristine cove where Vikingsholm—a thirty-eight-room rock castle built in 1929—embellished the shore with Scandinavian design. Big Spoon and I circled the mansion, peeking through the stained-glass windows and admiring the dragon-carved beams. Then we picked a place in the sand of Emerald Bay, stripped to our underwear, and ran into the lake.

The cold water soaked me to my sweaty bones. It was stirring and great. I swam out to where I couldn't stand but could still see the bottom, and I ducked under again and again to scrub my hair and skin. I opened my eyes beneath the water and saw Big Spoon swimming at me. He grabbed and kissed me in the depths. Then we swam down the dazzling bay—a fantastic change of stride from hiking. Not until evening's chilling shade replaced the late-afternoon heat did we return to the shore.

Tall streetlamps outshone the stars as Big Spoon circled the Walmart parking lot selecting a place to park. This vacant land of pavement would be our sleeping place for the night. We had driven here after Emerald Bay. It was forty miles east in Carson City and the closest Walmart around. In the morning, we would resupply at the low-priced supercenter. But tonight, we would save money on lodging by sleeping in the car.

"So, we're more like vagabonds with wheels," I had joked on our pitch-black drive into Nevada.

Big Spoon parked beneath a light post, away from the slumbering herd of RVs. We crouched behind the car on the asphalt to brush our teeth. Back inside, we cracked the windows, lowered the back seats, and unrolled our sleeping bags. It was an uncomfortable night's sleep— hard and hot—but it worked. Besides, after spending the last eighty-odd nights on the ground, what was it to us to sleep in a car?

Saturday and Sunday unraveled in nonstop activity. We strolled through art galleries on the main strip, listened to free rock concerts in the streets, filled up on tacos at casino buffets, and played the mesmerizing slot machines at Montbleu. That was Sunday at noon before we journeyed back to the trail. Montbleu speared the open sky amid the other casinos, dominating this strip of US 50. I had never gambled at a casino before and wanted to try my luck. The inside of the resort was dark and smelled like spilled bourbon. We stepped into the line at the front desk to exchange our cash for chips. Dance music blared. Inside the gaming area, waitresses in tight dresses slid between the felt tables and flashy machines, balancing full trays of drinks.

Big Spoon and I bet fifteen dollars each at the slots. I lost everything. Big Spoon gained two dollars. The

thrill of it lasted about twenty minutes before my re-
morse seeped in over this waste of money and time. In
the bold light of day, it struck me that I was among those
whose change purses clung to their hips as they sat in
the saturating dimness, pouring coins into the erratic
machines and waiting—just waiting—for each wishful
spin to hit the jackpot.

"I don't like it here," I told Big Spoon as he stood
counting his scant winnings next to a table of focused
poker players.

He looked up from what he was doing and nodded.
"This place is excessive."

"Yet it sucks you in. All the vibrant hype." I sighed,
causing a poker player to glance up from his cards.

"But you know the truth," Big Spoon said, slipping
the money into his pocket.

"What truth?" I asked.

"That it's not real. It's all a gimmick. Frills to fill a
void."

"Do you think it works?"

We looked around, surveying the shadowy circus
driven by human want.

"Backpacking has taught us a lot," Big Spoon said.

I nodded. "Everything we need to live fits inside our
packs."

"And look how far we've gone like this and all the
incredible things we've found. We need very little. We
need shelter. We need food and water. We need love.

The rest is all luxury," he said, taking my hand and leading me out of the darkness.

Later that afternoon, after we'd returned our rental car, a high school geography teacher named Deb gave us a lift back to Echo Lake. She picked us up on the side of US 50 as we fought to keep our thumbs raised in the grueling heat. Deb was fit and bright. On the drive, we learned she was an avid outdoorswoman and advocate for what she called "stepping out of bounds."

"What you're doing right now is teaching you to live in uncomfortable situations," she said as we roved beyond civilization. "It's teaching you to survive the hard times that will never fail to come. In my opinion, if you make it through the trail, you'll make it through anything."

The hard times that will never fail to come. I contemplated Deb's words as Big Spoon and I took to the rugged roots. "If we make it through the trail, we'll make it through anything," I repeated.

Was that true?

Big Spoon didn't respond.

Regardless of the answer, our path was about to take a very abrupt turn.

CHAPTER 29

THE SHIFTING WINDS

B ig Spoon and I had fallen behind because of the time we'd taken off the trail. As a result, at Echo Lake—within the demanding granite rocks—we calculated that we needed to hike twenty-five miles a day to finish the PCT before the October snows of Washington fell and blocked our path. Less than two weeks were left in July when we determined to increase our mileage. Over the next 104 miles through the Desolation and Granite Chief Wildernesses, we marched through a war of storms from dawn until dusk, stopping only to eat, never waiting a second longer than necessary to drink in the majestic power of the wild.

This trudge, which marked our entrance into Northern California, dampened Big Spoon's spirit. When the sun appeared after many days of rain, he kept his eyes on the muddy trail instead of lifting them to whatever the light touched, as he usually did. No longer did he bend to smell the wildflowers in our path. No longer did he step off the trail to explore what was beyond. Rather, he speared the soggy pinecones he passed with his pine stick—his means of distraction from the toil.

My spirit also sagged. When the clouds finally cleared and the trail opened to breathtaking views of glassy lakes and sylvan hills, I didn't stop to look. Instead, I continued behind Big Spoon, my feet operating like machines, my mind fifteen hundred miles ahead in Canada—where this journey would meet its end.

By the time we reached Sierra City at mile 1,198, our journey had morphed into a monotonous cycle of merely making our daily miles. It was the evening of July 23. The trail intersected with Wild Plum Road on the outskirts of town. Jagged brown buttes stabbed the sun before us as we ambled up the pavement. The light diffused into the darkening air.

Yuba River Inn marked the junction between Wild Plum Road and CA 49. We stepped up to the main lodge and scanned the empty highway. We were starving but saw no glimmer of a restaurant sign. A pear-shaped man wearing light khaki shorts that blended in with his pale legs walked over from his log cabin to where we stood, having seen us from his porch.

"I know the area pretty well if you need any help," he said, puffing a cigarette, his voice soft and shrill.

Just then, the innkeeper walked out from the main lodge. "You kids looking for the Methodist church?" he asked, his voice gritty as sand.

"What Methodist church?" Big Spoon asked.

"You know...the one where you hikers can sleep in the parking lot and shower in the public bathrooms. I'd offer you a room here, but we're full."

"Where's the church?" I asked.

The man smoking the cigarette pointed to the highway. "Not but a hundred yards or so up the road on your right," he said, winking at me.

"Is there a place where we can get dinner?" Big Spoon asked.

"Herrington's is the only restaurant open at this hour," the innkeeper said. "But it's way outside of town. The grocery store just closed about twenty minutes ago."

I glanced at Big Spoon's watch. It read 7:23 p.m. The day was Thursday. How could everything already be closed?

Later I'd learn that Sierra City had a population of only two hundred.

Silence lingered as Big Spoon and I thought over what to do. The only food remaining in our packs was peanuts. But after hiking twenty-five miles, our bodies begged us for a full meal.

"All right, you two, come with me," the man with the cigarette said. "I have leftover steak from earlier. And I can whip up some toast."

He seemed harmless, but I had a strange feeling about this man. Apparently Big Spoon did too, because he asked, "Is anyone staying with you?"

"Just my kids," he said. "Come along."

We leaned our packs against the outside of the man's cabin. He took a final drag of his cigarette and then flicked the bud into the gravel. "Call me Roy," he said after exhaling the smoke.

Inside the lamplit space, Roy introduced us to his kids, Kate and Tommy. They were a little younger than Big Spoon and me, sitting on the living-room couch and squinting their eyes to watch a TV show that materialized in hissing waves of static.

"We're from the Bay Area," Roy said, dropping two pieces of white bread into the kitchen toaster. "I own a used-car dealership there and retreat here every summer to fish with my kids at Jackson Meadows Reservoir. It's nice to escape where no one can find me." He said this as if he were a criminal on the run. "Let me say, I don't know what it is about the wilderness that makes a person so *ravenous*. When we got here this afternoon, I instantly drove to the store and bought all this steak. As you can see, it was too much for us. Please, dears, help yourselves."

He pointed to the dining-room table, where two plates of half-eaten steak glared back at us. There were salad remnants on the plates and dirty forks resting on the meat.

He's feeding us the scraps, I thought, mildly disgusted, hating that he called us "dears." I tapped Big Spoon's foot with mine as a way to say, Let's leave.

"Well, go on. Don't be shy. Sit down," Roy demanded.

To my dismay, Big Spoon did. Then he looked up at me with hungry eyes that said, "What else are we going to do?"

"It's a little overdone," Roy said as I reluctantly took my seat. "But I'm sure hikers like you are just happy to have home cooking."

Overdone was an understatement. The steak curled up on all ends and tasted tough as wood. Roy even burned the toast, but he gave it to us anyway, belittling us even more. To make matters worse, when Big Spoon and I had nearly finished the gnawed-up beef—every bite disagreeable, almost as if it were spoiled—Roy rummaged through the refrigerator and then brought out his last bottled beer for us to share. It had already been opened and drunk from. He set it on the table and watched eagerly for us to sip.

This crossed the line.

"Thank you, but I don't drink," Big Spoon lied. "And neither does my wife."

"Yes, thank you," I said, pushing my plate forward. "I'm very full."

"But you haven't eaten everything," Roy said, slapping his hand on his lumpy hip.

"Time for us to go before it gets too dark," Big Spoon said, as if the darkness bothered us. We ditched our manners and stood to leave. Roy followed us out the door. Kate and Tommy never once looked up from the foaming TV.

"Do come back, dears," our odd host said, lighting another cigarette on the porch while we gathered our packs.

"Never again," I said, almost gagging, as soon as our feet hit the road.

The stars stained the night sky white. Big Spoon and I were still famished and ate our peanuts in the Methodist church parking lot. Then, with our stomachs continuing to growl, we laid out our sleeping gear and cowboy camped beneath a stained-glass window of Jesus breaking bread. A handful of hikers wandered in as we fell asleep. I didn't recognize their voices, but it was comforting to know that Big Spoon and I weren't the only ones in this deserted place.

Which was how it had started to feel—as if we were the sole travelers left on a long and forsaken road. The next day, after Big Spoon and I resupplied and gorged ourselves on one-pound burgers at the Sierra Country Store, I dreaded returning to the trail. With our stomachs bloated and our packs weighed down with ninety miles' worth of food, we lingered outside the store, attempting to hatch our plan to hitch nine miles up a four-wheel-drive road to the Sierra Buttes Trailhead instead of walking the half mile back to where the trail had coughed us out last night.

We hadn't tried to skip a section of the trail until now. The idea had come about mere minutes before as we ate our burgers on the country store's sun-faded front porch. Even if it was only nine miles, the thought of doing that made me sick. It was like I was cheating. Like I was betraying my beloved trail. The alternative was to endure the notorious ascent from town to the Sierra Buttes. It started at 3,925 feet above sea level and harshly climbed to 7,007 feet. The thought of gaining 3,000 feet of elevation over the span of nine miles tormented me more than the thought of simply skipping that ongoing drag. Especially with the sun burning through the day like fire.

I hadn't said any of this out loud. My nature was to push through no matter what. It was Big Spoon who unfolded the map on the front porch and followed the brown line with his finger from our location to the top of the buttes.

"This dirt road goes by a PCT trailhead," he said, pointing to the map. "I know you want to hike every mile, but what if, just this once, we skipped ahead?"

His question carried me back to the conversation we'd had the night he caught up to me at Mission Creek. By the fire, he'd told me he wanted to skip ahead to the different sections on the trail. He didn't have the mind-set like me of walking every rugged inch to validate his thru-hike. I'd hardly known him then but had persuaded him to endure his unbroken hike. Now, as my husband waited for my answer on that porch, his deep-blue eyes pleading with me to say yes, I realized he had molded his mind-set to match mine. He was hiking the whole PCT in one continuous go because that was what *I* wanted.

Or used to want.

After many minutes of considering Big Spoon's proposal, I finally agreed to omit the dash of trail from Sierra City to the buttes.

A young guy named Max, who answered the call of our thumbs not long afterward, agreed to drive us to the trailhead in his battered pickup truck. He wore a muscle tee that displayed his strong, tattooed arms, and he was friendlier than he looked, telling us on the rocky drive up all about his profession as one of the last gold miners around.

"Must be awesome to strike gold," I said, sitting in the middle of the tool-cluttered truck, touching shoulders with both Big Spoon and Max.

He shrugged. "It can be. But I've been doing it since I was a teenager, and it's kind of gotten old. I loved it at first, don't get me wrong. But now it's just a job. If my dad wasn't my partner, I'd quit."

"It's crazy that people have such power," Big Spoon said as Max stopped in front of the trailhead. "The power to keep you doing something when you know you've had enough."

Dust kicked up behind Max's truck as he drove off after we'd gotten out. Big Spoon and I stared down the empty path that cut through the sharp-edged buttes. Some time went by before we actually stepped upon it.

As we hiked into evening, I wondered what it was that had now made the trail seem so unbearable. I couldn't pinpoint it. But my desire to walk the PCT had run dry.

CHAPTER 30

SHARP RIGHT TURN

"Honestly, I'm done," Big Spoon said, his voice harsh, his eyes ablaze.

It was the day after we'd left Sierra City. We were eating lunch on the side of the trail atop a wooded bluff. Big black flies swarmed around us, diving in to steal bites of our peanut butter. Since being dropped off by Max, each step we'd taken had felt heavier than the last, as if our feet were turning to stone. Our next stop in Belden was sixty-eight miles away. The sun spit down like dragon's breath.

Merely a week before, the trail had rattled us with storms. Thunder snarled and hail bit us as we'd hiked, like these flies were doing now. The nights had been so cold that I'd traded sleeping bags with Big Spoon. His was rated to keep a person warm in zero-degree weather, whereas mine was only effective in temperatures above fifteen. During that haul, frost littered the land in the mornings. My blood flow slowed as I cleaned up camp; my toes and fingers went numb.

Still, through these bleak and icy days, we kept on. We kept on. We kept on.

Until now.

Now it was as hot as hell.

"What do you mean you're done?" I asked, my tongue flinging the words like daggers.

Big Spoon had hardly eaten his sandwich. He stood, dusted the crumbs off his frayed pants, and walked over to the edge of the cliff. A lush, green valley gushed below.

"Do you want me to answer truthfully?" he asked, looking out. The gravity in his voice sounded as if someone had died.

"Just say it."

He sighed. "I want to get off the trail."

Now *his* words were the daggers—sharp and fast. They cut me to the core. They sliced my very soul.

I couldn't say, though, that I hadn't seen them coming. Earlier that morning, when we'd begun our routine slog, Big Spoon had suggested we skip more sections on the trail, like we did from Sierra City to the top of the buttes.

"Only where we can," he said. "A few miles here and there to give us little boosts."

I'd said I didn't want to do that because it was a slippery slope—one skip would lead to a bigger skip, and so on. It wouldn't be a pure thru-hike then. We had made it this far, so why slack off now?

Deep down, though, the idea of ditching miles to cut ahead enticed me. I had become quite miserable on the trail.

But why? I mused over it that morning after Big Spoon had proposed the boosts. It wasn't like I'd developed a meniscus tear or fallen ill with giardia. It wasn't like I was homesick and wanted to go home. It wasn't like I was alone. I had Big Spoon as a companion.

Then it hit me.

I had Big Spoon, and that was all. It had been this way for weeks. All the hikers we'd started with in April—Purple Princess, Donezo, the Oregon brothers, Splat—had dispersed on the trail like ripples in a lake: they'd gradually disappeared ahead. I didn't even know anymore where Saltlick and Pandora were. I realized I missed them—my friends, my Tallyhos. They had fired me with the motivation I didn't get from Big Spoon, because he hadn't come on the trail to hike the whole thing like the Tallyhos and I had. He'd come to see and experience the West. I'd come to walk in the wild. Without my friends, who—having my same mentality— would push me to endure this grueling grind the trail now presented, I'd lost all desire to resume.

My fire had dwindled to dust, and I couldn't relight it on my own. Especially considering how dismal Big Spoon had become. I knew that in his heart, he was finished with the trail. But I'd suppressed this truth for days because it killed me to give up.

Now, on the bluff, Big Spoon moved toward me. I was sitting in the dirt and couldn't look at him. "I know you want to walk from Mexico to Canada," he said, "and I've tried to honor that. But I came out here to explore the West. I saw the PCT as a neat way to do so, but I only planned to hike it as long as I saw fit. I didn't need to walk seven hundred miles in the desert to see what the desert was all about. Fifty miles would've sufficed. Then I would've jumped ahead."

It was true. The trail had become as redundant as a conveyor belt. Day after day, it lugged us through pine after pine as we crept nearer and nearer to Oregon's Cascade Range. I had started counting down the days until this trip would end. Three months of hiking, and we weren't even out of California. Nor were we halfway to Canada. We had more than thirteen hundred miles to go in all—a little over two months left on the trail at the pace we were walking.

Like Big Spoon, I was over it, but I had no intention to quit. When I set out to do something, that was what I did. To quit was weakness and fraud. To quit when you had dedicated yourself so much to something was betrayal. My joy in the journey was gone, but to quit was not an option. I would bear it out to the bitter end.

"That breaks my heart to hear," I finally said, as if accepting the news after the shock of a loved one's death.

Big Spoon crouched next to me and drew a deep breath. "I don't want your heart to break, Claire. I know how important this trail is to you. When I met you and we got married, I saw your passion for it and told myself I'd stay on it for you. And mark my words, I'll continue to stay on it for you. It's only a few months in the grand scheme of things."

A tear snaked down my cheek as he continued in a more vigorous tone.

"But the truth is, I've had enough of this *damn* trail. I've had enough of hiking through the waking hours, day after day after day. We've been doing this for three months—three solid months. I know how to thru-hike now. I know how to walk all fucking day."

He spoke with emphasis, his lips trembling as he tried to steady his voice, which grew louder and louder.

"I know how to pick a good site to set up camp," he said. "I know how to make dinner on my stove and take a shit in the woods. I know how to get a hitch into town and resupply. There's nothing new to learn now. There's nothing new to figure out." He swatted at a fly that had landed on his face. It flew off stunned but okay.

"You know," he said, shaking his head, "I used to see a unique formation off the trail and walk over to it to explore. That was something I loved to do. But now, when I come across something cool and different that's not on the trail, I pass it by. Why?" He stared into my tears.

"Because if I take the time to go check it out, then I'm losing time to make my miles. And it's all about making our miles now. It's all about making our fucking miles. Otherwise, if we don't make our daily miles, then we fall behind. So, if I want to see something amazing off the trail, I can forget it."

It looked like he wanted to cry.

"It's like we're on a cross-country road trip, speeding down the highway, missing everything that's off the road," he said. "It takes more time and effort to take the back roads where all the scenery is, just like it takes more time and effort to view something great—something worth seeing—off the trail."

He paused, and his silent desperation hung in the air.

"But you know what, Claire? I've reached the point where I don't want to work that hard anymore. And you know what else? That's pathetic." He spat the word with disgust. "It's pathetic, Claire, and it's this trail— walking it nonstop without time to take anything in— that's inflicted this indifference on me. It's as if the trail has been too much of a good thing. And now it's poisoning me."

Big Spoon looked tired. More tired than I had ever seen him. His weary face begged me to understand.

Instead, I attacked his vulnerable confession. "How long have you felt this way?" I asked, sounding like a hissing snake.

"Awhile," he admitted. "On and off since Tehachapi."
I did a quick calculation. "That was almost seven
hundred miles ago, Caleb. And *now* you're bringing this
up?"

He took a deep breath. "I didn't say anything because
I know how much you want to finish. But I can't keep it
in anymore. I don't want to upset you. It's just...I don't
even like backpacking. To walk all day carrying a heavy
load from one place to the next isn't as enjoyable to me
as setting up a base camp and exploring around that
area for several days. That's what I like to do. I mean,
when I think about it, it's crazy to me that I came on this
hike at all. But something kept pushing me—something
in my gut that said I *had* to go."

He pierced his eyes into mine, holding them there a
moment, to let me see what he saw.

"Now I know why I'm here," he said.

"Why?"

"You. Claire, I'm here because of you."

For some reason, I hadn't expected this answer.

"What else do I need from this trail now?" Big Spoon
declared. "I got a wife out of it. Others will say they got
Canada. I get to say I got my *wife*. I don't have to prove
anything to anybody by making it two thousand six hundred and fifty miles up. And I know we've been told
that if we make it through this, we'll make it through
anything. Well, as far as I'm concerned, we've already
made it through this. We've walked over twelve hundred

miles. We've already thru-hiked the PCT." His impassioned spirit blazed through his speech. "So, why draw it out?"

My tears slipped steadily down now. "But we'll be failures if we don't finish."

"Not in my eyes," Big Spoon said, employing his tone of certainty. "In my eyes, it doesn't make sense to keep doing something if my heart isn't in it. I know I can do it, but what's the point? What am I gaining by walking all the way to Canada when I know I've already found what this trail had for me to find?" He gripped my hand, indicating that it was me he'd found.

"I think we can both agree that this trip is an intense magnification of life," he said. "With all the wonders and hardships we've encountered, it's like we've lived twenty years in three months. But this trip isn't over, and so it makes me ask, *how* do I want to live this powerful stretch of life? Do I want to live it just so I can say I walked from Mexico to Canada? Or do I want to live it for something more, something that excites me and brings my spirit to life?" The fire flickered in his eyes.

"But I know it's different for you. I know you want to finish. And don't worry. I'll finish this trail with you," Big Spoon said. "But if I'm being honest, if it weren't for you, I would've dumped this thing months ago."

I didn't know what to say. I simply sat in the dirt, silent. My tears had run dry. The only sound was the buzzing flies. Big Spoon tried to put his arm around me, but I pushed him away. I was disappointed, yet I understood. I'd set out to hike the whole PCT. Not to one day *say* I'd done it, but to live a more meaningful life *right now.* To extricate myself from the suffocating box of a life I had slipped into and submerge myself in the wide-open world of the wild, where everything, even the flies, lived boldly—as if today was all they had.

So, I'd gotten out of the box. I'd gone from east to west, from a corporation to the great outdoors. In this new life, I'd met the man who soon became my husband. Our lives as one began on the trail. How exciting, how new, how tremendous was this life! Big Spoon had become my permanent mate. How much better was the journey now that the life of love joined it.

In that moment on the bluff, I started to see that Big Spoon was right when he said the trail had become too much of a good thing. What began as something like my marriage—exciting, new, tremendous—no longer satisfied my hunger. Like Big Spoon said, there was no longer anything new to gain from the trail. It was like eating my favorite fruit as my main meal every day. The sweetness of it was starting to make me sick.

And it was starting to affect my life with Big Spoon. How ironic, I thought. The trail that had brought us together was now cutting between us like a knife. Big Spoon wanted off. I wanted to stay on. But why? I wondered. For my joy in the journey was like Big Spoon's— gone. Like his, my spirit was being choked by its confining way. So, why stay on it? Why continue to put our life of love at risk?

With this thought, I started to see myself for who I really was. I started to see how prideful I had become to want to persist on this perilous path for the sake of following through with *my* original intent. I saw how stubborn and selfish I had become, too—so much so I had never sensed that Big Spoon had kept on the trail for me. He was sacrificing his desires for mine, and I hadn't seen it. My ambition to make it to Canada at all costs had blinded me to the truth. Big Spoon loved me more than he loved himself.

This realization ripped me to my soul.

"I'm so sorry you've felt this way," I finally said. "Caleb, I'm so, so sorry."

I reached for his hand, and his eyes welled up with tears.

"It's okay," he said.

That was the first time I'd ever seen him cry.

This wasn't one of those things we could sleep on to see how we felt in the morning. Big Spoon was done with the trail. He had been done for hundreds of miles, and—honestly—I had been done with it, too.

This was one of those things we had to make a decision on today.

"What would we do if we got off the trail?" I asked, face to face with Big Spoon.

He wiped his eyes and grinned. "Remember when we first got into the Sierra and sat beneath the bridge where the swallows had built their nests?"

"Yes."

"And remember how you asked me about the purpose of life, and how I said it was to experience as much as possible?"

"As if life was like a library where we could read from any book."

"Exactly. Claire, if we got off the trail, we would start a new experience. We would open a different book."

The idea rushed through me like a refreshing breeze—if we got off the PCT, we could do something else. We had the means to do it. Our money was holding out. How had I not realized this possibility until now?

"But I'm torn," I told Big Spoon. "I'm tired of the trail, too. But we've worked so hard and come so far. The PCT has become our *lives*. If we get off, will we regret it?"

"I know I won't," Big Spoon said in a way that made me feel the weight of this truth. "But we're different in that way. You know where I stand. Take the next few miles to think about it."

And so I did.

⚒

Fifteen miles later, instead of walking on toward Belden, Big Spoon and I stopped on the trail before Quincy La Porte Road. It was the remote road crossing Big Spoon had located on the map several hours earlier while we still sat on the bluff. The trail continued straight ahead.

But the road took a sharp right turn down the mountain, coiling for twenty-two miles through the Plumas National Forest to the town of Quincy.

"If anything, it gives us options," Big Spoon said on the bluff before we'd moved on.

During the hike leading to the road, I'd said nothing and pondered everything. I feared getting off the trail. I feared the unknown that came with that choice. This whole trip, though, had been a walk into the unknown. Which made me think, what—if anything—had this trail taught me if not to be bold in the face of the great unknown, walking bravely into it and believing in my soul that I would be provided for—no matter what—in great and unimaginable ways?

Mile 1,236 marked the road crossing. I placed my hand on the triangular metal emblem nailed to the evergreen growing where the trail and road merged.

"Pacific Crest Trail," I said, reading the words on the cool emblem. "Okay. Let's do it. Let's get off the trail."

Big Spoon turned to me with widened eyes. "Really? Are you sure?"

"Yes," I said. "It's for the best."

He dropped his pine sticks and embraced me. "Thank you," he said. "Thank you."

We stepped onto the road. Thick gray smoke gathered in the sky from a wildfire miles away. I could smell the burning land. The setting sun cast a blood-red glow onto the potent haze.

"It's like the trail is smoking us out," I said, unstrapping my pack and sitting down against the guardrail. We were the only ones in this place of pavement and trees.

"No," Big Spoon said. "This is just the trail's way of sending us on." Then it dawned on him. "Claire, we won."

"What do you mean?" I asked, feeling utterly defeated.

"We won," he said again, standing in hitch position beside me. "We realized before hiking another thirteen hundred miles that the PCT isn't all there is. So, take heart. Our journey isn't ending just because we're getting off the trail. It's changing. That's all. The world is our trail now. We *won*."

"The world is our trail," I said to myself, peering down the road. With my desires and hopes so wrapped up in reaching Canada, I couldn't see then the journey beyond this one calling me to come.

"The world is our trail," I whispered again, reaching for the Herkimer diamond around my neck, feeling its distinct prisms of light.

Big Spoon and I would determine our next move once we arrived in Quincy. As I slouched against the guardrail, it struck me that Big Spoon was right. We weren't ending our journey by getting off the trail. Instead, by altering our course, we were keeping our journey alive.

CHAPTER 31

SURPRISE GUESTS AT THE FORESTRY CAMP

No one traveled Quincy La Porte Road where the PCT intersected it. The twenty-two-mile hitch into town was "unlikely." That was how my guidebook put it. I had pulled it out to read as I leaned against the guardrail while Big Spoon stood partway in the road, listening for cars. It would be dark soon. I felt dark inside over the fact that we were getting off the trail. Even though I had made the call to do so, it felt like a landslide had suddenly crashed down, blocking the light at the end of the long, hard tunnel we'd been traversing.

And now what?

What would we do?

"Let's make our way up to Alaska," Big Spoon suggested, one hand cupped to his ear. "That's a place I've always wanted to go."

An image of the northern lights flooding the night sky fired through my mind. I untied my lucky bandana from my oily hair, unfolded it, and gazed. The northern lights in their neon pinks and greens whooshed across that cotton scarf between the painted stars. This wasn't the first time Big Spoon had mentioned his desire to one day travel to Alaska. Maybe this had been my destiny all along.

"I like that idea," I said. And I did. "But how would we get there?"

A blue truck backfiring down the mountain appeared in the distance before Big Spoon could answer.

"Hurry! Get up! Someone's coming!" he cried.

I jumped to my feet and waved my bright bandana. The truck slowed to a stop before us. The mustached man in the driver's seat carried a full family load. "You can cram in the bed," he offered when we told him we were going to Quincy.

Twelve minutes had passed from the time we'd stepped off the trail to the time we achieved a ride. Not bad for the road deemed unlikely for a hitch.

"Everything has worked out for us so far," Big Spoon said, raising his voice above the wind as we sailed down the road, sitting with our packs in our laps in the truck bed filled with tires. "That won't stop just because we're off the trail. Besides, we've learned a lot about how to get from place to place these last few months. If we want to get to Alaska, there will be a way."

I nodded, staring out at the diminishing mountains, taking every icy slap of wind on this last hitch of the trail. The driver sped down the whole twisty way, making the thousand evergreens we passed blend into one giant flash of the place I used to live.

"Good-bye, trail," I whispered, my words flying up into the wind. "Good-bye, my dear friend."

There was no turning back now.

Our driver dumped us on the outskirts of town in the midst of a shopping center, where Round Table Pizza was the only restaurant open. Big Spoon and I entered the arcade-style pizzeria, ordered a large pepperoni at the counter, and then grabbed a crumb-covered booth in the back. Besides the staff, we were the only ones there. As we ate our greasy pie, we tried to figure out accommodations for the night. It was Saturday. A multitude of phone calls revealed that every hotel in town was booked solid.

I laid my head on the dirty table while Big Spoon made a second round of calls. Several minutes later, I awoke to him shaking my shoulder.

"Time to go," he said. "Round Table's closed."

Outside, the sky was blacker than coal. We still didn't have a place to sleep—even after having asked the restaurant employees on our way out if they could help us.

They had shrugged their shoulders and averted their eyes. So, outside, Big Spoon and I resolved to walk toward downtown until we found a park or field in which to stealth camp. As we stepped off the sidewalk, a short guy with glasses and dark, wavy hair ran from the lighted parking lot toward Round Table.

"Ask him," I whispered to Big Spoon.

Understanding what I meant, Big Spoon stopped the guy in midstride, explained our situation, and asked if he knew someplace we could stay.

"Allow me to pick up my pizza before they lock the door," he panted in a thick accent. "But please wait here. I will help you."

He left and returned shortly afterward carrying a pizza box. "I am an environmental scientist from Italy living at the UC Berkeley Forestry Camp for the summer," he said, his voice lyrical and rich. "The camp is eight miles from here down Bucks Lake Road. There I research carbon levels in the charcoal produced by the wildfires." He spoke proudly and with great delight. "Filippo is my name. If you desire, you both may come with me. The camp has hot showers and much land for your tent you speak of. I do not think the students will mind."

Seconds later, Big Spoon and I sat packed inside the forestry camp's F-150 as Filippo drove us down a dark back road. Yellow hard hats and technical field instruments occupied the truck, which smelled like baked dough mixed with dust. When Filippo turned onto a gravel road and pulled into the rustic camp, I then smelled a campfire and saw some Berkeley students huddled outside the main lodge, ringed around a flaming pit.

They were roasting marshmallows and talking academics when we approached them. Filippo introduced us as the PCT hikers he'd discovered while picking up his pizza pie. Intrigued, the students invited us to join them by the fire. I sat in the dirt while Big Spoon stood with the rest. A beautiful Russian girl handed us two sharpened sticks along with a half-empty bag of marshmallows. Filippo set his pizza on a stump, left, and came back with three Coronas. He passed two of the glass bottles to Big Spoon and me before cracking his own bottle open and gulping from it.

I didn't want to drink a beer. I didn't want to roast a marshmallow. All I wanted was to go to bed. I wanted to fall asleep and hide from the shards of disappointment that stabbed me from breaking off the trail.

But I had to play along. If this was where I would sleep tonight at all, I had to be polite. Not until the fire died and the students scattered to their century-old shacks did Filippo show us the field, where we immediately pitched our tent. Next to the dimly lit bathhouse we slept, splashed by the light of the full moon that spotlighted my tossing and turning. At last, I flipped onto my stomach and buried my head in my sleeping bag, my attempt to blacken out even the night.

In the morning, Filippo stopped by our tent as we broke it down. "I have work to do in the lab just now," he said, holding a steaming mug of coffee. "But I can drive you into town at lunchtime." He wore a royal-blue Berkeley T-shirt that complemented his olive skin and eyes. "Please, make yourselves at home. I will get you what you need."

With our packs reloaded, Big Spoon and I walked to the still-smoldering fire pit and sat on one of the wooden benches set before a chalkboard. Birds chirped high in the pines as the sun peeked up from the violet horizon. I fixated on the glowing coals in the fire. The fire was dead, but the coals burned on.

Filippo brought out a tray of toast, jam, and coffee from the main lodge. "Do you like cream and sugar?" he asked.

We shook our heads.

Before the trail, I would have said yes. But now, the desire for such treats had been stripped from me. Simple black coffee with its bitter, hot sip sufficed.

Our hospitable host placed the tray next to us and then headed down the gravel road toward the lab. Big Spoon asked how I was, and I said I was fine.

"I know this is a hard move for you, but I really think we're doing the right thing," he said.

I drank the coffee and didn't respond.

Because it was Sunday, the students were slow to awaken. One by one, they moseyed from their shacks to the lodge for breakfast. An Asian boy in baggy sweat-pants noticed us on his way.

"Are you the thru-hikers who came in last night?" He yawned and then sucked from his waning cigarette. "My bunkmate said he talked to you by the fire. He said your story is insane."

I didn't know how to answer his question. We used to be thru-hikers, I thought I could say. But before I did, Big Spoon confirmed, "Yes. That's us."

The boy's eyes gleamed. He hopped onto the bench next to us, stubbed his cigarette out in the gravel, and pitched question after question to us about our trip. Another student joined the conversation, followed by another, and then another. Within minutes, the bench-es were alive with Berkeley students who were eager to listen and discuss as Big Spoon and I led an impromptu class on the PCT.

They inquired about a variety of trail aspects, like what food we ate, how we sourced our water, where we slept, and how we used the bathroom in the woods. The Asian boy gazed at us in admiration when we said we had hiked over twelve hundred miles. He exerted his mind, voicing aloud his contemplation, to understand the reality of walking this far.

"How are we to truly comprehend that distance?" he asked. "I mean, it's easy for you to say you walked twelve hundred miles. And it's easy for me to hear you say it. But do I really get what that means?" He stared off, appearing to calculate something in his head. "There's a one-mile trail up from the camp—uphill pretty much the whole way. I hiked it the other week and it took me almost an hour. I thought that was a really long time to hike. And it was only one mile. But what you guys did—with packs on, no less—would be like me doing that trail over a thousand times." His eyes widened. "That's ridiculous when I think about it that way. I don't even want to walk that trail twice."

All eyes were on the Asian boy as he pictured, with his words, the incredible distance Big Spoon and I had covered. Not until he related it in this way, using his analogy of a one-mile trail to gauge a thru-hike, did I feel proud of my and Big Spoon's accomplishment. We didn't finish the trail. But we had hiked over twelve hundred miles. *Twelve hundred miles.* That was like walking from Denver to Detroit, I learned later on. And as we sat with the students, I realized this distance, on foot, was huge.

The morning slipped by, and Big Spoon and I continued to educate the students on everything we knew about trail life. One girl brought her backpack and gear out for me to inspect. "I'm hiking the PCT after graduation," she said, looking at me as if I were a hero.

"You should," I told her. "It wrecks you for life. But in the best way." These were the same words Buffalo had said to me the day I flew into San Diego. At that time, I didn't understand them. But now they made sense. In a profound flash, the trail had changed everything. It had thrown my world upside down in a way that I never wanted it to be right-side up again.

The students asked more questions, and Big Spoon and I opened up about the selfless generosity of trail angels, the funny stories behind trail names, and the powerful friendships the trail formed. We talked about the beauty, the freedom, and the trials the trail cast us into every day. We talked about how we'd started on the trail alone, how we'd met and gotten married, and how we were now leaving the trail to explore something new.

The students sat entranced, as if they were watching magicians.

"You got *married* on the trail?" they all asked.

One student said she admired our decision to step off. Another said he thought we should finish.

"What will you do next?" asked the girl who'd showed me her backpack.

"We're going to Alaska," Big Spoon said, and the crowd stirred.

"What will you do in Alaska?" the Asian boy asked.

"We don't know yet," said Big Spoon.

"How will you get there?"

"We don't know."

The students, whose days revolved around the strict structure of a schedule, became silent.

"What we do know," Big Spoon went on, "is that we have the power to choose our fate. We realized the trail wasn't our master. We realized we were free to follow our truer path. Which is what we're doing by departing the trail and seeking greater heights."

"Are you scared?" the Asian boy asked.

Everyone leaned in.

"I am," I blurted out. "Making the decision to get off the trail killed me. The trail had become my life, the foundation for my days. Now, it feels like that life has crumbled to ash. That life has died, and it's alarming." The coals from the fire caught my eye. "But in my heart, I know it was the good kind of death. The sacrifice for something more. The fire that raged only to die, creating coals that hold the power to ignite a bigger, hotter, more beautiful fire than the one that came before it." My soul was speaking through me. "Things don't always go as planned," I said. "But I'm learning to let go of my blinding expectations to let destiny—the supreme trail—unfold. There's two parts to all of this—fate and choice. Like Big Spoon said, there's a higher calling for us that we're choosing to answer. That course is still unclear. But our time on the trail was like a blazing fire that birthed our red-hot coals. Now, we must build upon them to light our way." A flame flickered from a coal in the fire pit. "And we will," I acknowledged. "All we have to do is take the next step—keep taking the next step— to grow our new fire until it soars."

Passion burned through me as I spoke, dissipating the darkness inside me. It was like a ray of hot light blasting through. It was like being struck with the truth that something greater than I could ever dream truly existed beyond what I knew. My time with the forestry camp students let me see this. It was like the dousing of the trail—a searing event—for the ignition of the grander walk.

"We're going to Alaska," I said to Big Spoon later that day as Filippo drove us to town.

"There's no doubt in my mind," he said, sparking the first flame of what would be our magnificent quest into the great beyond.

CHAPTER 32

BUILDING ONTO THE FIRE

"I have to use the bathroom *right now*," I told Big Spoon, who was looking up the cost of Amtrak trains on his phone. Filippo had dropped us off minutes before, and we were sitting in the shade of a maple outside the Plumas County Courthouse, strategizing our next move.

Maybe it was the pizza from the night before. Maybe it was Filippo's toast and sugary jam. Whatever it was, in the midst of the sunny day, my stomach tossed and then tugged at me to take it to a place of release.

The Plumas County Museum was across the street from the courthouse. Big Spoon accompanied me as I power walked to the quaint white house of history. The curator behind the desk in the gift shop greeted us when we stepped in. Her name tag read Jane. She had sky-blue eyes and cloud-like hair.

"You two are certainly fresh faces!" she said, beaming like the sun. "What brings you to Quincy?"

"The bathroom for me," I said, smiling awkwardly and bouncing up and down, my pack rustling against my back.

Jane pointed to the hallway past the Mountain Maidu and gold-mining exhibits, where a wooden door opened to my rescue. When I returned from the restroom, I joined Jane and Big Spoon's conversation.

"We were on the PCT, but now we're thinking of shooting up to Alaska," Big Spoon was saying.

"But we don't know how we'll get there," I said, butting in.

Jane's eyes brightened. "My friend's son lives in Alaska. His name's Jason Clark—the friend, not the son. Everyone knows him. He's the carpenter in town and lives right up the road. I bet he could help you." She reached for the phone. "Let me just give him a call."

"Destiny," Big Spoon whispered, leaning in to me as a man answered Jane's call.

She told him we were PCT hikers looking to go to Alaska. "They'd love to pick your brain."

The man on the other end didn't hesitate. "Wonderful! Send them up," I heard him say.

Jane hung up the phone and then gave us directions to Jason's house. "He lives at the top of the hill from the museum. It's the big log house on your right. You can't miss it. He said to come now if you can. Jason's a great guy."

"Water, beer, or wine?" Jason asked when we met him in his backyard. He was bent over in his vegetable garden, dripping sweat into the soil as he pulled up weeds. He wore grass-stained jeans and a Clark Construction T-shirt that revealed his tanned, muscular arms. When he stood, he pulled off his blackened leather gloves and motioned us to sit at the round iron table beneath his fruit-bearing apple tree.

"Water, beer, or wine?" he repeated as we removed our packs and reclined. For a total stranger, he felt like a friend.

The afternoon sun mixed with the aromatic garden in a way that called for wine. Jason entered his garage and returned seconds later with three stemmed glasses, a corkscrew, and a bottle of Cabernet Sauvignon.

"I fermented it myself," he said, opening the bottle and pouring us each a glass. "It's from the grapes growing up the lattice in the front of my house."

"Cheers," I said, raising my glass.

Everyone clinked glasses and sipped.

"So, you want to go to Alaska," Jason stated with zeal. "That's a special place, my friends. A very special place. My son is a fishing guide up there in the teensy town called Aleknagik. I try to visit him once a year. The majesty of that world is immeasurable. I don't think there's any place like it—Alaska. Tell me, what draws you two there?"

Big Spoon and I looked at each other for the answer. "We don't exactly know," I responded for both of us. "We've never been, but something seems to be pulling us there. Maybe it's the wild grizzlies or the massive glaciers or the northern lights."

Jason stroked his bearded chin with his forefinger and thumb. "I see," he said. "I see. When I was a pilot in my youth, I traveled all over the world. It was the air that drew me to Alaska. It's as pure as it gets. My, what a pristine place." He paused, looking us in the eyes. "If that's where you wish to go, the way will open up for you."

I thought he might go into more detail on cities to visit and ways to get there, but that was all Jason really said on the subject of Alaska. As we drank our wine at the iron table, he moved on to other things, like how he'd built his house when his children were small from the trees he'd chopped down to clear the land. His house was beautiful with how it coexisted with nature. Evergreens rose around it, and dark-green vines crawled up the lattice along the outside walls. Bees worked to make honey in a hive on the deck. A porch swing hung from a sturdy limb over his yard of blueberry bushes and sunflowers.

"My wife and I used to sit on that swing together, swaying back and forth for hours just watching the mountains," he said, the shift in his tone letting us know his wife was gone. "Life is something where you never quite know what you'll get." He looked to the swing. "But, you must keep on. You must stand firm like the mountains and *grow* through life rather than just *go* through it. The day you stop growing is—I believe—the day you start to die." He looked at his watch. "And with that, my friends, I have to go. I'm camping tonight up at Bucks Lake, helping a friend tear down his rotted cabin walls. And then we'll rebuild." His voice regained its fervor.

Big Spoon and I took this as our cue to leave. We finished our wine, scooted back our chairs, and stood.

"But you two are welcome to stay here tonight," Jason said, standing with us. "I built my home for people to use, so please feel free to stay. I have eggs and bacon in the fridge from my neighbor's chickens and pig, and you can pick anything you like from the garden. Just don't forget about the wine." He winked. There was half a bottle left.

"I'll be gone until tomorrow night, but do make yourselves at home and stay as long as you need. My door is always unlocked."

"We'd love to stay here," Big Spoon said, reading my mind. "That would be a tremendous help."

"Wonderful!" Jason exclaimed. "Then follow me."

He led us into his house, where the sun streamed through the windows in every room. Upstairs, he showed us his son's old bedroom—decorated with moose antlers and vintage snowshoes—and told us we could sleep there.

The bathroom and laundry room were down the hall. "I know it's been a while since you've used these facilities, but I'm sure you know how they work," Jason laughed, pointing out the obvious. Big Spoon and I stank.

"Everything else is self-explanatory," he said once we were back downstairs in the kitchen. "Relax and enjoy. My only request is that you feed my cat in the morning. Her bowl is by the broom closet. Her food is under the sink."

Then he left, trusting his home, possessions, and cat to two odorous people he had met thirty minutes before over an afternoon glass of wine.

He was either crazy or the most charitable man I'd ever met.

Warmth wafted through the evening air as Big Spoon and I strolled through the garden, eating wild blackberries off the vine and collecting a variety of planted treasures, like squash, zucchini, carrots, radishes, cherry tomatoes, and lettuce. In the kitchen, we used Jason's cast-iron skillets to fry the squash and zucchini, cook the bacon, and scramble the eggs. With the rest of the vegetables, we made a beautiful salad. Then we fixed our plates, grabbed the wine and our glasses, and returned to the iron table under the apple tree.

"Can you believe this?" Big Spoon said, trying his best to let the bacon that melted in our mouths last.

"Hardly. This is the most beautiful house I've ever been to." I blew on my fork.

"Lets me know we're on the right track, too—you know, for something like this to happen the day after we get off the trail."

I swallowed my bite of egg. "Huh. Wow. And it's all because I had to go to the bathroom."

"The higher plan," Big Spoon said, and we laughed.

After dinner, we swayed back and forth on the swing with our wineglasses in hand. The sun slipped behind the mountains as we swung. The morning would bring a day of delving into the complex logistics needed to move us on. But tonight, we savored the simplicity of where we were. We drank our wine to the last drop.

CHAPTER 33

BEYOND REALMS

On the three-hour flight to Alaska, I slept. It was Friday, August 14. Over the last two and a half weeks since meeting Jason, Big Spoon and I had applied our trail knowledge on living resourcefully to traveling on an adventurous dime to Seattle, from where our one-way flight to Anchorage departed.

We'd booked it while at Jason's, choosing this particular flight because of its astoundingly low fare of one hundred dollars per passenger. Thus, after days of careful planning, we bused from Quincy to Redding, took a train from Redding to Seattle, and then rented a car for the days remaining until take-off to embark on a road trip to the volcanic lands of Mount St. Helens, the mesmerizing blue of Crater Lake, and the goliath trees of the redwood forest. During this time, we camped in

church backyards, next to active volcanoes, within towering redwoods, and beneath the Pacific coast stars. When
we returned our rental car, we had driven a round-trip
distance of seventeen hundred miles.

Then it was the morning of our flight. Although
we were off the trail, we'd remained in continual motion. As a result, when we boarded the plane to Alaska,
I crashed.

The pure white peaks of the Chugach Mountains
beyond my small rectangular window woke me. It was
just minutes before landing. The mountains escalated
in rolling layers above the Gulf of Alaska, the snow atop
them so brilliantly white that it glowed into the air.
Jason had been right. The air seemed purer—clearer
almost—as if the veil separating earth and the great beyond had been lifted.

After retrieving our backpacks from baggage
claim, we rented a red Nissan Frontier from the airport Enterprise booth and headed north for an hour
to Wasilla. The Alaskan day at this time of year was lasting upward of eighteen hours, causing darkness to fall
around midnight. It was evening, but it felt like noon
when Sienna and Nelson opened their door to us on
Discoverer Bay Drive. The museum curator and her
husband—the science professor at the local college—
were connections we'd made during our San Francisco
stay when one morning Autumn had asked us what we
planned to do after the trail. Big Spoon had voiced his

desire to travel to Alaska. Autumn grew excited, saying that Mia had a high school friend, Sienna, who now lived there. She gave us Sienna's contact information, which Big Spoon and I had used to connect with her after determining to travel that way. Now, forty days after that fateful conversation with Autumn, Sienna and Nelson were welcoming us into their home. Yet another example of how our path to our ultimate destination had been paved long before we knew where it would lead.

A flock of sandhill cranes flew up off the water and cawed overhead as Big Spoon and I slipped off our tattered boots and dirty socks before stepping inside. Their home was inviting, with open windows and a cream-colored carpet that soothed my callused soles all the way to the back bedroom, where Big Spoon and I would sleep for the night. Our hosts provided dinner, and the four of us spent the pink-and-yellow evening conversing at the dining-room table. The neckline of Sienna's summer dress accentuated the ivory pendant resting against her chest. Sky-blue forget-me-nots were painted on the ivory.

"They're Alaska's state flower. The ivory was carved from walrus tusk by a Native," Sienna said when I voiced my admiration of her necklace.

I turned my attention to the black-and-white photo of an Inuit woman mounted on the wall before me. In the photo, the woman carried her sleeping baby in the hood of her fur coat. The woman's eyes were compassionate, and her body was strong. The child lay against its mother's back in peace. When I pointed out the picture, Sienna said the woman was a symbol of survival in the harsh arctic conditions—the dark subzero days.

"A symbol," Nelson added, "of unyielding life."

The two continued to impart their Alaskan knowledge until sundown. As a result, Big Spoon and I left Wasilla in the morning with a rich and exciting itinerary. It was a misty Saturday, silver and damp. We drove north to Hatcher Pass, a scenic road and recreational area carved within the Talkeetna Mountains. Trucks and other four-wheel-drive vehicles stuck out from the rugged pull-offs. People were outside in rain jackets and rubber boots, bent over in the rolling fields with buckets at their hips.

"What are they doing?" I asked Big Spoon as we slowly drove by.

"I think they're picking berries," he said.

He parked at the next pull-off, and we got out. Sure enough, beside us in the emerald mountain meadow were blueberry bushes growing close to the ground. Big Spoon stooped over, picked a berry from a bush, and popped it into his mouth. The next one he plucked, he gave to me. Its juices bled into my tongue when I bit down. Its bitter sweetness sank down my throat.

From Hatcher Pass, we traveled north, entering the one-road town of Talkeetna two hours later. Here, foot traffic prevailed over cars. Tourists floated in and out of the log-cabin shops full of jade necklaces, caribou antlers, and ivory carvings of whales and moose. Big Spoon and I spent the rest of the day perusing the stores and eating fish 'n' chips at the local pub. Then we trucked sixteen miles down a lone road to the Montana Creek Campground.

"The Silvers Are In!" read the sign outside the camp. It was nine at night and as bright as day. Fly fishermen and women tromped in heavy waders from their RVs through the campground to access Montana Creek. Big Spoon and I had the only tent set up, and we were the only ones not fishing. During the lasting light of night, we watched from our tent door as those in wet clothing returned from the creek with fly rods over one shoulder and long silver salmon dangling from stringers over the other.

When I fell asleep, the salmon swam through my dreams. They reeled from the river where they were born out into the big, mysterious sea. I swam with them and watched them grow to their full size in the beautiful ocean until it came time for them to return to the river to spawn.

━≺⊦⊹≻━

"You have to get out on the tundra," said the general-store clerk the next day as Big Spoon and I resupplied on food before entering Denali National Park.

"If you don't get out on the tundra," he said, "you've wasted your time here in Denali."

As a result, we shot straight to the ranger station to attain backcountry permits that would allow us to, in the clerk's words, "get out on the tundra." I read the park brochure while we waited in line. Denali, also known as Mount McKinley, meant "the High One" in Native Alaskan. It was the tallest mountain in North America at 20,310 feet above sea level. Ironically, considering it was the grandest crag around, tourists, even locals, rarely saw its dominating peak because of the ever-present clouds that shrouded it.

This was the case for Big Spoon and me. We never saw Denali—we only felt its powerful presence.

"The grizzlies are eating up to forty thousand calories a day on berries before winter hits, so watch your surroundings on the tundra, and avoid hiking in places of dense hedgerow," the ranger said when we reached the front of the line. Her mandatory safety talk listed the aspects of the backcountry—like bears, lightning storms, and aggressive moose—that Big Spoon and I would have to be vigilant about once we entered its domain.

My heart pounded as I signed the contract that stated the park was not at fault if something happened to me. Big Spoon and I obtained our permits for an overnight backpacking trip on Primrose Ridge. The permits were free, but the catch was this: in order to preserve Denali's land, no trails were cut through the backcountry. Hikers had to make their own way. This scared me. Even in the most remote places on the PCT, I'd had a distinct path to follow. But in the enormous Alaskan wild, I had to bushwhack my own trail? What if I lost the way?

Standing in the station with these swarming thoughts, I remembered my dream of the salmon. It was true—I'd read it in the brochure—that when salmon reached a certain age, they journeyed from the river—their native home—to the sea, where they had never been. They left their comfortable realms to reach a greater world they somehow knew existed—regardless of the risk. This, I determined, would be my course as well.

The ranger handed Big Spoon and me two bottles of bear spray—an extremely potent mace used to thwart charging bears—as we left the station. We readied our packs in the visitor parking lot and then caught the Savage River Shuttle to Primrose Ridge. An hour later, we stood before the painted ridge surmounting fifteen hundred feet over Savage River.

"Do you hear that?" Big Spoon said after the shuttle had vroomed away, leaving us starkly alone.

We stood on the empty road, listening as a mass of howls rang out.

I gulped.

"Wolves," Big Spoon said.

The air was very still. The lime tundra spread before us to the base of the rocky ridge. Garnet mountains and teal flatlands surrounded the tundra. It was early evening. Several hours of daylight remained for us to make our climb. The howling ceased, and it was time to go.

I was about to get in over my head.

CHAPTER 34

PARALYZED ON THE MOUNTAIN

"What are we doing?" I cried out to Big Spoon, my hands trembling as they clung to the loose rock. My legs shook as if I had hypothermia. I wouldn't let myself look down the steep mountainside on which I was stuck.

Several hours before, Big Spoon and I had analyzed the map of Primrose Ridge we'd bought at the ranger station. From where we'd stood on the road, it was a two-mile climb to the top. We'd examined the mountain we would ascend and picked a path that seemed doable and safe.

Then we stepped onto the wet, spongy ground of the tundra. A hundred yards later, tall, thick brush swallowed us. The shrubbery hadn't seemed so tall or thick from the road. Big Spoon and I could no longer see our chosen path. I could hardly see Big Spoon, who was ahead of me, from ten feet away. The ranger had warned against this: "The grizzlies are eating up to forty thousand calories a day on berries before winter hits," she'd said, "so watch your surroundings on the tundra, and avoid hiking in places of dense hedgerow."

I was scared, but I continued to follow Big Spoon, who continued to push on, up through the tangled wood.

"We should reach a clearing soon," he kept turning back to say.

"Hey, bear! Hey! Hey, hey, hey!" I yelled over and over to ward off the berry-eating beasts.

The brush grew worse. It was a wild wall of saplings, thorns, and sticks built to keep us out. Half the time, I crawled on my knees, muddying my pants. My hands bled from thorn stabs. My hair fell in hectic clumps from where it kept getting caught in the twigs.

It was a fight I was losing. Then the ground rose suddenly and steeply, giving me hope that the clearing was near. I fitted my trekking-pole straps around my wrists and let them dangle behind me as I grabbed the limbs of shrubs and trees to pull myself up the mountain. Finally, three hours after battling one mile through this mess, the forest opened up to the bare mountainside.

The sun was starting to set, casting its final light on something I didn't want to see. Big Spoon and I, in our scrubland blindness, had gotten off the track we'd selected down at the road. Instead of being on the far right side of the mountain where the grade was gradual and smooth, we were situated in the center of its sheer, serrated slope.

Leaning boulders and loose scree devoured the terrain ahead. But Big Spoon was confident we could make it all the way without having to backtrack.

"We've been on stuff like this on the trail," he said as we faced the intimidating incline. "This is nothing new. The only difference is we'll have to cut our own switchbacks."

I was terrified, feeling unprotected and insecure, the bitter wind whooshing against me. One wrong step and I could tumble down the mountain. I could die up here, I thought, creeping up the wobbly stone behind Big Spoon, moving slower than a three-toed sloth.

Then my foot landed on a rock that couldn't bear my weight. The stone swayed, crackled against the other rocks, and then slid out from under my boot and fell brutally down the rise. An even greater fear slammed into me, paralyzing me where I was.

"What are we doing?" I cried, gripping the scree, my panic spilling out.

Big Spoon turned and rushed my way. Globs of gravel from his hurried steps rattled down. When he touched my distressed self, he took off my pack.

"Sit here," he said after clearing a spot with his foot and setting my pack atop a rock.

I did as he instructed, releasing the clenched weight of my body onto the vertical earth.

"What happened?"

My hands still trembled. "I don't know. I can't keep going. I feel so stuck."

Big Spoon crouched beside me. "Listen. I know you're scared, but we're not in a life-or-death situation. We got off course. This stretch is more demanding, but we'll be okay. You're more than capable of doing this. Stay calm and trust your abilities. Step by step."

He pulled the map from his back pocket and unfolded it. "The ridge can't be more than a quarter mile away. It looks like camping is limited where we're headed now, though."

With darkness encroaching, Big Spoon decided to dart up to the top without his pack weighing him down to see if any accessible campsites existed. He told me to stay seated on the slope and watch the packs until he returned. Sitting alone, I watched the sun dip into the tundra and blend its golden shine with the jade and emerald shades of that land. I was calmer now but perplexed, wondering how Big Spoon could stride up this extreme and exposed ground without an inkling of fear.

Meanwhile, the heavy stomp of my heart marched to the pit of my throat, where it paced like one unsure of what to do. After all of this, I thought, after all of this—the trail, my marriage, Alaska, over one hundred days of travel and thousands of miles of exploration—and now I'm stuck.

What was I going to do? Where would Big Spoon and I go? Our adventure, like the sun, was diminishing before my eyes. What would become of us when it was gone?

I'd fought these fears before—when we got off the trail. And although I'd conquered them for a time, they were back, wrestling against me now without mercy, locking me in a chokehold from which I struggled to break free.

"We have to go back down," Big Spoon said upon his return from the red stone peak, disrupting my inner battle. "It's too narrow up there—and windy. There's no good place to pitch a tent."

"Okay," I said, harshly exhaling my relief. I shakily stood, pulled my pack back on, and then started my downward scuffle. It didn't take half as long to go down the mountain as it had to come up. Back on level ground, we walked along Savage River until we found a patch of dirt, where we set up camp, ate dinner, and waited outside for the stars.

When the sun was completely gone, the darkness should have swept in. Instead, a lime-and-violet glow gradually appeared across the sky. The lights were faint but different, so very different from anything I'd ever seen in the sky, and so absolutely striking that although they were dim, unless I was blind, there was no denying what they were.

"Whoa," Big Spoon said, straining his neck as he gazed up.

"The northern lights," I murmured, almost in disbelief. I didn't think Big Spoon and I would get to see them, because earlier that day, as we'd filled out our backcountry permits, the ranger had told us we were too far south for the aurora borealis to reach Denali this late in the summer.

However, staring up at this waving path of light, I had no doubt this was it—the aurora borealis, the marvelous northern lights. The beauty was divine—a masterpiece on a black canvas, a doorway to a new and wonderful world.

"Thank you," I whispered up to the lights. "We're going to make it through."

"Of course we are," said Big Spoon, who'd heard me. "Just remember—step by step."

We sat side by side in the immense Alaskan wild with our heads cocked up, contemplating it all—the tundra, the river, the mountains, the painted night sky, the boundless glory of life—until our eyelids grew heavy, draping farther and farther down, prompting us to slip inside our tent and fall asleep.

———

Snowcapped volcanoes protruded from the gulf that ran parallel to Route 1. On the other side of the road, two male moose grazed in the vast, verdant fields beyond the guardrails. Big Spoon and I spotted the regal creatures the morning after we left Denali. We had slept in our truck's cab the night before, parked on a high-way pull-off after passing back through Anchorage. At sunrise, we returned to the road, not seeing another car for a hundred miles as we made our way to Homer, the halibut-fishing capital of the world on the southern tip of the Kenai.

I drove with the windows rolled down to let in the misty morning air. The highway took us along the Kenai River—like a melted aquamarine running through the mountains—over which the white mist hovered. About a mile down the river, several people were outside their cars, leaning against the guardrail. I figured they were looking at the color of the water, as spectacular as it was. Then Big Spoon pointed out a woman with binoculars.

"There's something down there on the bank," he said, motioning me to stop on the side of the road.

The quiet crowd stood motionless as they looked down the steep embankment.

"What do you see?" I whispered to the woman with binoculars.

But before she answered, I saw what it was and be-came as silent and still as the rest.

Just beyond the guardrail, down the dirt mound, were two grizzlies romping around on the riverside. My heartbeat hastened for being so close to these fierce ani-mals in the wild. I grabbed the guardrail and watched. The grizzlies were active, strong, and free. They roamed

the riverbank like gods and goddesses—powerfully—
their majestic russet coats shining in the sun.

One waded into the water, walking deeper and deeper in until she could no longer stand, causing the current to sweep her down. All I could see was her bobbing
snout as she swam diagonally with the water's flow to
the other side. The other bear watched his companion
drift before dashing down the bank and sprinting in
after her. Together again, the grizzlies started to fish,
standing up in the river with their paws outstretched
and claws extended—at the ready to strike. Every few
minutes, they returned to the bank to shake out their
burly fur. At one point, they exchanged spirited barks
and splashed each other with the water.

"They're playing," I said to Big Spoon.

"They're like us," he said and winked.

"They're so alive."

"They're free."

CHAPTER 35
SOARING

The owner of the Alaska Horn and Antler Gift Shop had white, wiry hair that stood up from his head in all directions as if attracted by some powerful energy swirling about. He wore a red-flannel shirt and was sitting on a stool at an industrial table with the desk lamp on, chipping away at an antler, when Big Spoon and I stepped in. I felt the calluses on his fingers when he set his carving aside and shook my hand, introducing himself as Jeremiah, an electric twinkle in his eye.

Minutes before, after seeing the grizzlies, Big Spoon and I had stopped here off Sterling Highway. The hundreds of caribou, moose, and elk antlers stacked outside the shop had drawn us in. As Big Spoon studied the horns, I could see the desire in his eyes for the massive brown moose rack with the white skull still attached. We hadn't bought an Alaskan souvenir yet. This wouldn't be the one. From its longest point hung a price tag: eight-hundred dollars.

Plastic bins of rocks, crystals, and gems jutted from the walls inside. The far back wall showcased Native Alaskan art, like glossy black baleen carvings of hunters spearing walruses. Baleen, I had learned, was a thin, tough plate in the upper jaw of certain whales. Also known as whalebone, it grew in a tooth-like series to filter food such as plankton and krill. Since being in Alaska, I had also learned that the Natives were the only ones allowed to collect baleen, along with ivory, to use for art.

Jeremiah reiterated this law when he noticed me examining a tiny yet impressive ivory statue of an Aleut holding a fishing rod in one hand and a salmon in the other.

"Yep," he said in a whimsical voice, "I sell most of the artwork here, because, you know, being that I'm not indigenous, they tell me I can't make it myself. Well, that's okay. I don't mind. I carve antlers. Me and my friends, we collect the sheds around this time of year. We know where to go, you know." He winked. "Make a ritual of it. It's not much, carving antlers. But I love it. I do. Gives me my purpose."

He put down the horn he was working on and moseyed over to a glass case that displayed a decorative array of ulus.

"You travelers might like these," he said, summoning us over.

"Do you make them?" Big Spoon asked after we joined the shop owner by the case.

Jeremiah grinned, sparking the light in his eyes. "Not the blades, young man. Just the handles."

Tan polished bone made up the handles for the odd-looking knives.

"Could we see one?" Big Spoon asked, enthralled.

Jeremiah opened the case and chose the only ulu that had a soft-pink tint gleaming from the handle. He placed the sharp, curved object on the counter, explaining that ulus were special knives that had been used for thousands of years by female Eskimos to skin the fish and animals their men hunted and killed.

"Everyone uses them here now," he said. "Your everyday kitchen knife."

It looked like a contemporary artifact. Big Spoon picked it up, swiped his thumb across its convex blade, and grasped its handle in the way he would if he were slicing something. He handed it to me to do the same. The grip was solid and smooth; it felt good in my hand.

"It's caribou antler," Jeremiah said. "The handle. A buddy of mine made the blade from a carbon-steel saw. This isn't one of those mass-produced ulus with the stainless-steel edges and wooden handles that won't last. I never understand why people invest in something that won't last." He grasped the lovely knife. "This is the ulu the Natives use. So long as you work with it right, it'll withstand the test of time. If you let it sit, it'll tarnish. You have to put it to use. You have to let it do what it was made to do. And it will shine forever."

We left Jeremiah's shop minutes later with the ulu. It cost seventy-five dollars—an investment in quality and style.

"Remember to use it," Jeremiah had urged as we walked out the door. "Never let a good tool go to waste."

Fields of bright-purple fireweed flamed up from the side of the road the rest of the way to Homer. Before reaching the town, we stopped in Ninilchik, a compact fishing community on the gulf, where views of the Cook Inlet volcanoes—Mount Spurr, Mount Redoubt, Mount Iliamna, and Mount St. Augustine—evoked our awe. We beheld the snowy volcanoes from the grassy overlook at the Russian Orthodox Church built by Russian settlers in the early 1900s. The Ninilchik River snaked through the settlement into the inlet that spread to the volcanoes. The narrow river ran into the ongoing sea, and it was comforting. At the end of the river, the river didn't end.

I wondered if this would be the case for Big Spoon's and my journey. It was close to running out. In four months, we had traveled almost four thousand miles by foot, car, and plane. From the border of Mexico to the edge of Alaska, we had merged our very lives. It had been the greatest period of my life. I would be sad to see it end.

However, watching the river enter the inlet, I knew this journey wasn't all. This journey was our river run. What awaited us now was the sea.

Down by the harbor, the smell of dead fish and sea salt fanned through the air. Apart from some fishermen unloading salmon from their boats onto the dock, no one was out. Something stout and dark was perched atop the rusty parking sign we were nearing.

"Could that be...is that a..."

"Bald eagle," Big Spoon confirmed.

He wheeled up to the sign and shut off the truck. The eagle raised its silky white head and stared at us with round, golden eyes. Seeing that we weren't a threat, it returned to pruning its long, refined feathers, plucking with its yellow beak, clutching the old sign with its black talons.

Bold and radiant beneath the blazing sun, it was a living symbol of freedom.

A fish delivery truck rumbled by, rousing the eagle to action. It unfurled its sleek wings, lingering on the sign as if to show us their bright and brawny span. Then it jumped up and flew off, soaring over the shimmering sea toward the volcanic horizon, rising higher and higher into the beautiful beyond, not slowing down, not looking back, but flying forward, onward, until it had reached new heights.

"What's wrong with them?" I asked Big Spoon, gaping into Resurrection Bay at the school of sick, gray salmon that half swam, half floated in the shallow water close to shore.

It was our last night in Alaska. We were in Seward, another town on the Kenai Peninsula three hours north of Homer. Homer had been a blast. Windsurfers swept across Kachemak Bay as float planes landed on the water next to the port where both battered fishing boats and elegant cruise liners docked. Big Spoon and I saw all of this the day we arrived as we slid in and out of the boardwalk gift shops along the Homer Spit—a four-and-a-half-mile strip of land dribbling from the mainland into the bay. In the mermaid-inspired store, Stella's by the Sea, a wooden sign hung next to a driftwood anchor that spelled out in fanciful lettering: "At the end of the road, Adventure begins."

It felt this way the night we tried to relax at Homer Spit Campground. It was too windy to make a fire where we tented on the round-stone beach. Big Spoon and I double-staked our home with rocks as whitecaps broke against the shore and water flung itself at our site. I cuffed my pants and waded into the troubled bay. It was painfully cold, especially with the wind. But it was terrific. Navy mountains powdered with snow lined the cyan sea. The sea waved far ahead—a whole other entity, a whole other realm, a whole other depth of mystery.

And I was standing partway in.

We fell asleep, bundled tight in our sleeping bags, to the swishing lullaby of the waves. At dawn, we woke to the trickling hum of high tide. The sunrise splattered the sky with fiery orange and magenta. On our way out of Homer, we stopped at Three Sisters Bakery for their famous sticky buns. The sky transformed from rose red to the blue of a Himalayan poppy as we sat on the bakery's back deck, letting the hot and gooey bread make a mess down our fingers as it melted in our mouths.

We made Seward later that day after stopping on the outskirts of the town and hiking three miles up a fertile mountain in Kenai Fjords National Park to view the crevasses and ice of Exit Glacier. Facing the massive glaze, I was blown away that this dense bulk of fire-blue ice was constantly moving. Although it looked as still as stone, the glacier sprang from the Harding Icefield in the Kenai Mountains, covering an area of four miles as it slid slowly, slowly off the frozen field like a paused waterfall, splashing into the valley below where it fed Resurrection River—where it gave another body life.

We camped for the next two nights on the bank of that river, huddled within some leafy trees off State Highway 9 next to a beach of silvery silt. On our last full day in Alaska, we indulged in a four-hour whale-watching tour through Resurrection Bay. Big, brown sea otters floated on their backs in the sapphire cove. Sea lions sunned themselves at the base of ashen cliffs. Porpoises raced our boat. Near the end of the tour, a flock of black-and-white puffins glided inches above the water toward something splashing in the open. Big Spoon and I stood on the bow of the cruiser with the masses. I seemed to be the only one who heard and saw the splash.

"Look!" I cried.

A humpback whale exploded from the water like a rocket ship. She spun in the air as she flew, her heavy black blubber taking in the heat of the sun before she crashed back into the frigid sea. The creature was colossal—forty feet long and sixty thousand pounds, the tour guide guessed as the whale swam off, flipping up her powerful tail as if to wave good-bye.

Back on land, Big Spoon and I wandered down the shore of the bay, ultimately sighting the salmon that looked like sea zombies with their bulging eyes and faded skin.

"What's wrong with them?" I asked.

"They're dying," Big Spoon said.

"They're dying? How do you know?"

"I read it in one of the brochures at the tour office. It said now's the time of year when the salmon spawn. And after they spawn, they die."

"After they spawn, they die?" I asked, troubled.

Big Spoon nodded. "That's what it said. After they spawn, they die."

The salmon bobbed like ghosts to and from the water's surface. They didn't struggle in any way but floated in place, waiting as if they were already dead for death to take its toll.

"How terrible," I said, frightened by their indifference. "They bring new life to the rivers and streams and then they have to die? Do you think they're ready to die?"

Big Spoon put his arm around my shoulder. "Is anyone or anything ever ready to die?"

I didn't know.

He continued, "I think, for these fish, their purpose here is complete. They've traveled to the ends of the sea and returned to this bay, where they were born, to continue the cycle that let them live at all. They've accomplished what they were created to do. Now, it's time for them to move on."

"But they look so dead already," I said, staring at the one with its puckered mouth partway out of the water. "They're not dead yet, but they look so *dead*."

I couldn't understand. Why live a whole audacious life only to die in the shallow confines of death? If you were going to die, why not die in the deep and stirring grandeur of life? Why not stand up to death? Why not charge it with ferocity and grit, with your utmost life, instead of getting caught up by it, trapped like a feeble creature, limp, in death's claws?

"They're ready, Claire," Big Spoon said. "To answer your question, I think they're ready. Maybe what you see in them is their peace. Maybe they know something we don't about what awaits them next."

What awaited us next was the Anchorage International Airport, where we'd booked a flight to Newark, New Jersey, after a lengthy discussion on the Homer Spit on what we should do. We returned our truck on Saturday, August 22, and then waited several hours at the congested gate for our night flight back east. In the morning, I'd meet Big Spoon's family for the first time, and two weeks after that, we'd drive his truck down to Chattanooga for him to meet mine. A couple of weeks beyond this, I would hear from Pandora. She would call with excitement to tell me that she and Saltlick had made it to Canada, that they had touched the wooden monument at the Northern Terminus of the Pacific Crest Trail.

Big Spoon and I would still be in Chattanooga at this time, gearing up to move into a one-bedroom apartment and begin our new and temporary jobs—Big Spoon building power-line equipment, me writing for a local paper. We would have a traditional wedding celebration months later. I would wear a wedding dress and Big Spoon would wear a tux as our loved ones surrounded us on the back deck of an old catfish restaurant on the Tennessee River. The April wind would whip and the sun would beam as Big Spoon and I stood by the rooted oak reaching out to the water, vowing before everyone and God to love and stay true to each other for the rest of our days.

And then we would leave. A year to the day of our marriage on the trail, we would load our packs into Big Spoon's truck and travel on, this time to Oregon to find what this realm contained—our way of keeping on our path and striving to spend our precious hours on experiences that brought us, and those around us, entirely to life.

I couldn't have known any of this as Big Spoon and I waited at the gate at the Anchorage airport. He held my hand the whole time as I watched plane after plane outside the wall of windows speed down the airstrip, zooming as fast as they could before taking off to cross unseen borders.

At sunset, a shrill screech sounded from the overhead speaker. The gate attendant was calling our flight to board.

I looked up at Big Spoon. "This is it."

He kissed me on the forehead. "This is it."

On the plane, we buckled our seatbelts and waited. Facing the cockpit, we sat on the right side. Big Spoon sat by the window. I sat still, uncertain of what lay ahead but confident that whatever it was, it would be our glorious destiny.

The plane streamed down the strip. Its pace crawled at first and then grew, gradually and deliberately, into a sprint. When it had gained maximum speed on the ground, it had no other course but to fly. It rose into the sky, flying up for many miles, soaring past the dying light of day and boldly into the darkness.

I leaned over Big Spoon to look out the window, remembering the sign in the gift shop that had said, "At the end of the road, Adventure begins."

The night blacked out the view.

It seems like the end of our journey, I thought, peering out.

Big Spoon pressed his head next to mine and tilted his ear to the roaring engines propelling the plane on.

It seemed like the very end. Yet, I knew the deeper truth. It was the beginning—not the end—of a new adventure of life.

For here we were, soaring boldly on.

ACKNOWLEDGMENTS

Writing a book and then getting it published is a long and intricate process that requires help from many hands in order to get that book into yours. That being said, I'd like to thank the many "hands" who helped bring *Mile 445* to fruition.

Thank you, Caleb Miller (aka Big Spoon) for your exquisite eye for detail. Your feedback and sharp memory regarding our grand adventure helped make *Mile 445* a richer and more captivating tale. Thank you, Kathaleen Hughes—my beautiful aunt who introduced me to backpacking when I was twelve—for being one of the first persons to read the manuscript during the editing phase, and for teaching me during this time that "ice cream Sunday" is actually spelled "ice cream *sundae*." Margaret Cooke, thank you, my dear friend, for also reading *Mile 445* through an editor's eyes and for being gracefully honest with your feedback on "info dumps."

To the CreateSpace team who worked on the book's cover, interior formatting, marketing copy, and editing, you all did a fantastic job and were very professional and enjoyable to work with. Furthermore, thank you to the business entrepreneurship class, LAUNCH, and specifically to my facilitator Linda Murray Bullard, for teaching me how to confidently and effectively get my book out there in the world.

Thank you to my parents, Peter Henley and Jennifer Ward, and to my siblings, Eric and Locksley Henley, for your constant love and support (even when I married a man I'd known for less than thirty days). You are all bright lights in my life, and I love you all more than you'll ever know. Also, thank you Barry and Ave Miller—my father-and-mother-in-law—for your help and encouragement throughout this project. Ave, I'm so glad you are not afraid to go up to total strangers and promote the book, because I do not have that skill!

Additionally, a big thanks to the Pacific Crest Trail Association for working to beautifully preserve the PCT so people like me can take a hike. Thank you, trail angels, for taking a chance on some of the dirtiest and smelliest people on earth. Your hospitality is more valuable than gold. To all the thru-hikers Big Spoon and I met on our journey, thank you for your friendship, fun, and genuineness. It really is the people who make this journey great!

Thank you to the rest of my friends and family who were "there" throughout the PCT-hiking and book-writing process. Your uplifting love is divine. You know who you are.

Last but not least, thank You, God—my Heavenly Father, Savior, and Friend—for being with Big Spoon and me every step of this incredible journey—without Your love and guidance, we'd be lost.

ABOUT THE AUTHOR

 Claire Henley Miller was born in Tennessee and has since lived in the Loire Valley of France and the Colorado Rockies. She holds a bachelor's degree from the University of Tennessee-Chattanooga in creative writing and, in 2016, worked as a journalist for The Chattanoogan.com. She is also the author of a children's story, *The Land of the Living Sunrise*, and a book of poetry, *The Infinite*. She currently lives with her husband in Bend, Oregon.

38534364R10223

Made in the USA
Middletown, DE
21 December 2016